New Approaches to Teaching Elementary Social Studies

with Illustrative Units

by
Donald L. Barnes, Ed. D.
Ball State University
Muncie, Indiana

and
Arlene B. Burgdorf, Ed. D.
Hammond Public Schools
Hammond, Indiana

Burgess Publishing Company

426 South Sixth Street • Minneapolis, Minn. 55415

FOREWORD

In attempting to develop an effective social studies program, perceptive social studies educators consider the learner, his social milieu, and the knowledge and understandings which make up the social studies discipline. Today, the learner and the social studies educator exist in a world which continues to be marked by national and international tensions, numerous and varied technological developments, a rapid rate of change, an explosion of knowledge, and a mobile population. In this book Dr. Barnes and Dr. Burgdorf emphasize social studies programs and teacher competencies necessary to meet today's needs.

As the authors point out, recent research has produced evidence relating the importance of attitude formation, individual value judgments, and group interactions to the acquisition of knowledge. Scholars continue to give attention to the improvement of techniques in problem solving, critical thinking, and teaching strategies that provide other new focuses of attention. Dr. Barnes and Dr. Burgdorf have keenly recognized the dilemma confronting practitioners: How does a social studies educator synthesize these disparate elements into an integrated whole, with sequence, continuity, and direction? In confronting this question, the authors provide valuable assistance to those involved in social studies education.

The beginning chapters on curriculum planning, current issues, and types of social studies programs provide an overall picture of the present situation in social studies. In Chapter II, "Separate Disciplines in the Social Studies," the authors have selected basic generalizations from each discipline and have shown the relationship of each to three specific social studies topics. The attention given to the development of the relationships among the social science disciplines and elementary social studies topics is characteristic of the practical treatment Dr. Barnes and Dr. Burgdorf give to all topics included in their book. Granted, it is not enough to state that we cannot, and should not, give children ready-made answers. The next step is to provide them with ways of finding and using information. In the portions of this book that deal with problem solving, fostering creativity, critical thinking, reading and study skills, the authors take up the need for providing the learner with the basic tools of investigation, analysis, and evaluation. Over the years, much has been written about the need for a differentiated curriculum, and it is commonplace to find a chapter devoted to individual differences in a social studies methods book. Dr. Barnes and Dr. Burgdorf have wisely chosen to discuss differentiation in an integrated fashion, giving attention to the topic with reference to questioning, reading, and study skills, as well as devoting an entire chapter to meeting needs of individuals. A particularly fine chapter is the one on teaching strategies useful in the clarification of values. Questions are explored pertaining to particular values, value change, and the study of values.

The capstone of this book is made up of carefully constructed units which illustrate how the "parts" of the social studies, treated in the previous chapters of the book, go together in practice to make the "whole" of the social studies. Throughout this book, the authors seem to have anticipated the areas in which teachers, teachers-to-be, and curriculum planners most need help and have illuminated these areas in a clear, explanatory style, often utilizing practical and meaningful classroom situations. The result is a book that should be a valuable aid in social studies education.

Joan Schreiber, Asst. Prof. of History, Ball State University

INTRODUCTION

Social studies is basically a study of man's well-being. This has been, and continues to be, our most pressing problem. Our work in social studies should help us better understand the causes and consequences of human behavior, the problems of group relationships, and man's use and misuse of his natural environment. Stated more specifically, social studies should: (1) assist learners in their quests for personal meanings and understandings in life; (2) develop an awareness of man's struggle to fulfill his basic needs in group and institutional settings; and (3) develop the intellectual capacity to use key generalizations and viable processes established by specialists in exploring social behavior.

PROBLEMS AND PARADOXES

Although the above explanation may appear, on the surface, to be relatively simple, it is not without difficulties. At this point, for example, we are not quite certain whether social studies teachers should be half teachers - half guidance counselors, well-informed scholars in history, geography, economics and the behavioral sciences, or all of these things. Jarolimek has pointed out:

> The problem of selecting content for elementary social studies is confounded by the more basic problem of defining exactly what constitutes achievement in this area of school curriculum. Just what achievement really is in the social studies seems to be one of the least well answered questions in elementary education.[1]

Social scientists are far from agreement regarding the responsibilities they will accept in the modification of human conduct and human affairs. This problem is treated in some detail in Chapter IV.

We also have the problem of emphasis or focus. It is obvious that no human being can become even casually acquainted with the whole of man's experiences. Some important choices need to be made. Young children often best understand human activities within their immediate surroundings; yet if topics are restricted to local studies, we may find them ill-suited to our highly mobile society. The problem of content selection is further complicated by the fact that children today are learning a great deal more from a broader world than we thought. Frazier[2] reviews several studies which suggest that sixty per cent or more of our primary children may already be familiar with traditional topics outlined for second grade social studies.

[1] John Jarolimek, "Curriculum Content and the Child in the Elementary School," *Social Education,* Vol. XXVI, No. 2 (February, 1962), p. 117.
[2] Alexander Frazier, "Lifting Our Sights in Primary Social Studies," *Social Education,* Vol. XXIII, No. 7 (November 1959), pp. 337-338.

In addition, we have the problem of individuality and conformity. This is not a new dilemma. The conflicts among individuals, groups, institutions and governments make up the story of much of recorded history. In the classroom the drama is simply played out on a more abbreviated scale. What emphasis and recognition shall be given to individual interests, individual effort, and unusual or incompatible expressions of social behavior? And how much shall we push for cooperative group effort, involving the subordination of individual desires? How much importance shall be attached to individual creativity? How much to basic fundamentals? These questions are treated in Chapters VII and VIII.

Finally, we must face the problem of competition within the school program. At the primary level particularly there are forces which militate against the development of meaningful and viable social studies offerings. An obviously serious limitation is the tacit repudiation in some primary classrooms of the social studies as having any basic relevance, particularly as an organized area of the curriculum. In these classrooms other subject areas, notably reading and arithmetic, are considered so much more important that they usurp much of the time that might otherwise be devoted to social studies.

Some primary teachers rationalize the lack of form and substance in social studies by explaining the genuine belief that this subject is expressed in the day-to-day atmosphere of democratic living within the classroom. There is no denying that every opportunity should be taken to make this area of study directly applicable to ongoing social situations. It is, however, shortsighted to leave to chance the development of major social concepts and generalizations. A similar notion is that because no area of the curriculum is, in a sense, independent of social studies, it should find its major emphasis in correlational activities with art, music, literature and language arts. Thus social studies becomes the fodder upon which other subjects feed. This is a rather modest calling for a subject area that deals so basically with man's total being.

EMPHASIS UPON FINDING AND USING
INFORMATION INTELLIGENTLY

A great many philosophies have found expression in American education. Some have emphasized creative expression, problem-solving, and critical thinking; some have stressed knowledge of fundamental disciplines, prudent use of data, and closely reasoned arguments; still others have focused on basic social or vocational competencies tailored to contemporary life. Despite the fact that each philosophy is built on different assumptions about the nature of man and knowledge and the essential conditions of learning, all recognize that man must know how to find and use information efficiently and judiciously in whatever tasks he sets for himself. It is this task of finding and using information in problem-solving situations, creative endeavors, and value studies that is stressed throughout this volume. We cannot, and should not, give children ready-made answers. But we can, and should, provide them with the basic tools of investigation, analysis, and evaluation.

Finding information and using information are, unfortunately, not unitary skills; they are composites of more than fifty interrelated competencies, some of a relatively high order. The locational skills involve:

1. A wide knowledge of informational sources — the organization and uses of many basic references and reference tools.

2. Mastery of specialized skills relating to the efficient use of parts of books (indexes, footnotes, tables, sub-headings, etc.) and reading skills (skimming, identification of key ideas, relationships, etc.) important to the intelligent study of printed materials.

Using information includes:
1. Competencies in the analysis and evaluation of information collected.
2. Organizational skills related to the assembling and synthesis of data.
3. Interpretive skills used in judging the significance, relevance, and importance of information.

Helping children develop these interrelated skills and understandings is a tremendous job! Our hope is that there will be many teachers who care enough about children and the future of man to carry out this intricate task thoughtfully and thoroughly, yet with a clear and pervasive sensitivity to the children they are teaching.

TABLE OF CONTENTS

Chapter I

CURRICULUM PLANNING– EVERYBODY'S BUSINESS

"Speaking generally, education signifies the sum total of processes by which a community or social group, whether small or large, transmits its acquired power and aims with a view to securing its own continued existence and growth."

John Dewey in *Cyclopedia of Education*

National leaders, journalists, social scientists, individuals associated with special interest groups, and many others have long recognized the fundamental role of educational institutions in molding the basic competencies, understandings and social consciousness of youth. These individuals and groups, along with other forces, have had an important effect upon the development of school curricula. Their influence has often been greater in one period of time than at another, depending on political, social, and economic trends.

What are some of these forces which play a part in molding final decisions related to curricular matters? One of the strongest is *tradition*. Curricula based on tradition have stood the test of time; they apparently have been workable in the estimation of many. Teachers are already experienced with these courses of study; they feel secure with them. The word "tradition" often carries connotations of reverence, desirability, and stability.

Change with its many ramifications, intrudes upon all areas of life. Urbanization, mass transportation and mass media, automation, and other recent innovations have a wide national impact. Nevertheless, the continuing interest in preserving and protecting individuality and local autonomy makes it inevitable that regional and ethnic differences will continue to persist in many areas.

Mass media have tended to play a larger part in molding public opinion about education than in the past, if for no other reason than that they have become so ubiquitous. Some special interest groups, sensing the importance of this development, have become more militant in combating the influence of mass media on education. Political parties give attention to education in their campaigns. Parent-teacher and other lay groups have often made careful studies of curricula in order to make their voices heard above the clamor of competing interest groups.

Commercially produced learning materials exert an influence rather directly because they are used within instructional programs. These materials include texts and workbooks, programmed devices, films, filmstrips, tapes, recordings, newspapers, maps, charts, etc. The tendency is for this instructional material to perpetuate the existing curriculum because immense costs involved in production and time required for processing make it difficult to incorporate changes rapidly. Yet, authors and publishers are alert to trends; in fact, to retain a share of the market, it is essential that they be sensitive to and cognizant of important curricular modifications.

Contributions in the form of research and instructional aids emanate from *colleges and universities.* These institutions are influential, too, in determining the content of high school curricula because of the entrance requirements they establish. Academic and professional course offerings likewise exert a continuing effect on curricula in earlier phases of education. College faculty members often serve as consultants on curriculum committees. Universities frequently operate curriculum laboratories and serve as instigators of or resource people for curriculum projects. Closely related to the above are accrediting associations which dictate what is acceptable for particular types of certification.

Professional educational organizations are interested in curriculum decisions and generally formulate statements of their positions with regard to various aspects of curricular change. These recommendations may vary greatly, since organizational orientations and purposes are often quite different. While some are national in scope, others are local, subject-oriented, or related to specific types of learning programs (for example, programs for the deaf or orthopedically handicapped).

Agencies, foundations, and special interest organizations support and promote various aspects of curricular programs. Foundations underwrite projects in particular subject areas; they also grant scholarships and fund special training workshops. Government agencies have become increasingly influential in the specific areas in which they operate. The United States Office of Education, for example, serves as an advisory body. One of its functions is to provide publications, including those on recent curriculum developments. Certain other national organizations, such as the National Chamber of Commerce and the American Legion, often prepare materials which they distribute free of charge to schools and citizen groups.

Testing programs affect the content of the curriculum by their emphasis on particular facts, skills, and understandings in selected subject areas. This is particularly true if the tests are national in scope or are required for entrance to a school or college.

Parents, if they are actively engaged in school affairs, may make their desires known through the PTA or other specially organized community groups. When they are militant enough to join forces with other national or state organizations, their impact may be substantial.

A growing trend toward *specialized curriculum studies* has served to draw attention to this aspect of the educational program. By providing broad guidelines and recommendations, their efforts have aided in a better understanding of the process of curriculum construction as well as a clearer picture of the elements which make up its basic ingredients.

State legislatures and departments of education also grant funds and set up requirements for eligibility. Legislatures may, likewise, pass measures which have an indirect effect on curricular decisions. State departments of education issue guides in many curricular areas as well as standards for school certification.

Implementation of curriculum guides comes from *classroom teachers*. Thus, ultimately, it is the teacher who determines the day-to-day content. Additionally, classroom teachers often serve on curriculum committees. *Administrators, supervisors,* and *curriculum consultants* also have a very direct and immediate effect on the curriculum in their positions of leadership. Members of *boards of education* may serve on curriculum committees or receive reports from these committees. Since the Board of Education has control over most of the broad financial aspects of education, it is in a position to affect not only purchases of materials, but the granting or withholding of funds to finance curriculum research.

In the social studies area *social scientists* furnish most of the basic facts, ideas, concepts, generalizations, and topics for study. Results of social science research furnish a vast storehouse of information on which social studies curriculum workers may draw.

Their problem is one of abstracting, sorting, simplifying, and reorganizing information suitable for elementary children, then synthesizing these materials with the objectives of both the specialized field and the larger curriculum in mind.

Curriculum Planning has frequently been defined as the orderly study and improvement of the instructional program in the light of criteria provided by objectives. Unfortunately, objectives in social studies are often vague and usually much too numerous. In fact, researchers have found that their number runs into thousands, though there is a common core of objectives for each of several periods in the past.

Present trends appear to relate to the fomulation of objectives as well as to the nature of the objectives themselves. Trends in formulating objectives suggest:

1. More joint participation of many groups in determining objectives.
2. Increasing integration within the total school program.
3. Less theoretical and more functional orientations.
4. Shorter lists of objectives.
5. Statements of objectives expressed in behavioral terms.

Trends related to social studies objectives themselves indicate these (1) should be concerned with the individual and with society, (2) mirror the changing nature of the social sciences, (3) emphasize critical thinking, (4) show concern for skill development, (5) require greater teacher responsibility.

Criteria for improving the social studies curriculum were outlined by the Committee of the National Council for the Social Studies in 1962[1]. They suggest:

1. Emphasis on ideals and values of the American people.
2. Understanding of all peoples.
3. Attention to unsolved issues.
4. Provision for critical thinking.
5. Use of newest insights from each of the disciplines as well as new knowledge from interdisciplinary studies.
6. Rigorous selection when developing courses and units, with a focus on understanding of contemporary society.
7. Taking account of maturity levels of children.
8. Use of a wide range of learning experiences, materials, and media.
9. Insuring continuity and consistency in the program.
10. Providing each individual with the stimulus, skills, and familiarity with resources that will enable him to continue to learn independently.
11. Provision for carefully planned and evaluated experimentation.

Even though all the above-mentioned factors may play a significant role in the total process, the final decisions on curricula in each school area are left to the person or persons responsible for the school program. The local unit for making curricular decisions will normally involve the superintendent of schools, supervisors, teachers, and members of the board of education. It may also include parents, other lay people, and children. In larger school systems there may be an assistant superintendent in charge of curriculum or a curriculum director as well as department heads. Any or all of these many serve as members of a curriculum team. Lay members, however, should normally restrict their comments and suggestions to policy matters. The overall objectives of education are the responsibility of the public; the implementation of policy should be the responsibility of professional members of curricular study groups.

[1]Dorothy Fraser and Samuel McCutcheon, "Basic Considerations in Revising the Social Studies Curriculum," in John Gibson, ed.*New Frontiers in the Social Studies,* Vol 2, pp. 260-268.

The curriculum in small schools may encompass no more than plans written for the guidance of one class. In larger systems a curriculum is often outlined in a series of detailed curriculum guides, usually updated every few years. Later these may be supplemented by alternate or enriched programs. The written guides may be suggestive, mandatory, or merely supplementary. These guides frequently incorporate directives from the state level.

Ideas may take many forms. An idea comes to life only after it has found an appropriate mode of expression.

The tendency in curriculum construction is to involve a large number of people. This not only provides the benefits of several points of view, but also results in more general acceptance of the final product. Concurrent with this trend is another which aims at delineating, in so far as possible, the precise sphere within which any given segment of curriculum makers can and should operate, in order to avoid unnecessary duplication of effort.

Efforts of the National Committee of the Instructional Project have resulted in these guidelines:

1. Local school faculties should make decisions within state and local requirements.
2. Local school boards should operate with the leadership of the local superintendent. The responsibilities of board and superintendent should be clearly delineated and understood.
3. The state authorities should establish standards, provide resources, and furnish dynamic leadership.
4. The state legislature should set forth goals, provide financial support and delegate broad powers to state and local educational authorities.
5. The federal government should provide general financial assistance. The Office of Education should encourage and stimulate experimentation and innovation.

6. Efforts of nongovernmental groups related to experimentation and innovation should be encouraged. Scholars in academic and professional fields should be involved in the effort.
7. Promising findings of curriculum projects should be incorporated in the curriculum.
8. Time and money should be allocated by school systems for experimentation and innovation as well as staff participation in the evaluation and improvement of the program.

Using all of the resources at their disposal, committees are directing their efforts toward organizing content in social studies around a cohesive set of ideas, whether it be expanding horizons, cycles of content, in depth studies, or some other specific orientation. McAulay suggests:

" An examination of the newer courses of study for the social studies in elementary schools reveals a trend toward more complex content from a wider and more diffuse selection of sciences."[2]

After the content has been chosen, it is so structured that students grow in their ability to use key concepts in analyzing information, formulating hypotheses, relating ideas, and organizing data. The broad outlines established by the committee are often supplemented by a written curriculum guide which covers the area in more depth and which often contains many suggestions for implementing the program at various instructional levels. The teacher then further modifies the plan and adapts it to his particular teaching situation. With new disciplines and new strategies finding expression in the elementary social studies curriculum, today's elementary teacher must be increasingly imaginative, resourceful, and flexible. Weber and Haggerson echo the thoughts of many curricular workers when they suggest: "If emerging trends are at all indicative of future developments, the social studies curriculum of the future will be much different from what we have today."[3]

[2]J. D. McAulay, "Social Responsibility – A Modern Need of the Social Studies," *The Social Studies,* Vol. LVIII, No. 3, (March 1967), p. 120.

[3]Del Weber and Nelson L. Haggerson, "Broad Trends and Developments in the Social Studies Today." *The Social Sciences,* Vol. LVIII, No. 1, (January 1967), p. 6.

Chapter II

CURRENT ISSUES
IN THE SOCIAL STUDIES

Although the movement toward revitalization of the social studies was slow in gathering momentum, the current state of involvement promises exciting developments for the future. There is evidence that the pace of reform and change has increased perceptively in the past years. The dominant trends have their roots in past experimentation, but present exigencies have forced the incorporation of ideas and strategies into forms which are useful in educational programs. Reforms in science and mathematics curricula, the proliferation of social problems as the world continues on its course of rapid change, and new insights into behavior and learning have all combined to create challenges which the new social studies is confronting with a variety of fresh insights.

At present, reform tends to remain fragmented. An analysis of all aspects of the social studies is essential in discovering which elements are useful and necessary. While this concentration on narrow segments of the whole leads to greater knowledge of each part, it also produces specialization and segmentation. In attempting a synthesis of these diffuse factors, a communications gap has become evident, and, unfortunately, the proper place of the individual disciplines within the social studies continues to be an issue of major importance. Concomitant with the trend toward specialization is that of rigorous scientific method. Here the "hard-nosed" social scientists (those who choose to be allied with natural science) and the traditionalists come to a distinct parting of the ways regarding the fact-value syndrome. The "Hard-nosed" social scientist prefers to consider himself relatively value-free, while his humanistically-oriented colleague is concerned that scientific impartiality is a mask for indifference. Hence, integrating the diverse elements remains a problem of major proportions.

In any attempt to create a coherent program, the clarification of goals and objectives is a paramount issue. Shall the social studies concentrate primarily on creating good citizens or on developing knowledgeable students? Or can both of these goals be achieved within the time allotted to social studies in the elementary school? Some social science educators believe that the social studies cannot do both equally well; that an *informed* populace is essential to the development of citizens of the highest caliber. Others are convinced that it is not the responsibility of the social studies alone to develop citizens; that this should be undertaken in all curricular areas.

Objectives for the social studies often proliferate to such a degree that confusion over basic aims is rampant. The ranges of expectations are totally unrealistic. To clarify the scope of objectives and establish some broad bases for operation, it has been suggested that objectives be classified under three headings.

    1. Knowledge.
    2. Inquiry.
    3. Attitudes and Values[1]

---

[1]Edwin Fenton, *The New Social Studies.* New York: Holt, Rinehart and Winston, Inc., 1967.

Under these headings there would be ample opportunity for growth and change, yet provision would be made for a broad and complete social studies program. There would be unlimited possibilities for teacher experimentation and for contributions to a continuing improvement of the social studies program.

As social studies educators view the developments in their field, the reality of social change is one that persistently impinges on their planning. There is a continual duel between the realities and occurrences of the past and the emerging social and technological changes. One offers security and reasonable certainty; the other introduces doubts and confusions. Planning a program based on known factors is quite different from attempting to structure a course of study which incorporates changes whose impact cannot be fully assessed and whose duration in their present forms is unpredictable.

The explosion of knowledge adds another dimension to the structure of all disciplines. Those working in social studies, in common with other areas, must be alert to newer developments and prepared to incorporate promising innovations and insights. Recent research has produced evidence of the importance of attitude formation, individual value judgments, and group interactions in the acquisition of knowledge. Many of these findings are particularly applicable to social studies. Continued attention by scholars to the improvement of techniques in problem solving, critical thinking, and teaching strategies provides other new focuses of attention. The refinement of basic concepts and generalizations provides rather definite foundations upon which to build. The dilemma confronting practitioners is the synthesizing of all of these disparate elements into an integrated whole with sequence, continuity, and direction.

The curriculum, upon which most other issues in social studies ultimately converge, may be thought of as an issue of prime importance. For it is through the curriculum that the actual dissemination of information takes place. While the issues already mentioned indirectly affect the curriculum-making process, there are other matters with a more direct and immediate bearing on the composition of a social studies curriculum.

As a community is faced with the task of setting up a course of study, some immediate concerns must be resolved in order to proceed. Old teaching approaches are giving way to new models of organization. Some schools have retained their expanding environments design in social studies and simply added new components; others are focusing upon two or three disciplines at all levels with varying degrees of complexity. Fused programs, including concepts and generalizations from an ever wider group of disciplines, are also being initiated. Whatever type of program is chosen, the question of how many disciplines may be included and what areas of each discipline are suitable at any particular level must be resolved. Furthermore, a decision must be effected on the feasibility of a wide coverage of materials or a thorough, in-depth treatment. Planners need the courage to exclude the irrelevant and the wisdom and imagination to include a judicious selection of the emerging elements which were unnoticed or even unknown a generation ago.

As the social studies program is delineated, the problem of balance intrudes and requires judicious deliberation. The desirability of a differentiated curriculum for the various intellectual levels becomes apparent when one considers the growing complexity of social science offerings. Agreement on this aspect of the problem is fairly general; implementing it operationally becomes a difficult task. Also confronting the curriculum maker is the impact of outside forces of many kinds. Contributions of groups such as national committees, state departments of education, federal agencies, parents, spokes men for mass media and many others must be weighed in the balance and judged intelligently.

Another issue which looms very large relates to teachers — the preparation of teachers, in-service education, and involvement in the process of curriculum construction and evaluation. It is now generally conceded that the teacher is in a prime position to secure the success of any program. It is he who actually translates challenging material into a form which is understandable to the students. In recognition of his strategic situation, efforts are being expended toward improved training and planning. Concurrently, serious educators are attempting to discontinue the practice of assigning whatever teachers happen to be free at a particular period to the social studies class.

Social attitudes are fostered through group participation.

One of the primary focuses of attention in the improvement of teacher preparation is the methods professor. It is he who guides the single most important course for elementary social studies teachers. It is within his power to acquaint his students realistically with goals, objectives, criteria for content selection, materials, grouping, enrichment, and emerging trends. He can serve as a model of stimulating instructional practices. Only if methods courses and practice teaching experiences measure up to their promising potential is it possible to develop elementary social studies teachers who are able, enthusiastic, informed, and eager to teach social studies so that each elementary student is personally involved. The achievement of these objectives on the part of the methods professor has been hindered in some instances by limited informational resources. Many of the social sciences themselves are of very recent vintage and thus have not had time to mature and develop effective methods of inquiry. Nor have we always involved the scholars in these fields with a view to fostering promising avenues of inquiry. Thus, development in this area is an issue with crucial implications.

If we are fortunate enough to prepare our fledgling teachers adequately, we are still faced with the retraining of teachers who have not been exposed to recent methods and developments. Decisions must be effected relating to in-service training of the kind that may be most useful, the possible need for differentiated training for teachers in differing school environments, the length and duration of such re-education programs, and the need for observation of newer techniques in operation. To aid in the process of keeping abreast of developments, it may be desirable to develop reporting systems which will more adequately apprise teachers of ongoing research. Additionally, the involvement of classroom teachers in research projects may further facilitate educational progress in this area.

Teaching strategies which meet the challenges of new facts, ideas, insights, concepts, and generalizations are required if the social studies are to continue as a vital force in the educational program. Devising new methods and revising existent ones must be a continuous process. Sensitivity to barely perceptible alterations in social relationships requires ingenuity and dedication. The periodic resolution of these small issues results in gradual shifts in teacher strategies so that the classroom procedure does not become stagnant.

Publishers and their products constitute yet another area of concern. Traditionally, caution has pervaded the industry, and thus changes of any magnitude have been almost impossible to effect. The situation is presently compounded because of mergers with related educational materials suppliers. It is anticipated that in the future one complex will control an entire related set of educational materials including textbooks, maps, atlases, globes, films, filmstrips, tapes, records, and allied educational aids. Their potential for influencing the ongoing social studies program is obviously a factor of considerable importance. An issue closely related to this is that concerning the state adoption of textbooks. In the light of rapidly changing content, many believe that this custom inhibits skillful, imaginative, and resourceful teaching.

The changing structural organization of school buildings to meet educational developments has affected teaching patterns. Materials centers often offer possibilities for large-group instruction similar to those of the Stoddard plan. Team teaching offers other approaches to programming. In the elementary grades the benefits to be derived from subject specialists must be balanced against possible impersonalization and more limited teacher guidance. The stimulation gained from a meeting of many minds must be weighed against the matter of readiness to absorb new experiences.

Parent involvement in school situations also requires the attention of thoughtful social studies planners. If children are to participate in first-hand experiences such as trips, parent aid is generally considered desirable. The decisions relating to parental participation may be crucial to the success of the program. Encouraging parents to be responsible for some of these extended experiences may prove to be the difference between enthusiastic participants in social studies experiences and onlookers who do not become interested or involved. Informing parents and gaining their interest in innovations in the social studies field may aid in fostering better understanding and community support.

Increasingly, the social studies are becoming engulfed in the ever proliferating sphere of the mass media. Educating children to cope with the bombardment of stimuli from several sources is a serious task. Inventing teaching techniques to match the subtle sophistication of propaganda experts is another of the challenges facing social studies. Adapting or adopting some of the highly successful practices of the mass media may offer other fruitful avenues of development.

The issues confronting the social studies, then, are numerous and diverse. Their resolution offers challenges to both practitioners and scholars. The consequences of today's decisions will be of far-reaching significance.[2]

---

[2]A list of innovative social studies projects throughout the United States is included in the appendix, "A Directory of Social Studies Projects."

Chapter III

SEPARATE DISCIPLINES
WITHIN THE SOCIAL STUDIES

Social studies has, in the past, been considered as a collection of separate subjects. The specific subjects to which this collective term originally applied were history, government (political science), and geography. In the course of time sociology and economics were added. More recently anthropology, psychology, philosophy, and law have also been included. The tendency at present is to consider the social studies as a discipline in its own right, one which can synthesize the various elements of the separate components into a cohesive whole.[1]

What do we mean by a discipline? McCutcheon defines it as "a pattern of values which imposes a pattern of behavior on its diciples."[2] Thus, each of the areas named above possesses its particular pattern of values and behavior. This pattern in every instance is applied to content and results in organized, systematic frameworks. When each of the frameworks is analyzed and compared, the lines of demarcation between areas are found to be indistinct, for the basic foundations of research, scholarship, and critical assessment of materials are common to all.[3] While each may employ distinctive terms, its subject matter is not necessarily unique. Every discipline contains elements of each of the others to a greater or lesser degree. All are concerned with man and his relationships with his fellowmen.

In considering recent social studies programs in the elementary school, one notes a trend toward an interdisciplinary organization of programs. Curriculum guides tend to include materials from all the social sciences in a fused or integrated pattern, often with no reference to the separate disciplines. Concurrently, we find scholars reappraising and clarifying the concepts, generalizations, and unique contributions of each discipline.

If teachers are to conduct a fused or integrated program, they will need to be aware of the point of view from which each social science approaches man. Unless teachers have this basic training, they will lack the framework on which to build critical thinking and to evaluate learning.

In order to relate the basic concepts of each discipline to specific areas, three possible social studies topics will be considered: an Eskimo tribe, England, and Thailand. If any of the three areas were studied separately, several or all the generalizations would be encountered, depending on the scope of the unit. Since generalizations apply rather widely, they can often be identified and clarified within different cultural settings.[4]

---

[1]Samuel P. McCutcheon, "A Discipline for the Social Studies," *Readings for Social Studies in Elementary Education,* ed. John Jarolimek and Huber M. Walsh, New York: The Macmillan Company, 1965, p. 116.

[2]*Ibid.*

[3]John U. Michaellis and A. Montgomery Johnston, "The Social Sciences: Foundations of the Social Studies," *The Social Sciences,* ed. John U. Michaelis and A. Montgomery Johnston, Boston: Allyn and Bacon, Inc., 1965, p. 8.

[4]An extensive list of Social Science generalizations is provided in the appendix, "Major Generalizations Within the Social Studies."

Stressing generalizations does not eliminate the need for factual information. This would be acquired as a necessary condition of understanding the general statements. An increasing knowledge of factual data would enable the learner to interrelate the concepts within each discipline, as well as to make possible comparisons with other disciplines.

GEOGRAPHY

Geographers consider their area of concentration both an art and a science. As an art it presents descriptions and representations of regions of the world. As a science it furnishes us with concepts and theories of space relating the physical, cultural, and biological factors. Geography has a strong kinship with the physical sciences, particularly geology, but most geographers consider their field of study within the social sciences. Unless geographic concepts are handled judiciously, children are likely to develop the notion that geography is made up of long lists of exotic names used in identifying political regions, land forms, and bodies of water. Modern geographers, however, feel that the physical features of the earth are closely associated with attitudes, motivations, skills, and other aspects of man's culture. Lillian Stimson suggests that geography offers four rather distinct emphases:[5]

1. spatial references
2. area studies
3. man-land relationships
4. earth-science considerations

In the elementary social studies program spatial concepts are dealt with in learning directions and in using maps. Area studies are frequently used as the basis for the organization of the curriculum, as in studying the United States. The man-land tradition (ecology) is concerned with the way in which man uses his environment and is exemplified in a concern for resources and conservation. The earth-science tradition has received primary emphasis, especially in the elementary school. It deals with the earth, bodies of water, and earth-sun relations. Actually, these different aspects of geography are not taught as separate entities, but are usually interrelated.

Preston James suggests that

" by inserting the framework of geographic concepts into the social studies, much needed unity and coherence are provided. . . . The perspective of geography, added to that of history and to the concepts of human behavior, can bring the world into focus and illuminate the world ahead.[6]

One generalization relating to physical geography states: *the shape of the earth causes the unequal distribution of sunlight, which in turn influences circulation in the atmosphere and differentiates climate and natural vegetation into regional types.*

A consideration of the natural habitat of the Eskimo reveals that the distribution of sunlight has a profound effect on his working habits. Time available for hunting and fishing in winter is much shorter than at other times. The lack of sunshine is a contributing factor to the intense cold, which in turn requires a different kind of clothing and habits than would be necessary in a more temperate climate.

---

[5]Lillian W. Stimson, "Geography," John U. Michaelis and A. Montgomery Johnston, "The Social Sciences: Foundations of the Social Studies," *The Social Sciences,* ed. John U. Michaelis and A. Montgomery Johnston. Boston: Allyn and Bacon, Inc., 1965.

[6]Preston E. James, "Geography," *The Social Studies and The Social Sciences,* American Council of Learned Societies and the National Council for the Social Studies, New York: Harcourt, Brace & World, Inc., 1962.

England, being farther south than the homelands of the Eskimo, has somewhat longer days in winter. However, England's climate is an illustration of another of the generalizations: *climate is determined by sunlight, temperature, humidity, precipitation, atmospheric pressure, winds, unequal rates of heating and cooling of land and water surfaces, ocean currents, and mountain systems.* Warm ocean currents moderate the climate of England and make it more humid than other areas so far north.

Thailand, being farther south, has a more equal distribution of sunlight in the various seasons. This helps account for a more even temperature and a hotter climate. Thailand also illustrates another generalization: *major climatic regions coincide approximately with major vegetation zones because vegetation is related to climatic conditions.* The warm, moist climate is accompanied by luxuriant, tropical vegetation. This generalization could be applied equally well to Eskimo lands or to England.

A generalization relating to cultural geography states: *man constantly seeks to satisfy his needs for food, clothing, and shelter and his wants; in so doing he tries to adapt, shape, utilize, and exploit the earth to his own ends.* The Eskimo exploits his natural environment by hunting animals to provide food, clothing, shelter, and fuel. The natives of England and Thailand grow crops to provide food, cut wood for shelter, and raise animals and plants for food and clothing. In England and Thailand waterways have been altered and utilized to transfer commodities from one place to another.

Another contribution from cultural geography states: *man's utilization of natural resources is related to his desires and his level of technology.* In the Eskimo culture the technology level is not as advanced as that in England. Hence the Eskimo is generally satisfied to exploit only the animal resources, whereas a mining engineer from England might be more interested in exploiting the mineral deposits below the surface of the soil. Two sample units, "How Rivers Affect the Lives of People" and "Canada," have been included in this text. Both have a geographical orientation.

HISTORY

Whether we consider history as the panorama of the past or as a record of past events, we assume it has some relevance to the present, that it provides insights into the actions and decisions of humans, and that it provides a stabilizing force to counterbalance our rapidly changing world.

Historians state that history may be used as a base line in understanding the present; there are often useful precedents for deciding current problems. A caution should be observed in actually applying such a theory, however. Past happenings occurred in the context of situations which existed earlier, and final outcomes were dependent on total factors operating within each specific situation. Furthermore, it is not possible to be cognizant of all these diverse factors; thus an accurate analogy between any two events is not really possible. Yet broad guidelines for action may be drawn from situations having somewhat similar features.

History may contribute the broad backgrounds which serve both as the basis for understanding present institutions and for stimulating critical thinking. Reading history uncritically may provide the sequence of events leading to the establishment of modern institutions, but it cannot result in the reader's *understanding* of the evolution of any organization. For this he needs to be able to weigh the relative effects of the various happenings at each stage of development in the light of conditions prevailing at that time.

Projects add dimensions of understanding and frequently
help to clarify basic ideas.

History may contribute to an enlightened patroitism. Here the key word is *enlight-ened.* An enlightened patriot is sensitive to both the strengths and weaknesses of his nation. He is not blinded by the fanfare and flags which capture the hearts of zealots, but he does take pride in the basic achievements of his country. At times he serves as his government's loyal opposition, offering criticisms and suggesting alternate courses of action.

History may assist in fostering attitudes of tolerance and acceptance of others. It may furnish components on which to base value judgements. Thorough, critical reading from a wide variety of sources *may* help individuals achieve this goal. Evidence provided from many times and places often contributes to attitude formation and the development of value judgments. On the other hand, reading without involvement will not serve this end.

The reading of history may serve as a springboard to new ideas by extending and widening the horizons of the individual. This very general statement could well be applied to almost any of the social sciences. It is an idea worthy of consideration, for a continual replenishing and enlarging of ideas and concepts is necessary if the individual is to grow intellectually. The scope of history is immense and the horizons almost unlimited. History can help readers place current events in broader perspective. What may appear to be unique, especially tragic and threatening in the present, will often seem less severe, less traumatic in historical context. Every age has had its prophets of doom and gloom who would strip us of all hope, all dreams, all expectations of a better world.

One of the generalizations of history states: *the historical past influences the present. The present cannot be adequately understood without knowledge of the past. Life goes on against the intricate tapestry of the past.* England can undoubtly be cited as one of the best examples of this statement. The Magna Charta has influenced not only the granting of rights to all people in that country, but also the acquisition of rights in other countries.

We can see that Thailand illustrates this generalization by noting that centuries of development of art forms in temples, styles of native dress, and other matters continue to influence the Thai, even though he might be largely Westernized. It might be somewhat more difficult to understand the Eskimo customs were it not for the fact that minimum contact with the outside world left untouched the ways of living that previously were common to a wider degree in the world.

History also postulates: *space and time form a framework within which all events can be placed. All of man's experience has occurred within a space and time framework; however, the same relationship does not necessarily apply to events as they have occurred in various parts of the world.* This truth can be easily understood if we take a ten-year period in history as 1940-1950 and assess the happenings. If we were comparing developments within an Eskimo group, we might well find that much had happened in a particular group because an airstrip had been built nearby. In another ten-year period the changes would perhaps be less noticeable.

If one were to compare areas with one another, it might be found that an advanced civilization (such as England) was relatively static in a specific period whereas activity was heavy before or after. A civilization such as Thailand's might have temporarily passed a peak period of development and be in a resting stage.

History reveals a degree of homogeneity in mankind of all periods of recorded time. Environments in many places and regions have been altered physically, but human motives or drives within them have remained nearly the same. Whether one is referring to the flooding resulting from the thaws in the Artic or to a marauding tribe that nearly decimates a small group, the instinct for survival and for progress, however meager, remains intact. In a more highly civilized society the ravages of war, of tornadoes, and other catastrophes temporarily alter, but do not wipe out, human drives to rebuild. After the bombing in World War II, for example, the English repaired, restored, and rebuilt both the material and the spiritual evidences of their civilization.

Thai temples, like Egyptian pyramids, illustrate the historical generalization: *although certain historical customs and institutions have characterized individual civilizations or nations of the past, men in every age and place have made use of basic social functions in adjusting themselves to their world.* Yet the Netsilik Eskimos have also adjusted themselves to their world. In place of special symbols such as the temple and pyramid, they have used the basic institution of marriage as one method of adjustment by arranging for these ceremonies as social events of the long, monotonous winter season. The English perform a similar adjustment to winter by scheduling more shows and plays in London in the season when it is less congenial to engage in outdoor pursuits.

POLITICAL SCIENCE

Political science concerns political systems and the institutions of government. It does this from four viewpoints or perspectives.
1. Processes, behavior and institutions.
2. Relations among political systems.
3. Public policies.
4. Ideas and doctrines about government and the political system.

Political science, dealing primarily with the contemporary world of human activity, necessarily involves important value questions. Although history may delineate the development of political institutions, political science deals with a critical understanding of them. In comparative government the student is permitted a clearer view of his government by checking its salient points against those of other governmental systems. Political parties, another of the topics dealt with in political science, requires decisions on the merits (or values) of political points of view and the ability to compare party positions on continuing social issues.

Law is still another area of political science. Children in elementary schools become familiar with this aspect of human activity early in their lives through rules and regulations. In applying these rules, values are developed about fair play, respect for the rights of others, self-discipline, leadership, and group action. As children study groups of people, they learn that a system of prescribing law and order is necessary.

From the standpoint of the elementary child, political science may be thought of as having a concern with citizenship, voting, and government. Yet, one of the generalizations relating to government states: *government is but one of the institutions serving society. The state or government is essential to civilization and yet it cannot do the whole job by itself. Many human needs can best be met by the home, the church, the press, and private business.*

While a society such as England's has need of a complicated system of government, its best efforts come to naught without the support of home, church and press. Although the monarchies in both England and Thailand are generally treated with respect, the king and queen are too far removed from the daily life of the individual to be very helpful. While the government to a large extent consists of unwritten laws among Eskimo tribes, it still constitutes a reasonably effective form of management. Here the home is of paramount importance.

Another generalization in political science states: *two essential functions of government are to serve and to regulate in the public interest. The ultimate responsibilities of government fall into five big fields: (1) external security; (2) internal order; (3) justice; (4) services essential to the general welfare; and (5) freedom (under democracy).* Governments like those of England and Thailand provide armies for external security, a police force for internal security, a judiciary for justice, and various special agencies for welfare. In England the welfare system is more paternal and extensive than it is in Thailand.

In cultures such as that of the Eskimo, all men are obligated to be a part of the external security. Internal order is a responsibility of the family and internal tensions are often worked out through ceremonial dances. Welfare is an extension of family responsibilities.

That the decisions, policies, and laws of a given society are based on the traditions, beliefs, and values of that society is another political science generalization. Tradition has decreed that Thailand and England shall have a modified monarchial form of government rather than an elected head. At the same time the policies and laws reflect the needs and interests of the people. In a like manner, the able tribal elders of the Eskimos provide for those under their charge in a way consistent with their own value system.

ECONOMICS

"Economics deals with that aspect of human behavior which has to do with individual and group activity related to the production, exchange, and consumption of goods and services i.e. making a living."[7]

[7]Ronald H. Wolf, "Economics," *The Social Sciences, op. cit.*

It is commonly divided into micro economics and macro economics. The first deals with the individual business and with specific product prices. The latter is concerned with total output and total price level. Each may be national or international in scope.

In the school, the study of economics contributes to an understanding of the economic problems of society and the economic processes with which each of us deals. The central and most important economic problem according to Lewis is, "How shall we use our limited resources in the light of our unlimited desires?"[8] All other problems stem from this central one at particular times and under particular conditions.

In carrying out the role mentioned above three questions are central to the task. These may be enumerated as follows:

1. *What* shall we produce with our material and human resources?
2. *How much* can we produce and how fast should the economy grow?
3. *Who* shall get the goods and services produced?
4. *How* can we bring disadvantaged subclasses into the main stream of our economy?

The three questions *what, how much,* and *who* are the focal points of any economic system. The answers should lead to the goal of economics, i.e. the establishment of an economic order which maximizes the satisfaction of human needs.

An important generalization in economics states: *productive resources are scarce and human wants unlimited. Since man cannot satisfy all of his desires, he must make choices.* In an Eskimo economy the range of choices is not as wide as those in England or Thailand. However, choices must be made. For example, if meat is in short supply, it may be necessary to forego the convenience of dogs to pull sleds in order to avoid human starvation. In England land is not available for unlimited agricultural production and therefore must be used "economically." Another generalization asserts: *the economy of a country is related to (1) natural resources, (2) quality and availability of the working population, (3) capital for investment, (4) organizing skill of managers, and (5) the existence of a free trade area.* In polar regions the natural resources are sometimes available but difficult to exploit; the working population is often not sufficient for a division of labor; the capital, organizing skill, and trade area are not sufficient for an expanded economy. Thailand possesses natural resources; she has normally suffered from an insufficient supply of qualified technical workers and capital; trade areas have sometimes been cut off by war.

England does not contain all the necessary resources but does have the necessary transportation facilities to obtain them. For centuries she also held widely scattered colonies which provided raw materials. In each of the other areas she has been in a favorable position to excel. Hence her economy has been more advanced, yet the loss of her colonies and her inability to enter the closest trade area (the European Common Market) as a full partner has had a depressing effect upon her economy.

SOCIOLOGY

Sociology may be defined as the study of society or social systems. These systems are composed of:

1. Small voluntary and often short-lived groups as gangs, clubs, associations, etc.
2. Larger, more permanent groups as a family, school or industry.
3. Stratified groups, such as classes and castes.

[8]Ben W. Lewis, "Economics," *The Social Studies and the Social Sciences, op. cit.*

Sociology studies value systems and interactions as well as group environmental factors involving rural or urban populations.

Sociological processes afford another focus of attention, *social conflict,* whether within the family, in the business world, or in the political sphere. Social problems, too, fall within the realm of sociology. It is a highly fluent field, but has been involved with certain long-standing problems such as crime and delinquency, mental health, and minority-group relations. Social change is a major element of recent concern. It is based on changing patterns of life and problems relating to these changes. It often results in a serious social lag represented by institutions no longer adequate to meet the demands of modern society.

Sociology at the elementary level may contribute to an individual's understanding of his role in society and the larger social context within which he functions. It will aid in his understanding of complex social institutions and acquaint him with various facets of his culture.

A well-known generalization from sociology states that *the family is the basic social unit in the culture and the source of fundamental learnings.* In much of the Eskimo culture the family is virtually the only source of learning. However, one needs to recognize that "family" in this culture refers to an extended family. In Thailand this is also true in some areas. However, in crowded living sections, learning may not be confined to the family. In highly industrialized areas, such as those in England, the family is composed of a husband, wife, and children. Often the mother works outside the home. In this case many of the fundamental learnings are provided by other persons or agencies within the community.

All societies develop a system of norms, values, and sanctions, and set up a definition of roles. To this general statement could be added the fact that these role delineations, norms, values, and sanctions are different, even if only in subtle details, in each society and at various times in the same society. The role or roles taken by an adult male in each of the three societies discussed in this chapter will be widely divergent. Values and norms usually show a more rapid change in urban, industrial societies than in rural farming or hunting groups.

Two sample units, "How the People of the World Remember" and "Progress in Understanding Each Other," are included in this book. Both draw upon sociological generalizations.

ANTHROPOLOGY

A frequently quoted definition of anthropology is that it is "The study of man and his works."[9] Anthropology may, like some of the other social sciences, also be considered a biological science or a facet of the humanities. Its main branches include physical and cultural anthropology. Linguistics, ethnology, and archaeology are subsumed under cultural anthropology.

Anthropology attempts an understanding of man in the biological sense and in his adaptations to his environment. Generally these adaptations, including man's *views* of his environment are labeled "culture." While there is not much agreement on a definition of this term, some underlying presumptions about culture are accepted by most anthropologists. In general they would agree that culture is unique to man, learned rather than inherited, and an integrated system of behavior.

[9]Clyde Cluckhohn, *Mirror for Man.* New York: McGraw-Hill Book Co., Inc., 1949.

In elementary social studies the cultural branch of anthropology appears to be most useful. Cross-cultural studies provide insights into ways of behaving and models of various methods of solving human problems. Linguistic studies of anthropology have contributed insights into improved reading materials in the elementary school. Archaeology has made the study of other cultures come "alive" by providing actual models of their artifacts.

One of the generalizations of anthropology states: *the culture under which a person is reared exerts a powerful influence on him throughout life.* Another related generalization adds: *culture may be altered by human activities; norms are derived historically but are dynamic and thus may be changed.* In a relatively simple society like that of the Eskimo, there is unlikely to be planned change from within. However, change often comes about through the infiltration of the white man and his modern "conveniences." In highly developed societies as Thailand and England, technological change constantly modifies aspects of the culture.

Another related generalization states that *a major problem in the modern world is to discover ways in which social groups and nations with divergent cultures can co-operate for the welfare of mankind, and yet maintain respect for one another's cultural patterns.* Difficulties in cooperation might be evident between Eskimo ways of life and highly industrial nations because of the speed and mechanization of the latter. Highly developed nations are often impatient with other ways of life and much too eager to force their own ways on others.

An intermediate grade unit, "How We Learn About Early Man," may be found in the latter part of this book.

PSYCHOLOGY

From the standpoint of elementary social studies, psychology may be regarded as a field in which understanding of behavior is of prime concern. In one form or another it is relevant to all topics studied in social studies. Children are interested in many facets of behavior, and are immediately involved in behavioral understandings. Children are fascinated by personality and the forces that shape it. Simple understandings in this area are entirely possible. Toward the close of this book is a sample unit for early primary children entitled, "Learning to Know Yourself."

Learning theory is a major area of psychology. While this cannot be incorporated in elementary social studies as content; nevertheless the contributions of learning theory are invaluable in improving the presentation of the elementary curriculum and in providing clues to human motivation.

One pertinent generalization in psychology states that *human behavior is purposive and goal-directed. The individual may not always be aware of the basic purposes and needs influencing his behavior.* Psychology attempts to bring about a better awareness of reasons for behavior. Whether the human need is basic, such as slaughtering animals to secure food and clothing; or more complicated, such as attending a play for entertainment (with perhaps a hidden desire for identification) it is goal-directed. Psychology may help the individual partially understand his basic drives and motivations. An advanced or complicated society is not the only one that may be concerned with these underlying drives. The Eskimo, in his war dance, not only seeks to entertain; he may also be expressing aggression in a form that is recognized and socially accepted.

Another generalization of psychology states: *socialization processes such as child-rearing differ markedly in different groups. Personality structure and behavior are markedly influenced by these practices.* In an uncomplicated culture child-rearing is likely

We know now that simple exposures to stimuli are not enough;
children also need help with interpretations.

to be more consistent because the mother often has a closer association with the child. She is less likely to seek employment away from the home.

While it is difficult to state precisely how much emphasis should be placed on each discipline in an integrated program, there are some guidelines. In recent projects involving several disciplines, history and cultural geography appear to receive considerable emphasis, with cultural geography pre-dominant at the elementary school. Lesser attention is being given to political science, economics, sociology, and anthropology, but these are, nevertheless, an important part of many units.

The scope of the social studies program is obviously narrowed for the elementary grades. The concepts which form a part of the program are taught as related understandings. Thus the elementary child does not view social studies as a collection of related disciplines, but as a unified means of learning about his world.

SUMMARY

To demonstrate the interrelationship of the various social sciences, we may start with a single generalization from one discipline and note its associations with other disciplines.

economics	1. People have wants.
geography	2. These wants are related to the climate and topography of the region in which they live.
political science	3. As individuals attempt to satisfy their wants, they sometimes exploit others, and regulations or laws (child labor laws, for example) are developed.
sociology	4. As specific economic and subcultural groups (members of trade unions or the American Indians, for example) attempt to satisfy their wants, intergroup conflicts often develop.
anthropology	5. These ways of conducting group activities depend on patterned behavior (culture).
history	6. They also depend on tradition and previous experiences with similar problems.
psychology	7. The behavior of each individual in satisfying his wants is the product of his own personality.

A study of a particular country might include:
1. The geographic conditions,
2. The major historic events or highlights.
3. The economic patterns.
4. The political setting.
5. The culture within which the events take place.

The interrelationships of the social sciences are such that a reasonably comprehensive view of any particular segment of the world is certain to touch on several different disciplines.

Chapter IV

AN OVERVIEW OF SOCIAL STUDIES EXPERIENCES

Social scientists and social studies teachers differ widely in their views concerning the responsibilities they should or will accept in regard to pupil experiences. Arch conservatives believe that the social studies teacher's responsibility may be properly restricted to the presentation and analysis of fundamental information. Many reconstructionists, on the other hand, suggest that we should not only provide information, but encourage changes in individual and group behavior with a view toward modifying or reconstructing the social order. The classification, structure, and measurement of individual behavioral change is described in Krathwohl and Bloom's *Taxonomy of Education Objectives: Cognitive and Affective Domains.*[1] Individual pupil responses may range from a very simple awareness of a controversial issue to a strong and persistent conviction and commitment about any number of social problems.[2]

The elementary social studies teacher must make some basic decisions regarding the types of outcomes he hopes to realize through his teaching, for the long-range objectives he establishes in social studies will determine to a large degree the methods and approaches he will use in his teaching. Unfortunately, many teachers persist in deluding themselves in this important area of personal choice. They insist that they are building character or developing critical thinking through programs which are essentially teacher dominated and doctrinal in nature. Very elaborate analyses of social studies programs with anticipated outcomes may be found in text books and professional journals. For purposes of clarity and utility, however, virtually all of these may be grouped within four general classifications which are basically cumulative in nature. Each catagory tends to add a new dimension to the preceding one.

A. Category I - Programs primarily concerned with providing information about the people of the world, their historical legacies, differing environments, and basic activities.

B. Category II - Programs which emphasize, in addition to basic information, an understanding of continuing economic, social, and political issues and the factors which give rise to differences among people.

C. Category III - Programs which attempt to analyze a variety of cultural patterns and social issues and contrast these with persistent American customs and beliefs, providing a continuing reassessment of our own way of life.

D. Category IV - Programs which stress not only an understanding of others and ourselves but also the development of personal convictions and a willingness to grapple with social issues in action-oriented experiments and projects.

---

[1] Benjamin Bloom, et al *Taxonomy of Educational Objective, Cognitive Domain* New York: Longmans Green, 1956 and David Krathwohl et al, *Taxonomy of Educational Objectives,* Affective Domain New York: David McKay Co., 1964.

[2] An interesting summary of children's political attitudes may be found in Hess' and Torney's book, *The Development of Political Attitudes in Children,* New York: Doubleday, 1969, 331 pages.

If we could ignore the present structure and organization of school programs, the expectations of parents, and the wide variety of demands placed upon the teacher's time, we might step quietly into the fourth category and develop highly imaginative programs in elementary social studies. These might very well involve wide travel and focus upon a multitude of exciting first-hand experiences. They would likely include experiences with contrasting ethnic groups or subcultures, an acquaintance with a variety of natural environments and a first-hand look at some of our most sensitive social problems. Let us hope that in the very near future we will see many of these kinds of experiences become a natural and integral part of the social studies curriculum. For the present, however, most of us will need to settle for less than this. Time and budget considerations alone will preclude many of our most imaginative ventures.

There is, fortunately, a second world of excitement and adventure that is frequently overlooked. It is a world complete with characters and color, contrasts and conflict, convention and comedy. It is a world which offers us the real voices of real people, the authentic accounts of treasured events and candid glimpses into the lives of people everywhere. It is an exciting world that allows us to try life on for size. It is the world of pictures and stories, filmstrips and tapes, models and recordings that go together to make up the well-planned elementary library or materials center.

While one fourth grade teacher is ushering his children through pages 43-60 of the social studies text studying the principal regions of China with their products and population centers, another more imaginative colleague may be introducing his charges to the tragedies and triumphs of these same people - their foods and festivals, conquests and conflicts, legends and drama, music and art, discoveries and disillusionments. He may use forty or fifty books of various kinds (authentic fiction and non-fiction), a half dozen films, two or three recordings, atlases, charts, wall maps, and flat pictures as well as resource persons within his own or neighboring communities. It is not difficult to see that the more imaginative teacher is likely to have a much more enthusiastic response from children as well as a deeper and more thorough study of China.

THE INFLUENCE OF BOOKS UPON CHILDREN'S BELIEFS AND VALUES

Teachers who make wide use of library materials should not expect to fulfill all their dreams through carefully selected resources. We have come to recognize both the values and limitations of books. In the past we felt secure in our belief that good books with convincing ideas could do as much to change attitudes and beliefs as any other activity we might devise. Plato suggested that the reading of books had some effects upon character, and Napoleon tried to mold his own thinking by burying his thoughts, indeed his whole consciousness, in a literary study of Caesar's life. Books of many kinds were used by Germany and Russia for purposes of indoctrination. Relying heavily upon instructional materials, on biographies, picture books, primers and readers, the Russians and Germans developed in their youth a fanatical commitment to a way of life. Earlier, on this side of the Atlantic, the *McGuffey Eclectic Readers and Blue Back Spellers* attempted a somewhat more humane transformation. They helped to remind young readers of the wages of sin and wickedness. These books enjoyed almost universal acceptance in the United States between 1836- and 1900.

Several large-scale projects have also attempted to relate books to personal value change. In 1947 the University of Chicago Reading Conference focused its attention on "Promoting Personal and Social Development Through Reading." The published report included a book list, *Reading Ladders for Human Relations,* which was revised and expanded in 1955 and again in 1966. In 1957 the American Association of Colleges for Teacher Education commissioned Mate Gray Hunt to write the *Values Resource Guide,* an annotated listing of books, films, pictures, plays, poems and recordings related to particular aspects of character development and morality. Some character education programs have relied heavily upon these kinds of materials. The Detroit Citizenship Project utilized a variety of readings and controlled discussions, and the Louisville Public School's transition from segregated to integrated schools was initiated with the distribution of books on Negro culture and life. Some book companies have also issued new readers which stress moral concepts. Ullin Leavell has compiled the *Golden Rule Series* and the *Modern McGuffey Readers.* Neither has been widely adopted in public schools to date.

Stories can reinforce social attitudes.

As yet we have not been able to clearly determine the impact of books and other materials upon personal value formation. After a review of many such studies, Gray ("The Social Effects of Reading," *School Review,* LV, 1957) concludes that reading can and does influence the understandings, attitudes, interests, beliefs, morals, judgments and actions of readers. He states, however, that there is some doubt that books can give anything to a reader that is not already present in some measure. Books may, however, contribute to a complex of forces and factors which do build values and influence behavior. They, along with other types of learning materials, not only add appreciably to the breadth and depth of almost any study, but also afford a welcome change of pace and variety. They help to break the lockstep of chapter by chapter assignments and extend the scope of investigations within the social studies to a point where individuals and small groups must pursue parts of the study on their own.

If we cannot at present physically transport our elementary pupils to exotic lands, we can at least make use of the sensitive stories and acounts of those who have been there. If we cannot descend the dirty mine shafts to mingle with the miners or feel the reflected heat of glowing ingots being transformed into mile-long threads of steel, we can at least traverse the endless tunnels and giant founderies through the magic of films and recordings. Today's teacher has the world at her fingertips. Both the quantity and quality of library enrichment materials have exceeded the grandest imaginations of our early pioneers in library science. Almost a half million new titles are appearing each year, and many of these are suitable for children.

IMPORTANT CONSIDERATIONS IN THE PLANNING OF SOCIAL STUDIES UNITS

There is an old saying which suggests that nothing is certain but death and taxes. In our own lifetime we are finding that even the boundaries of death are being pushed back, and the tax structure moves like a sensitive cardiograph reflecting the pulsations and moods of our dynamic but fluid national economy. Statements of fact which are accepted today become obsolete tomorrow. New nations come into being almost overnight, and regions which were completely unexplored and unknown yesterday may be laid bare and analyzed in the course of a few short months through the use of aerial photography. Change is constantly nipping at our heels.

Social scientists have had to devise new approaches to accommodate accelerations in change which have become increasingly complicated by man's own inventiveness. In social studies, we are attempting to meet the challenge of change through a new and insistent emphasis upon problem-solving techniques and the use of basic generalizations - approaches which cut across the barriers of time and culture.

PROBLEM-SOLVING TECHNIQUES

The importance of problem-solving and its fundamental relationship to widely varying modes of inquiry have been recognized and at least partially understood by scholars since the time of the early ancients; but teachers have continued to view it myoptically. We appear to recognize its importance to some types of learning activities and not others. All of us, for example, seem to accept the fact that children can learn to swim only by getting into the water and having an opportunity to try out and perfect new strokes. We would need to search a long time to find an aquatic director who would be willing to conduct an instructional program without a swimming pool or water front. Yet many of us appear to believe that we can help children learn how to handle problems in social studies without any genuine, first-hand experiences in problem-solving. Far too many of us view planning, decision-making, evaluational procedures and other kinds of judgmental functions as a specific type of information an individual may possess rather than as a process, like swimming or drawing or reading, which he can learn only through personal experience.

Problem-solving involves a series of fairly complicated steps, and the basic nature of the problem-solving process itself appears to be somewhat different within the various disciplines. Problem-solving in music and art bears only a partial resemblance to problem-solving in geology and physics. The ground rules for verifying and substantiating information in the two areas of physical science and aesthetics are quite different. The social studies relate to both these areas, for they embrace the whole of human experience. They seldom approach the precision of physics, yet they enjoy a firmer base in the world of systematic inquiry than art or music, which appear to be more closely related to changing human preferences.

Problem-solving in elementary social studies will ordinarily involve six or seven steps: (a) identifying the problem; (b) clarifying the problem; (c) collecting data relevant to the problem; (d) analyzing and organizing the data collected; (e) determining possible solutions; and (f) evaluating the solutions which appear to hold most promise. Where possible, students may also implement the solutions they have formulated.

The first problem facing any class studying a country or a geographical region is frequently the task of sketching the broad outlines of possible approaches to the subject. This is not easily accomplished, for the children are, in essence, attempting to analyze a general topic with which they have little or no familiarity. How can a fifth grader propose interesting projects and sub-topics to be pursued in a small group study of the United Kingdom; for example, when he has never heard of this region before? His dictionary may point out that the United Kingdom is made up of Great Britain and Northern Ireland. An Atlas may help to clarify the problem further by showing the political subdivisions of England, Scotland, Wales, and Northern Ireland. He may also notice the names of a few cities which are vaguely familiar. The encyclopedia will give him a brief historical sketch of the region with statistics and commentary on terrain and climate, principal industries, government, population centers, etc. Gradually he and the members of his committee will extend their search to include the more intimate and interesting books on travel and geography.

Highly personalized and beautifully illustrated accounts of contemporary Britain, like *My Village in England* or *The Key to London,* will provide the loom upon which these children will eventually weave their own interpretations of English life. They will need to carefully weigh and sift the information for topics which are keys to understanding and genuinely representative of English political, social, and economic life. They will have to decide how much ought to be said about Stonehenge and Shakespeare, Tower Bridge and textiles, Windsor Castle and woolen mills, Coventry and the Commons. Once they have chosen topics, the teacher or librarian may help members of the committee locate some of the more subtle sources of detailed information. Those interested in ship building and shipping may find *Birth of A Liner* by Buehr exceptionally useful. Those with an interest in rulers and government may discover valuable accounts of British soverigns in *Kings and Queens* by Farjeon. *The Story of Weaving* by Lamprey may appeal to those in the group who are attempting to piece together a picture of British industry.

Two or three members of the group may prefer the kilts and customs of Scotland to the heather and hamlets of England. In addition to basic sources, they may find *Scotland* by Brodlie, *The Young Traveler in Scotland* by Finlay and *The Land and People of Scotland* by Buchanan of special interest. Again, however, the teacher or librarian may need to help with the more obscure sources where Scotland is not mentioned in the title. *Singing Streets,* for example, offered by the British Information Services, is a delightful kaleidoscope of Scotish tunes which may be easily overlooked.

Piercing together the fascinating facts about a great nation can be a memorable experience, an exhilarating kind of treasure hunt. There is, first of all, that vague, haunting feeling that, maybe, we picked the wrong topic. Maybe there is nothing in the library on your subject! Then comes the excitement of finding the first book with references to people and places that can be pursued beyond the edges of its own covers. There is a little bit of each of us in our own discoveries. We know it was there for anybody to find, but *we* were the ones that found it; it is *our* information, *our* contribution to the study underway. Then there is the fun of putting it together, the puzzling, but intriguing game of fashioning a vivid picture which represents our own feelings about the subject in the special ways we want to say it.

Far too many children miss out on the fun of problem-solving, and there are good reasons for it. Sometimes the topics or questions are poorly chosen, as was the case with one forlorn little fellow who was trying to find out who founded India. Each child had been given a country and a list of questions. The teacher, unfortunately, had not checked to see whether the questions were appropriate for each nation represented on the list. Often the teacher and the children give up before either has gained enough proficiency and confidence to see the project through to a successful conclusion. It takes a great deal of patience and persistence as well as encouragement and effort to complete the first project. Succeeding projects, however, become easier as the rough edges of basic skills and understandings are smoothed out. Teachers and children don't make as many mistakes the second and third time around. It is not unlike trying to learn a new song. When a person doesn't know how the tune goes, it is hard to follow the melody. But children do learn new songs, and teachers and pupils can also learn new ways of solving problems!

There ought to be something very special about the first project. It should be a relatively simple investigation, it should be something the children really want to study, it ought to be planned cooperatively, and it should culminate in an exciting activity - a play, tape recording, or other type of presentation which will give additional meaning to the study. Those children who are not capable of independent study should work rather closely with the teacher. There is a readiness for independent work just as there is a readiness for reading and writing. Not all children are ready for independent work at the same time. The teacher may also wish to provide a class progress chart to plot the step by step achievements of each group as they move toward the completion of their chosen assignment. Many teachers attempt to pair the weaker students with the stronger ones so that a committee of poor students doesn't get bogged down. It is wise to provide resource materials with specific page references for the first project and meet with the small groups everyday for a few minutes at the beginning and end of the study period to make certain that confusion is held to a minimum. It is usually necessary to give groups specific help and suggestions in how to organize their work and prepare it in a form suitable for presentation to the class.

If a textbook is available, it should not be ignored. The textbook can be used as a point of departure in the early stages of a new unit to help children gain an overview of the topic under discussion and establish a common background of basic information. Textbooks, however, are highly condensed and are written with the thought that teachers will supplement and enrich the study through the use of other materials. The textbook should not become the social studies curriculum. Far too many teachers who feel they must "cover the book" end up killing all interest and enthusiasm for the subject.

HELPING CHILDREN CONSTRUCT
VALID GENERALIZATIONS IN SOCIAL STUDIES

Recent medical studies of prenatal development indicate that a child can hear even before he is born. He very quickly begins to attach meanings to the many varied activities and objects which make up his environment. He develops his own ideas about which things are pleasant and interesting and which are threatening and displeasing. By the time he is five years old, he has developed a great many concepts about people and ways of behavior, objects and their uses, as well as abstractions and their meanings. He has also related concepts one to another and constructed generalizations which often take the form of rules or basic principles of operation. Many of his generalizations are inaccurate or incomplete because of his limited experiences and his imprecise methods of checking and validating evidence. The child is not unlike the adult in his need for certainty. He wants to straighten up the furnishings of his mind and sweep out the frustrating cobwebs of ambiguity as quickly as possible. In an attempt to achieve some degree of self-assurance, he frequently jumps to conclusions which are completely unwarranted. He concludes that Turks are bad people because he once read a story about a Turk who was selfish and mean. He decides that Florida and states near Florida are not very nice after spending a rainy vacation at Key West.

Individuals or groups attempting to construct valid generalizations must know how to identify and interpret key ideas; they must know how to establish criteria for use in making judgments; and they must know how to weigh evidence carefully and objectively. Above all, they must be able to identify or trace relationships between and among ideas. Every great thought that has ever entered into the conscious mind of man has involved relationships of one kind or another. These have been the indispensable keys to man's understanding. In social studies the basic generalizations often concern interrelationships between man and his environment; reciprocal factors involved in particular political, social, or economic principles and their applications; and relationships between ethical ideals or beliefs and particular social conditions.

The social studies teacher who wishes to help children develop and use basic generalizations must emphasize and reward clear thinking and logical reasoning wherever possible. He will not only sensitize his children to the elementary factors in each social issue, but he will also urge them to seek out clues, make judgments, and test their decisions in give and take discussions. He will often ask children to provide evidence in support of their conclusions, compare contrasting or similar situations, identify causes and outcomes, or decide between two or more courses of action which might be followed. He may ask children to describe the major characteristics of a particular group of people, outline the steps that might be followed in carrying out a program, or make judgments about the wisdom and justice of acts initiated by world leaders. In each case he is helping pupils sort out key ideas which may be combined into valid generalizations.[2]

A fourth grade class was recently trying to decide which of our two presidents, Theodore Roosevelt or Franklin Roosevelt, was the greater. The teacher decided rather early in the discussion that the class would not get very far until they agreed upon a few factors which they thought contributed to greatness. Without any agreed upon rule of measure they could not begin to reach a conclusion. Through this one suggestion the teacher not only clarified the issue and helped children see the importance of using criteria in making judgments, but also encouraged the class to develop an operational generalization concerning greatness. Their beliefs about greatness will change as they mature, but their beliefs about themselves and their ability to make sound judgments will hopefully grow with each new experience.

---

[2]A brief study of fourth grade children's attempts to identify Social Studies generalizations is included in the appendix of this book, "Experimental Study to Determine the Percentage of Fourth Grade Children Who Are Capable of Identifying Generalizations."

Chapter V

DIMENSIONS OF THE
SOCIAL STUDIES TEACHER'S TASK

The American teacher does not enjoy the certainty of established educational patterns and relatively firm social traditions found in many parts of the world. Ours is an open society, for the most part, and American education, with all its strengths and weaknesses, represents one of the broadest and boldest social experiments of all time. Our educational system is marked by universality, mobility, and diversity. Since the early dawn of struggling settlements and uncertain nationhood, Americans have championed and cherished education as an open door to the good society. Their triumphant faith in learning and educational opportunity has been severely tested through war and reconstruction, immigration and civil strife, industrialization and economic disaster. Never has so much been required of a single institution. Even today, as each new challenge rises to public view, Americans turn to the educational institutions of the nation with the same expectations that transformed their earlier visions. Whether the problem is one of social disorganization, economic privation, or technological transition, education is seen as the major instrument of remediation, rectification, and hope.

It is not difficult to see that the social studies teacher's responsibility to the nation is a major one. The typing teacher may be primarily concerned with the refinement of specialized motor skills, and the music appreciation teacher may be principally interested in the development of aesthetic appreciations. But the social studies teacher must be vitally involved in the development of a whole galaxy of attitudes, skills, and understandings, for his domain of study encompasses virtually the entire spectrum of human social experiences.

The social studies teacher must have a keen sense of *purpose*, unusual *resourcefulness* in dealing with the great range of materials available to him, and *sensitivity* to children who have the difficult task of finding some semblance of meaning in a world of contradictions. The effective teacher is frequently one who is actively seeking personal enrichment through the lives of his children. Their triumphs are *his* triumphs, and their failures represent *his* dreams unfulfilled. A sense of purpose, resourcefulness, and sensitivity, however, are not the exclusive properties of effective teachers; good parents may have these same attributes. What differentiates good teachers from good parents is their ability to provide stimulating intellectual experiences for large groups of children. This is an enormous task, for children differ widely in background, in their interests, temperaments, and abilities; and the resources available to teachers in some communities are very limited.

The highly effective social studies teacher is usually an imaginative, creative individual who is reasonably well-informed in the basic disciplines upon which the social studies rest - history, geography, philosophy, sociology, anthropology, political science, social psychology, and economics. In planning his program he does not rely on children's interests alone, for children's interests are closely bound to the present and are often short-lived, diffuse, and fluid. But he does capitalize on pupil interests when they offer a real potential for learning and growth. Interests often need to be crystalized and expanded before they can assume importance and relevance. As interests are expressed, the creative teacher often explores with the class the likely consequences of possible learning experiences, their uses, and the personal gains which may be derived from them.

The successful social studies teacher recognizes that his role as planner and director or helper and sympathetic listener rests to a large degree on the nature of the activities pursued. He must make important decisions about (1) the extent to which goals have been established and clarified with students, (2) the ability levels represented in the learning group, and (3) the kinds of outcomes desired. Studies conducted by Flanders,[1] Calvin, Hoffman and Harden,[2] and Maier[3] suggest that where goals are unclear and, perhaps, unaccepted, or students are of limited ability, a large amount of structure and direction may be appropriate. Bright students with clear goals, on the other hand, often benefit from permissive learning environments. Clearly no one plan of operation or pattern of teaching is equally appropriate in all circumstances. The sensitive teacher knows how to change roles and modify or adjust his instructions to meet the needs of differing groups of children.

What children understand, they often remember. Those things which they don't comprehend are quickly forgotten.

[1] Ned A. Flanders, "Teacher Influence in the Classroom," in *Theory and Research in Teaching,* Arno Bellack (ed.). New York: Bureau of Publications, Teachers College, Columbia University, 1963.

[2] A. D. Calvin, F. K. Hoffman, and E. L. Harden, "The Effect of Intelligence and Social Atmosphere on Group Problem Solving Behavior." *Journal of Social Psychology,* XLV (1957), 61-74.

[3] N. F. Maier and R. A. Maier, "An Experimental Test of the Effects of Developmental vs. Free Discussions on the Quality of Group Decisions." *Journal of Applied Psychology,* XVI (1957), 320-23.

The skillful social studies teacher recognizes the interrelationships which exist among the understandings, skills, and attitudes he seeks to foster. He knows that children cannot solve social problems without some basic background information and a knowledge of at least a few elementary concepts and understandings in geography, history, government, economics, and sociology. He also recognizes that information which children view as unrelated to their own personal interests or cooperatively planned problems and projects is likely to be set aside and forgotten. A major part of his task, then, is to help children sense the relevance of basic information to the tasks they have chosen to pursue. Skillful teachers often use carefully chosen questions to open up new avenues of awareness and discovery. Questions are the pivotal points of discussions. They can restrict and circumscribe thinking; they can also stimulate new dimensions of thought and expression. If a teacher asks what policemen do, the discussion is likely to be descriptive; if he asks why we need policemen, the focus may be more analytical and introspective.

Questions are often categorized as rote, convergent, divergent, or value oriented.

Rote questions involve the simple recognition or recall of information. Rote questions usually require only simple identification on the part of the student. They do not involve an understanding of high level relationships or intricate applications of principles.

1. Where is the peninsula on the map?
2. What is the capital of France?
3. How many animals are shown in the picture?

Convergent questions call upon the student to identify or trace relationships of many kinds. Convergent questions may require the pupil to compare or contrast ideas, events, or conditions. They may call upon the student to explain procedural sequences, cause and effect relationships, or grounds for belief. Children may also be asked to cite evidence, select key ideas, relate basic principles to their applications and uses, or make judgments concerning the relevance or significance of information.

1. Why did this (city, activity) happen to develop here?
2. What prompted these people to do this? (settle here, start this war, divide the land in this way)
3. What are the three main characteristics (of this city, of these people, of the land in this area)?
4. What were the major problems? (in the establishment of the country, in working out a settlement)
5. What factors would one need to take into account in deciding? (what kind of crops to grow, how the United States can best assist South American countries)
6. What were the major outcomes? (of the Civil War, of the great immigration)
7. How were they alike? (these two people, these regions, these events)
8. What are the major steps (in manufacturing this product, in establishing a government, in getting to the root of the problem)?
9. What conditions were different? (with respect to geography, historical events, economic conditions)
10. How would you judge whether it is praiseworthy? (this expectation, this action, this outcome)
11. How many ways have we seen this exhibited? (this basic need, this kind of activity)
12. What differences (in customs, in interests) do we see in these two groups?
13. What evidences do you find in the picture to suggest (that the situation is confused, that these people have been here a long time, that these people have made clever use of their resources)?

14. What evidence was there in the story (that these people really had a hard life, that a policeman's job is difficult)?
15. Why is this so frequently the most difficult part? (getting the committee organized, making it interesting)

Divergent questions are related to imaginative or creative thinking. They normally involve speculations about actions which might have taken place in the past or may occur in the present or future. Since past actions cannot be changed, it is more useful to speculate about present and future issues than historical events. Divergent questions often call upon the student to imagine how something might be done differently.

1. How might we bring peace to the world?
2. What new plans might best insure the individual rights of citizens?
3. What can be done to guarantee an adequate supply of fresh water?
4. How can we help provide better safety on the highways?
5. What kind of homes might we develop in the future?
6. How can we eliminate the wasteful use of our resources?
7. How might we provide help for poor people at home and abroad?
8. What new ideas might help in the fight against crime?
9. How can we best care for our sick and mentally ill citizens?
10. What could be done to preserve our lakes and forests?
11. What types of transportation might serve our nation best in the future?
12. How can we provide more living space for our growing world population?
13. How can we develop a better school spirit?
14. What can we do to keep our school and the grounds around it cleaner?
15. How can we arrange our Lost and Found Department at school so it really works?

Value-oriented questions require the student to weigh and judge what he believes is most desirable - that which "ought to be." Most people recognize that what is desired may be quite different from that which is desirable. Value questions relate to our beliefs about wisdom, goodness, and justice.

1. Should anything be done to help the American Indians?
2. Are we justified in fighting Communism in Asia?
3. Should we curtail the growth of our national government?
4. What is the best kind of life to lead?
5. Should we try to beautify America?
6. Should world peace be our most important goal?
7. How should citizens help their country?
8. What would be the right way to handle criminals?
9. What should be the greatest contribution of the United States to the world?
10. How much power should the President of the United States be granted?
11. What would be the fairest way to handle offshore oil reserves?
12. Should we do anything about the increasing use of alcohol and drugs?
13. What is the most serious problem in our school?
14. Should pre-school children have rights as citizens?
15. What freedoms are most worth preserving?

Unfortunately, not all questions fit neatly into the four categories noted above. If we ask about the most important contributions to progress in a particular area of knowledge, we cannot know immediately whether we have a rote or value question. If the answer has been agreed upon by authorities, the question may relate only to the recall of previously studied information. If, however, the question is not settled, but open to dispute, it may call for a value judgment on the part of the pupil.

CRITICAL THINKING AND
THE USE OF LEARNING MATERIALS

In addition to the thoughtful and imaginative use of questions in class discussions the effective social studies teacher emphasizes critical thinking in the use of a wide range of learning materials. Critical thinking appears to involve not only basic tools of inquiry and learning strategy, but also certain habits of mind and levels of expectation. Unfortunately, there is little general agreement regarding the exact nature of critical thinking. Huelsman[4] has summarized critical reading skills mentioned in one or more of fifteen articles on the subject. His list is as follows:

1. To define and delimit a problem.
2. To formulate hypotheses.
3. To locate information bearing on specific problems.
4. To determine that a statement is important for a given purpose.
5. To distinguish the difference between facts and opinions.
6. To evaluate the dependability of data.
7. To recognize the limitations of given data even when the items are assured to be dependable.
8. To see elements common to several items of data.
9. To make comparisons.
10. To organize evidence that suggests relationships.
11. To recognize prevailing tendencies or trends in the data.
12. To judge the competency of a given author to make a valid statement on a given topic.
13. To criticize data on the basis of its completeness and accuracy.
14. To criticize a presentation on the basis of the completeness and logic of its reasoning.
15. To suspend judgment until all evidence is assembled and evaluated.

Some of these are highly sophisticated and normally inappropriate for all but the most astute elementary pupils, but they provide us with some indication of the size of the task. It is interesting to note that virtually all the points listed relate to aspects of scientific inquiry or logical reasoning. They are designed to promote objectivity and systematization which may, in turn, yield insight and understanding. Despite the magnitude of the task, however, some elements of critical thinking may be introduced in the kindergarten and first grade. Shotka[5] has delineated eight competencies which can be successfully introduced to many first graders. These include:

1. Recognizing and defining the problem.
2. Recognizing assumptions.

[4]Charles B. Huelsman, Jr., "Promoting Growth in Ability to Interpret when Reading Critically: In Grades Seven to Ten," in *Promoting Growth Toward Maturity in Interpreting What Is Read.* Supplementary Educational Monographs, No. 74 (Chicago: University of Chicago Press, 1951), pp. 149-153.

[5]Josephine Shotka, "Critical Thinking in the First Grade." *Childhood Education,* Vol. 36, No. 9, (May 1960), p. 405.

3. Formulating an hypothesis.
4. Reasoning from an hypothesis.
5. Gathering evidence from: reading, observation, survey, and experimentation.
6. Evaluating evidence: detecting bias, determining validity and reliability, evaluating significance.
7. Organizing evidence.
8. Generalizing and deciding.

Critical thinking is discussed in greater detail in Chapter VII. At this point we are simply indicating the range of the teacher's responsibility in this area.

FACTORS IN CRITICAL READING

Critical thinking is as much a matter of attitude as ability. Many children have the ability to think and read critically. In fact, they develop powers of discrimination long before they can talk. Any child can make judgments and evaluations. Even slow learners and mentally-retarded children make judgments on levels that are meaningful to them. Bright children often respond to ideas in a greater variety of ways, but a high level of intelligence in and of itself is no guarantee of success in critical reasoning.

Almost any kind of critical analysis involves the identification or tracing of relationships. A reader, however, cannot evaluate statements effectively without information. He also needs criteria or standards with which to judge. Simple criteria and information alone, however, are not enough; the reader must also have a background or context within which he can weigh the writer's statements and views. Significant experiences which lead to the formation of useful concepts and generalizations are basic to critical thinking and reading. Neither children nor adults can reason or interpret ideas in a void. In a very real sense, the formulation, clarification, and refinement of personal interpretations and judgments is a matching strategy. The reader or listener matches the ideas he receives against his own background experiences. Some ideas ring true because his experiences have led him to similar interpretations or conclusions; other ideas appear inaccurate or altogether false because they run contrary to his own personal interpretations.

A reader must *want to know* before he is receptive to ideas. And *what* he wants to know determines to a large extent what he will receive from a reading experience. Some children are happy with a simple, uncritical replication of what is read. These children know what the author *said,* but not what he *meant* by his statements. There is a simple, literal reproduction of ideas. Other children attempt to find the tone, the significance, the meaning *behind* what the author says. They are interested in the reasoning which led the author to his conclusions. They not only read the lines, they read *between* the lines as well. A somewhat smaller group of pupils read *beyond* the lines. They are interested in the implications and applications of the ideas offered. They seek to deal creatively with the thoughts presented. They try to absorb new ideas, observations, and interpretations into their personal view of life. They want to put the ideas to work.

Many elementary teachers plan directed activities which require children to make judgments and decisions, but only a small percentage provide developmental programs which systematically introduce children to increasingly sophisticated levels of reasoning. Even though most children in the primary grades do not read complex materials, much can be done to help them in weighing and interpreting ideas. Children can compare pictures in a number of ways. They can decide which is best to illustrate a story, judge which picture is most realistic, or which is most interesting. It is at this point that the teacher needs to ask *why* it best illustrates the story, *what* makes it more realistic or interesting. A picture may be interesting because of the action portrayed, the uniqueness of the setting, the types of characters involved, or for any number of other reasons. The beauty of the story may also center around characterization, setting, plot, style, word usage, or other factors. The teacher who is interested in developing critical thinking and reasoning will encourage children to figure out why they prefer one picture or story or explanation to another. As pupils become adept at making decisions of this nature and receive recognition for their efforts, they may seek further opportunities to analyze problematic situations and eventually prefer this more sophisticated intellectual task to simpler, less stimulating learning activities.

The foundations of critical thinking and critical reading established in the primary grades should be reinforced and extended in the middle and upper grades. The ability to react thoughtfully and creatively to the acts and ideas of others is a major objective of sound instructional programs at all levels. As basic reading skills develop, wider reading is possible. Children can begin to secure information from several sources, including different text books, trade books, encyclopedias, newspapers, and magazines. Children may note similarities and differences among the ideas discussed, select relevant portions and discard others. Gradually many students will learn to detect biases and general points of view. Some may even learn to identify basic assumptions and fallacies in thinking. The most sophisticated students may become as much concerned with the writer's purposes as they are with his ideas. The teacher can assist these students by pointing out that authors normally write for one or more of three reasons: to inform, to entertain, or to offer social criticism.

The alert, successful social studies teacher is concerned with much beyond the realm of knowledge and information. He is acutely sensitive to the modes of inquiry he is fostering and the attitudes children are developing about themselves, their competencies, and the world about them.

Chapter VI

TEACHING STRATEGIES
FOR THE CLARIFICATION OF VALUES

Although this discussion is most directly concerned with teaching strategies as they relate to the identification and clarification of personal values, some attention must first be given to definitions and purposes. Strategies are, after all, only means or catalystic agents which we may employ in working towards desired ends or outcomes. The strategies have little or no value apart from the ends they are designed to serve.

WHAT ARE VALUES?

Values have been defined in various ways, and in view of the complexity of the subject, several studies need to be cited. In the words of Fay L. Corey, "A value is an attitude, a standard, or a belief which the individual has selected and reconstructed from the many concepts that beset him in his environment and the feelings that struggle within him."[1] Blackwell suggests that "Values are the core of social institutions, the criteria and mainsprings of behavior and social action which are internalized for the individual and are binding on his personality."[2] Perhaps the most succinct definition, however, is the one in which the authors state that "The values of people are the rules by which they live."[3] These authors go on to clarify their meaning by listing the following functions of a value system:

1. It supplies the individual with a sense of purpose and direction.
2. It gives the group a common orientation and supplies the basis of individual action and of unified, collective action.
3. It serves as the basis for judging the behavior of individuals.
4. It enables the individual to know what to expect of others as well as how to conduct himself.
5. It fixes the sense of right and wrong, fair and foul, desirable and undesirable, moral and immoral.[4]

Louis E. Raths of Newark State College suggests that beliefs must satisfy six criteria to qualify as values:

1. *There must be freedom of choice.* Values must be freely selected if they are to be really valued by the individual.

---

[1]Fay L. Corey, *Values of Future Teachers: A Study of Attitudes toward Contemporary Issues.* New York: Bureau of Publications, Teachers College, Columbia University, 1955, p. 5.

[2]Gordon W. Blackwell, "Impact of New Social Patterns upon Education." *Teachers College Record,* LVII (March, 1956), 396.

[3]B. O. Smith, William O. Stanley, and J. Harlan Shores, *Fundamentals of Curriculum Development,* revised ed. New York: Harcourt, Brace and World, Inc., 1957, p. 60.

[4]*Ibid.,* p. 61.

2. *There must be a pattern or repetition.* A single utterance or a single incident does not constitute the establishment of a pattern or the presence of an established value.
3. *There must be prizing.* If an individual has established a habit which he dislikes, it is unlikely that his behavior would qualify as a value.
4. *There must be consideration of alternatives.* Impulse and hasty action do not generally reflect basic values. In the absence of some consideration of alternatives it is unlikely that the process of valuing has taken place.
5. *There must be thoughtful consideration of consequences.* A value can emerge only when consequences are considered.
6. *There must be relationship to life activities.* If stated beliefs are not reflected in life activities, we categorize them as conceptualized but non-operational values.[5]

Values concern those things which people consider desirable. It is important that we not confuse values with personal preferences, interests, needs, or drives. All -too-frequently these terms are used interchangeably. An individual may express a *preference* without believing that any of the alternatives open to him are actually desirable. He may simply be selecting the least undesirable course of action. *Interests* may also differ greatly from individual beliefs about what is desirable. A person may be extremely interested in riots and civil disorders within his own country without approving the activities. His interests may stem largely from fear and a concern for self-preservation. Psychologists have defined *drives* and *needs* as physiological and psychological dispositions to act. They represent physiological and psychological desires. It is when these desires and appetites come in conflict with an individual's beliefs about what is right, desirable, and good that feelings of frustration and guilt frequently arise.

WHY IS IT IMPORTANT FOR US TO LEARN TO DEAL WITH VALUES?

Whether we like it or not, life forces many decisions upon us. And the decisions we make in life determine to a large degree the quality of our experiences, the depth of our understandings, and the contributions we may or may not make to humanity. Van Cleve Morris has stated this point with clarity and beauty:

> Man is not only a "knowing" organism; he is also a "valuing" organism — he likes some things more than others, i.e., he has preferences. Man's valuing is perhaps an even more decisive characteristic of his behavior than his knowing. This is the view, for instance, of many people who believe that the *quality* of a person's life, i.e., what he cherishes, what he truly wants out of life, is a better measure of his humanness than the "quantity" of his life, i.e., how *much* he knows, how widely read he is, or how knowledgeable or learned he may be. We all know people who are highly educated and conversant on a great many topics but whose life values leave them, in our eyes, short of attainment of the humane and cultivated life.
>
> So likewise do we judge whole societies and cultures. The true meaning of a society, or even a whole civilization, is better looked for in what the society basically *wants*, rather than how sophisticated its technology may be or how efficient its political institutions are.[6]

Americans today are faced with many more decisions than Americans one hundred years ago. Life moves faster, and the number of options or choices available to us is much

---

[5] Louis E. Raths, Merrill Harmin, Sidney B. Simon, *Values and Teaching,* Columbus, Ohio: Charles E. Merrill Books, Inc., 1966, pp. 28, 29.

[6] Van Cleve Morris, *Philosophy and the American School.* Boston: Houghton Mifflin, 1961.

greater. Unfortunately, it does not appear that we are any better able to make wise judgments. Crane Brinton concludes in his *History of Western Morals* that there is no evidence to suggest that we are getting closer to the ethical ideals we have erected for ourselves. We have simply substituted more sophisticated methods of warfare for the duels, Roman spectacles, and clan feuds which monopolized our energies earlier in history. In our cities and towns we find that increasing crime rates are an accepted part of modern Americana. Fidelity losses paid by insurance companies have jumped 130 per cent in the last ten years, and shortages in American department stores have now reached two hundred million dollars annually — more than half of net profits. Crime is costing us $22 billion a year. This is ten per cent more than we spend for education across the entire nation.

The full damage cannot be seen in capital losses alone. We are paying a tragic price in warped lives and broken relationships. A Louis Harris poll published in *Newsweek* (June 22, 1964) reports that one family in six has a mentally ill member, one in six has an alcoholic, and one out of every six has severe marital difficulties. "Home Sweet Home" appears to be more of a dream than a reality for many Americans.

INITIAL STEPS IN THE DEVELOPMENT OF VALUES

As Erik Erickson has pointed out in *Childhood and Education,* the child comes into the school system with certain "ego virtues" which form the basic ingredients out of which value systems develop. The child has acquired a balance of trust and distrust; trust in himself and others, but sufficient distrust to make him want to test the world about him. He is unwilling to rely on blind faith.

Whether new values such as industry, courage, and sensitivity to others will grow, become refined, and allow him to eventually develop life purposes, self-respect, and the competencies necessary to make more sophisticated social judgments will depend to a large degree upon his school and community experiences. The mechanisms through which values eventually develop rest primarily upon identification, a growing consciousness of ideals, and conscious or unconscious desires to reach personal goals.

FIVE PSYCHOLOGICAL DIMENSIONS OF VALUE CHANGE

There appears to be a general feeling among Americans that the individual who is most poorly adjusted, the farthest removed from the norm, is the ripest candidate for change. Unfortunately, this is not true. The same principle applies here as in weight reduction. The very, very heavy person frequently makes no attempt at weight reduction. Our dieters are, by and large, people who are only a little overweight; the really heavy people have simply given up. Willingness to change is directly related to love of self. We sometimes call this "self-acceptance", but it is really more than this — it is more closely related to self-assurance, self-pride, and self-satisfaction. Suggestions regarding ways of building self-esteem and self-assurance may be found among the strategies listed in the latter part of this discussion.

A second psychological consideration relates to "insight" and "introspection". A child must be able to see differences in points of view and their consequences if he is to make judgments with any degree of consistency. Peck and Havighurst[7] found that only 25 per

[7]Robert Peck and Robert Havighurst, *The Psychology of Character Development.* New York: Wiley, 1960.

cent of the high school youths they studied had the psychological and intellectual requisites necessary for the examination of personal values. The psychological requisites related to personal security and self-assurance are described above; the intellectual requisites find expression in the child's ability to see relationships among ideas and between ideas and their behavioral counterparts.

Thirdly, we must recognize that there are a number of dimensions of human feelings and personal experiences which seem to defy expression. Edgar Lee Masters has described our dumbness and inadequacy of expression more eloquently than most:

SILENCE

I have known the silence of the stars and of the sea,
And the silence of the city when it pauses,
And the silence of a man and a maid,
And the silence for which music alone finds the word,
And the silence of the woods before the winds of spring begin,
And the silence of the sick
When their eyes roam about the room.
And I ask: For the depths
Of what use is language?
A beast of the field moans a few times
When death takes its young:
And we are voiceless in the presence of realities —
We cannot speak.
There is the silence of a great hatred,
And the silence of a great love,
And the silence of a deep peace of mind,
And the silence of an embittered friendship.
There is the silence of a spiritual crisis,
Through which your soul, exquisitely tortured,
Comes with visions not to be uttered
Into a realm of higher life,
And the silence of the gods who understand each other without speech.
There is the silence of defeat.
There is the silence of those unjustly punished;
And the silence of the dying whose hand
Suddenly grips yours,
There is the silence between father and son,
When the father cannot explain his life,
Even though he be misunderstood for it.

Certainly, there are many feelings which we can express only partially or indirectly. How many times have you seen a teacher corner a child and say to him, "You sit right there until you can decide why you did that?" Unless the child has very unusual insights, he probably doesn't know why he acted as he did. Many of our strongest motivations appear to lie deep within our subconscious minds.

A fourth aspect of value change concerns our personal need for structure — our need for an environment with stable and familiar forms. We may need an authority, a pattern of traditions and customs, creedal statements or familiar surroundings, for we feel ill at ease without them. Much has been written about our individual needs for structure or dogma in *The Authoritarian Personality, The Open and Closed Mind* and *The True Believer.* These studies reveal that persons who are given and accept large degrees of personal freedom have a wider range of perceptions and more accurate views of the world about them. They are more tolerant of ambiguity and uncertainty. They are more skillful in communication. They can say things in ways that permit their ideas to "get through" to others. They have positive self-concepts, feel that their ideas count, and that they are wanted by the groups with which they associate. They tend to attribute positive characteristics to others and enjoy giving and taking in full measure.

In any situation that requires a decision or in which an individual takes a position, there are relevant and irrelevant factors. These are related to the belief system of the individual. According to Rokeach, all persons have rational and irrational forces within this belief system. He states:

> All belief-disbelief systems serve two powerful and conflicting sets of motives at the same time; the need for a cognitive framework to know and to understand and the need to ward off the threatening aspects of reality.[8]

A final question relates to evidence of behavior change. It is difficult to know whether persons really change or whether environmental conditions simply call forth the expression of different behavior patterns at different times. Many psychologists believe that behavior is situationally controlled. We know that every individual is capable of many behaviors. He can be altruistic, cruel, selfish, kind, greedy, truculent, meek, harsh, gentle, savage, and benign. He can also develop "typical" patterns of response. That is, responses which are typical of *him*. The question of whether individuals really change is, at least partially, a matter of definition. We may wish to define behavior change as differences in overt responses; i.e., the way an individual's outward responses appear to change over a period of time. These responses, however, may result from a strong self-discipline rather than a natural disposition to act in this manner. On the other hand, we may define behavior in a way that suggests that a person's basic desires, preferences, and values have been modified.

The *Taxonomy of Educational Objectives: Affective Domain*[9] by Krathwohl *et al* delineates the range and intensity of responses that may find expression within an individual's behavior pattern. Note that values begin with a willingness to respond and end with conceptualization. (See page 41.)

SHOULD WE EMPHASIZE PARTICULAR VALUES?

All of us recognize that we cannot help but display many of our personal values in day to day work with children. When we chose teaching as a career, we revealed many things about ourselves, our values, interests, and preferences. When we suggest a topic for class discussion we are, in essence, saying that this topic is worthy of the attention of our students. Rather than ask whether we should emphasize particular values, we might better ask whether we should *consciously* and *systematically* emphasize particular values. We can find spokesmen for both sides of this issue. John Gardner in his now famous book, *Self-renewal and the Innovative Society*,[10] warns: (p.21)

> All too often we are giving young people cut flowers when we should be teaching them to grow their own. We are stuffing their heads with the products of earlier innovations rather than teaching them to innovate.

[8]Milton Rokeach, *The Open and Closed Mind.*
[9]David Krathwohl et al,*Taxonomy of Educational Objectives.*
Affective Domain, New York: David McKay Co., 1964, p. 37.
[10]New York: Harper & Row, 1964.

RECEIVING	AWARENESS
	WILLINGNESS TO RECEIVE
	CONTROLLED OR SELECTED ATTENTION

RESPONDING	ACQUIESCENCE IN RESPONDING
	WILLINGNESS TO RESPOND
	SATISFACTION IN RESPONSE

VALUING	ACCEPTANCE OF A VALUE
	PREFERENCE FOR A VALUE
	COMMITMENT

| ORGANIZATION | CONCEPTUALIZATION OF A VALUE |
| | ORGANIZATION OF A VALUE SYSTEM |

| CHARACTERIZATION BY A VALUE COMPLEX | GENERALIZED SET |
| | CHARACTERIZATION |

Julian Huxley in *New Bottles for New Wine*[11] also suggests that we should be emphasizing differences rather than conformity. He states: (p.41)

> Satisfaction comes through the fuller realization of possibilities. In the light of this concept, the sharp antinomies between the individual and society, between nation and mankind, disappear, for each has its claim to its own fulfillment, and all are complementary within the total process of the evolutionary fulfillment of life.

The Education Policies Commission, on the other hand, suggests that the basic principle of the *Importance and Dignity of the Individual* is fundamental to the American

[11]New York: Harper, 1957.

culture and provides the foundation upon which all other social, political, and economic considerations should be based.

Laswell and Kaplan believe that there are eight values found in all open and free societies.

General Value Term	Some of its Idices
1. Affection	Love, friendship, congeniality, loyalty, emotional security, fondness, tenderness, emotional warmth, devotion, liking.
2. Respect	Recognition, esteem, acceptance, reverence, worship, admiration, honor, consideration.
3. Enlightenment	Understanding, insight, discernment, clarification (of meaning), generalization, discovery, knowledge (functional), wisdom.
4. Skill	Talent (intellectual, social, communicative, physical, aesthetic), proficiency, craftsmanship.
5. Power	Decision making, influence, control, restraint, rule, leadership, capacity to act, authority, sway, jurisdiction, command.
6. Wealth	Economic security, goods and services, material culture, property, possessions.
7. Well-being	Health (physical and mental), comfort, happiness, contentment, relative freedom from fear, physical and biological bases of adequacy.
8. Rectitude	Moral, ethical, law-abiding, just, relative freedom from guilt, religious, responsible.[12]

We cannot resolve this conflict here. The question of whether instructors should feel obligated to teach basic American values or simply conduct open forums for the honest examination of all values will be debated for some years to come. A society without some common commitments relating to the right and diginity of individuals, however, would soon degenerate into chaos.

CONTROVERSIAL ISSUES

Controversial issues are quite different from basic American values. These are questions about national, state, and local problems around which no general consensus of opinion or historical agreement has been made.

When controversial areas are dealt with as a part of the school curriculum, some guides for the selection of the issues are helpful. The National Committee on the Instructional Program has suggested several criteria, no matter at what grade level these issues are studied.

1. The subject chosen should be suitable to the maturity and background levels of the child.
2. It should be related to the course objectives.
3. Materials should be available relating to various viewpoints.

---

[12]Harold Laswell and Abraham Kaplan, *Power and Society, A Framework for Political Inquiry.* New Haven: Yale University Press, 1950, p. 87.

4. The issue chosen should be important and of continuing significance.
5. The teacher should be able to handle the issue objectively.[13]

After the issue has been carefully scrutinized and the teacher is ready to proceed, he will need to: (1) Define the issue clearly and carefully. (2) Explore the issue so that the various aspects become familiar. (3) Suggest a variety of solutions. (4) Collect data. (5) Present data in as unbiased a fashion as possible. (6) Sift and appraise the data. (7) Relate data to suggested solutions. (8) Help children draw conclusions.

As the class pursues the study of selected issues, it may be desirable for the teacher to call particular factors to the attention of the class. Some points for children to consider in gathering information and making judgments are listed below.

1. Be certain to secure data on as many aspects of the problem as possible.
2. Be aware of the difference between fact and opinion.
3. Do not hunt for a fact to support an already-formed conviction.
4. Remember that open-mindedness and willingness to change are essential in using critical thinking.
5. Have the good manners to hear the other person out before clamoring to present your own view.
6. Refrain from attempting to force one's view on someone else.

The National Council for the Social Studies has suggested that effective study of controversial topics and problems requires straight and disciplined thinking.[14] They further state that intermediate-grade children should have frequent opportunities to identify and evaluate primary sources. During secondary school years students should be aware of differences of opinions among scholars as well as responsible and irresponsible efforts to mold public opinion.

The teacher has some responsibilities which he will need to assume as the study proceeds. He may need to work diligently for a desirable climate by setting an example of respect for others' rights and opinions. Children will need his guidance in learning to disagree courteously. His leadership will help pupils learn to comprehend values, relationships, differing viewpoints, the influence of personal attitudes upon final decisions and other factors basic to an unbiased study of the problem at hand.

The effective teacher will be careful not to indoctrinate his students. He probably will refrain from expressing an opinion until as many facets of the problem as possible have been presented. He may find it profitable to follow a suggestion made by Alice Miel:

> What is required above all is that teachers themselves become students of the significant movements in their society and that they care enough about the direction their society takes to care what kind of persons their children will be.[15]

SOCIAL STUDIES TEXTBOOKS AND VALUES

The social studies text would appear at first glance to offer the teacher her richest store of resource material for the study of values. Certainly there are enough important

[13]Project on the Instructional Program of the Public Schools, *Deciding What to Teach.* Washington: National Education Association, 1963.

[14]National Council for the Social Studies, "Criteria for an Adequate Social Studies Curriculum," *Readings for Social Studies in Elementary Education,* ed. John Jarolimek and Huber M. Walsh. New York: The Macmillan Company, 1965.

[15]Alice Miel, "Social Studies with a Difference," *Readings for Social Studies in Elementary Education,* New York: MacMillan Co., 1965.

social issues to keep social studies classes well supplied with topics for some time to come. If Ballinger's observations are correct, however, the classroom teacher cannot expect great help from the social studies text. Ballinger studied recent social studies texts and observed:

> With only one exception, the social studies textbooks examined failed to treat values and controversial issues to any substantial degree. . . almost all of the books examined stated explicitly or implied clearly that the central concern in dealing with controversial issues should be to assist students in getting the facts straight. . . it seemed to be assumed that if facts are correct, the questions of value, the questions of worth and desirability, will automatically straighten themselves out.[16]

Dr. Ballinger is a philosopher, and he knows that we cannot treat values as though they were scientific facts. And teachers and children should know this, too! It is probably safe to assert that to date we know of only one basic method of supporting (not proving) values. This is to convince one's protagonist or adversary that the value you support is, or will be, instrumental in arriving at an already agreed upon value; i.e. it will have desirable consequences (from your opponent's point of view). Thus, if you wish to establish more national parks, and you know that your opponent is concerned about juvenile delinquency, you try to convince him that more national parks will help reduce juvenile delinquency.

Men can agree on all the facts in a situation and still disagree about the value or worth of recognized outcomes. If they share no basic agreements on any values (even a common concern for mutual preservation), it is difficult to see how they could persuade each other of any action. A Red Cross worker and the commandant of a concentration camp might well agree on all of the facts relating to the deaths which had occurred within the camp and the manner of execution, yet disagree completely regarding the ethics and justice of the whole operation.

THE BASIC KEY TO THE STUDY OF VALUES

James Raths[17] believes that teachers now attempt to develop values by lecture, peer-group pressure, finding or setting examples, and through systems of punishment and reward. As teachers, we need to develop skills in raising issues, not providing solutions. Life is a quest, not a game of questions and answers. The effective teacher introduces her students to rich and varied experiences and encourages them to work out their own personal interpretations and conclusions. Teachers have frequently failed in the area of values because they have not encouraged exploration and discovery. In short, they have attempted to study values apart from the experiences which are basic to their understanding. Bower discusses the problems as follows:

> . . . if values are to be real and vital in the lives of children and young people, they must be *experienced.* That is why presenting them as abstractions and verbalizing *about* them are bafflingly ineffective, with little or no measurable influence upon conduct . . . Normal learning begins in experience and ends in experience. Ways of acting are the outcomes of dealing with concrete and specific situations. . . .They can never, except in the most general way, be predicted in advance of the specific circumstances. Thus, what is loyalty in one set of circumstances may be

---

[16]Stanley E. Ballinger, "Social Studies and Social Controversy". *School Review,* (Fall, 1963).

[17]James Raths, "A Strategy for Developing Values." *Educational Leadership,* (May, 1964).

quite different from loyalty in another set of circumstances. Instead of looking around for situations in which to "apply" an abstract and generalized trait, learning should begin with the situation and work itself through by analysis of the situation and its possible outcomes, the utilization of the end-products of past racial experience, choice among alternatives, and decision to the completed act. Only by some such creative procedure, can that most difficult of all lines in education — that between verbalization and action — be crossed. And only so can those incentives that are inherent in the purposive act be counted on to carry through.

This is true because values, like ideas, sustain a functional relation to experience. On the one hand, they grow out of experience; on the other, they re-enter it as factors of control in determining the ends of purposive action, in providing criteria for judgments, and in supplying motivation.[18]

EIGHT EMPHASES IN THE STUDY OF VALUES WITH ILLUSTRATIONS OF SUPPORTING CLASSROOM ACTIVITIES

Unless a teacher is convinced that the examination of values is important and that children can grow in their understanding of values, little progress is likely. Children who are accustomed to right and wrong answers in spelling and arithmetic frequently feel ill at ease in the "no man's land" of values. The relative certainty and feelings of personal adequacy which may accompany studies in science are virtually nonexistent in the study of values. Conflicts in values exist precisely because the issues have not been settled, and there is little expectation that the basic conflicts will be universally agreed upon in the forseeable future. There are at least eight emphases that may be considered in the study of values:

BUILDING SELF-APPRECIATION AND SELF-ASSURANCE

As was mentioned previously, children and young people must have a degree of pride and security *before* they can seriously consider initiating changes in their personal behavior. In our society we are judged by our demonstrated competencies. It is almost ludicrous to suggest that an individual is very important and deserving of status if he has extremely limited skills and competencies. A child needs to feel that he has some abilities that he can point to with pride. One of our jobs as teachers is to help him build self-confidence in at least a few areas of competence.

1. One primary teacher, over a period of time, had each child identify one or more areas of personal competence and then draw a picture illustrating his competence. These pictures were mounted on the fronts of the children's desks. They served as a reminder that, no matter how poorly a child performed in other tasks, he always had at least one status skill, an ability worth noticing and sharing with others.
2. Intermediate grade teachers often encourage children to change roles in their search for status. Poor readers have frequently gained tremendous confidence in themselves when allowed to assist first grade or kindergarten teachers in story hour, recess periods, or work skill games.
3. High school faculties have conducted talent searches among their students and uncovered some unusual competencies, generally unrelated to school work. These were featured in news articles, talent programs, craft displays and school fairs. One member of a high school faculty

---

[18]William Clayton Bower, *Moral and Spiritual Values in Education.* Lexington: University of Kentucky Press, 1952, pp. 61 ff.

explained recently, "A fellow has to be known for something and we'd prefer to have him known for his ability to handle snakes, draw cartoons or tear down an engine rather than his expertise in tearing down society."

WORKING WITH PARENTS AND OTHER COMMUNITY MEMBERS

There is strong evidence to suggest that parents should be involved in some way in any examination of values. They not only have an important vested interest in the values their children embrace, they also constitute the most important single influence on the young child. If parents hold values which are very different from those being examined in school, there may be serious confusion and even open conflict between home and school. If parents and educators can find common concerns and common interests, the study of beliefs and values is likely to be much more rewarding.

1. Organize a panel discussion involving parents and students to determine what parents expect of their children and what children expect of their parents in relation to study, duties at home, and other activities.
2. Ask a member of a community minority group to discuss the problems confronting his group. Can minorities ever enjoy full privileges? How?
3. Write a radio or television script which describes the conflict between the younger and older generations. Can you make it realistic and objective?
4. Conduct role-playing in which the parts of parents, teachers, students, etc., are portrayed. Do you know enough about how parents and teachers feel to portray their ideas clearly?
5. Children frequently feel that adults do not want them to participate in community affairs. Contact civic leaders to determine the kinds of activities in which teen-agers can participate. Also try to discover reasons why they are not permitted to participate in some activities.
6. Interview members of the school board or city council to find out what pressures they must meet. Try to discover from what general areas of society most of these pressures come. Discuss the ethics involved in these pressures.

FINDING MODELS

Since children and adults are highly imitative in their search for life patterns, it is often wise to seek out models which reflect some of the values being examined. It is important that the children have a strong voice in the selection of models and, when possible, have an opportunity to question the individual models about their beliefs and activities. The teacher should not be surprised to find a kindly school janitor serving as a model.

1. Ask a group of sixth graders whom they would prefer for a best friend: an actress, a politician, a judge, a doctor, or an Olympic gold medal winner. Ask the same question of your adult friends. Is there any relationship between the two sets of preferences? Do the results indicate that values change with maturity? Suggest hypotheses for any consistent difference between the choices of the two groups.
2. Talk with people in the community to find out who are considered outstanding persons. Interview these persons to find out what they believe with regard to religion, politics, economics, and social relationships. Are there any similarities among their beliefs?
3. Identify the person in your life whom you most admire. How does he meet his problems? Compare his beliefs regarding cooperation, tolerance, and self-reliance with your own. Are there differences? Are there similarities? Which of your beliefs or attitudes would you most like to change?

USING GENERALIZATIONS AS SPRINGBOARDS FOR DISCUSSION

All of us are looking for summarizations of life. We note that certain statements seem to ring true. They express our deepest feelings about life. Their crisp messages seem to tie together the many untidy, fleeting observations that have thwarted our attempts at understanding. Sometimes we can use broad value statements as springboards for discussion. As adults, how would you react to the following sixteen statements:

Agree	Disagree	
		1. Pleasures and displeasures grow with the growth of our spirit.
		2. A chasm will always exist between the ideal and the real, hope and realization, expectancy and fulfillment in human experience.
		3. Man is constantly threatened with nothingness.
		4. Often education simply systematizes our biases.
		5. Education can be judged by its consequences, ideal and actual, its capacity to enrich and sustain life, and by its contribution to the enlightenment of man.
		6. Our failings lie not in our errors but in possibilities we do not explore.
		7. Facts cannot be divorced from values. When facts are illuminated by values, they become alive and tend to transform human existence.
		8. Even though the term "good" may not be defined, its applications may be testable in terms of laws. It is similar to the term "love" in this respect.
		9. Men think they desire things because they are good; but in truth things are good because men desire them.
		10. The human problem lies in the values that we are going to put on graciousness as we struggle for efficiency.
		11. Man will not be satisfied with mere harmony: he desires discord as well. He desires everything: happiness and pain, harmony and discord, chance and issue.
		12. All men desire peace, but few desire those things which make for peace.
		13. Absolute certainty is a privilege of uneducated minds — and fanatics. It is, for educated folks, an unattainable ideal.
		14. It is difficult, if not impossible, for most people to think otherwise than in the fashion of their own period.

continued on next page

Agree	Disagree	
		15. Cruelty, selfishness, lust, cowardice, and deceit are normal ingredients in human nature which have their useful roles in the struggle for existence. Intrinsically, they are all virtues. It is only in their excess or their exercise under the wrong conditions that justly incurs our moral disapproval.
		16. The moralist may speak for others with authority when he knows them better than they know themselves, but not otherwise.

It is not difficult to see that some very interesting discussions could be developed around the provocative ideas listed above. Children in the primary grades, however, are more likely to be able to deal with statements like "Honesty always pays" or "Being fair in games is more important than winning." Beginning with statements such as these calls for deductive thinking, and it is less life-like than problems involving inductive thinking. However, generalizations may be used to add variety to classroom discussions.

EXAMINING ISSUES

The examination and study of basic, continuing social issues has been, and probably will continue to be, one of the most fruitful approaches to the study of values. Successful character education and citizenship education programs conducted by Jones,[19] Baugarten-Tramer,[20] Meier,[21] Wheeler[22] and Klevan[23] all had these elements in common. They involved an open and careful examination of social issues; they provided ample opportunities for reflective thought and discussion; and they emphasized feelings of mutual confidence and a high *espirit de corps*.

Some of the following might serve as a basis for class discussion:

1. Secure a large photograph of a typical social situation involving some type of conflict. Have a member of the class make up a story describing what has gone on prior to the present scene and how the problem should be resolved. Exchange the stories among the members of the class and have them list the values which seem to be reflected in the stories. Try to discover how individual values influence our interpretations of social situations.
2. Invite a city official (probate judge, councilman, or social worker) to discuss the values he feels are important to him in his everyday life, and why he considers these values to be important.
3. Ask a physician to discuss the effects of physical needs, stamina, and body chemistry upon behavior. How much should we demand in the area of social responsibility? In judging others, how much allowance should we make for differences in physical needs?

[19]Vernon Jones, *Character and Citizenship Training in the Public School – An Experimental Study of Three Specific Methods.* Chicago: University of Chicago, 1936.

[20]Franziska Baumgarten-Tramer, "Une Methode Nouvell D'Education Morale." *Enfance,* VI (1953), 153-57.

[21]Arnold Meier et al., *A Curriculum for Citizenship – A Report of the Citizenship Education Study.* Detroit: Wayne University, 1952.

[22]Eldon G. Wheeler, *Developing the Social Studies Curriculum for Citizenship Education.* Manhattan, Kansas: Kansas State College, 1952.

[23]Albert Klevan, "An Investigation of a Methodology for Value Clarification: Its Relationship to Consistency of Thinking, Purposefulness and Human Relations." Unpublished Ed. D. thesis, New York University, 1958.

4. Have each member of the class list the values or beliefs he thinks are worth fighting for. See if there are any similarities in these beliefs.

5. In America we like to believe that all wholesome work is good and of equal value. Is this belief evident in the ways in which various occupations are depicted in the movies and on TV? Why or why not?

6. Some of our problems in working with other nations stem from the fact that they have a different way of life. Give suggestions that might be used by Americans as they work with those in underdeveloped countries.

7. Should rules be set up for judging championship teams on the basis of sportsmanship as well as ability to win games? Why or why not?

8. Why is there frequently a difference in the attitudes of children regarding "What I want to be like" and "What I ought to be like"?

9. We often hear the statement, "Children must be taught to think." Does the local community desire youth who can think for themselves? What evidence seems to support or contradict this idea?

10. Study and compare the moral and ethical principles espoused by organizations such as (a) service clubs, (b) Boy Scouts and Girl Scouts, (c) Campfire Girls, (d) YMCA and YWCA, and (e) youth groups in churches.

11. Make a list of the values you think you accept and use on an everyday basis. Keep a record of your actions for a few days and try to determine whether you really act in terms of these values. Parents and friends may keep a similar record of your behavior.

12. Write a brief description of an important decision you have recently made. Try to think of the values you hold which influenced your decision. What are the sources of these values? Which of your values do you most consistently follow?

13. Make a study of representative cultures to secure information regarding the value systems which underline these patterns of behavior. *National Geographic, Life,* and books by anthropologists, or discussions by members of the community may prove helpful. What factors appear to give rise to these values?

14. Develop a list of issues or beliefs about which there are general disagreements in the area of personal living. Write out your own beliefs and then invite persons to discuss opposing views on the subjects of minority rights, economic issues, or duties of citizenship. Check your original statement. Do you still hold the same beliefs?

15. Ask each member of the class to clip one news item which represents a positive value and one news item which represents a negative value. Are there similarities among the positive ones? Are there likenesses among the negative values expressed in the news items?

16. In America we value cooperation, loyalty, responsibility, honesty, and courage. Are there situations in the school or community where these values are being overlooked? What can be done to make these values more functional?

17. Write and produce a play in which a character must make a choice between equally strong and important values. For example, a boy has strong loyalties to his mother and his friends, but the two disagree. How can he resolve his loyalty conflicts?

18. Collect several political speeches (either from current literature or from historical documents) given by a candidate seeking public office. Study these speeches for consistency of viewpoint. Do the statements change from community to community? Is an office seeker justified in changing his point of view to fit his audience?

19. Study John F. Kennedy's *Profiles in Courage.* Do you agree that each of the persons he describes deserves the recognition he accords them? What is the easiest type of courage? What is the most difficult kind of courage?

20. Try to establish some guidelines to good conduct and then test them in several problem situations. Do they hold up during application? How would you modify them?

21. Secure a statement of city or county laws. Compare these with the Ten Commandments. Are there any important differences? Why?

22. Collect a series of advertisements which are designed to influence our social and economic values. Analyze the values which are emphasized in each advertisement. Can advertisements change our attitude in ways which are inconsistent with basic beliefs? Why or why not?

23. In the Middle Ages the major concern of both serf and feudal lord was salvation of the soul. They expected life to be brief and filled with trials and tribulations. Today man is much more concerned with happiness and prosperity. How do you account for these changes in values?

24. What factors have been responsible for the changing attitudes in the United States regarding birth control, divorce, sterilization, and eugenics? Are these changes good?

25. Make a study of the changing values the government holds in providing for the needy, the unemployed, the aged, the blind, etc. in the Great Society. What brought about these changes?

26. Examine the methods used by political parties in their attempts to create a favorable attitude toward their policies and programs. What methods are most effective? What methods seems to be unethical? Outline a program for evaluating the claims of parties and candidates.

BUILDING ON INTERESTS

It is usually helpful to have some understanding of the interests of children at the outset of any study of values. Children's interests give clues to the setting in which the study of values may take place. If children are interested in high adventure, the stories and other activities used in the study may more profitably be related to these kinds of experiences. If, on the other hand, a stronger interest in the love and care of animals is expressed, values such as loyalty, justice and brotherhood may be more profitably pursued in this setting. All experienced teachers are familiar with ways of detecting children's interests. Some of the more common approaches are listed below:

1. Ask each child to tell about his favorite game, animal, story and school subject.
2. Invite children to describe their preferences as they relate to television shows, gifts they have received, and places they have visited.
3. Encourage children to bring unusual objects to school and watch the reactions of the class as these are displayed and discussed.

INTRODUCING CHILDREN TO THE PARADOXES OF LIFE

One of the reasons that we continue to have heated arguments and protracted discussions over values is because we have adopted many basic values which are inconsistent with each other. The Western world and parts of the East foster a hazy ambivalence regarding many aspects of community life. Facets of honesty and cleverness, faith and reason, nationalism and internationalism, humility and pride are interwoven into a crazy-quilt of contradictions. The problems inherent in these awkward compromises have been further confused in recent years by new and insistent world-wide demands for human equality and freedom. An imaginative teacher can, through stories and descriptions of value predicaments, introduce children to some of our value inconsistencies relating to:

1. Competition and cooperation.
2. Individuality and conformity.
3. Efficiency and worker welfare.
4. Judging on intent and judging by consequences.
5. Artistry and practicality.
6. Tradition and innovation.
7. Public service and care and protection of one's own family.

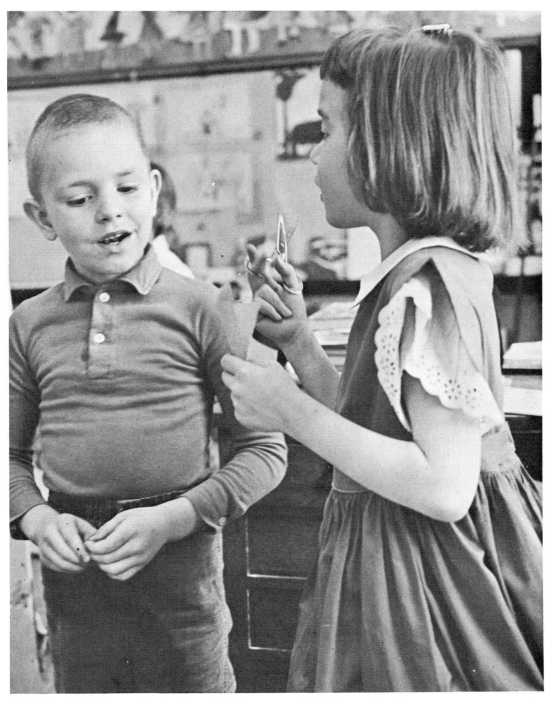

Children invariably learn a great deal from each other.

8. Justice as impersonal and objective and justice in which the human dimension is given prominence.
9. Freedom of expression and national security.
10. Social equality or recognition of individuals according to their status or contributions.
11. Jacksonian democracy and Jeffersonian democracy.
12. Emphasis upon feelings and sensitivity vs. an emphasis upon rationality and reason.

PERSONAL GOALS AND THEIR SYMBOLIC REPRESENTATIONS

Ernest Ligon and others associated with character education projects have found that the setting of personal goals is basic to the development and strengthening of individual values. When children choose a goal freely and affirm it in their daily life activities, value changes are frequently more genuine and longer lasting. Teachers should not anticipate highly imaginative goals reflecting levels of idealism which are not readily apparent in society. Children's goals are usually procedural and often pragmatic.

There is a good deal of evidence to suggest that these personal or group goals may need to be reflected in symbols of some kind. Ernest Cassirer[24] has traced the function of symbols in human activity. His findings suggest that many abstractions must find expression in outward form in order to survive. Ideals are, of course, abstractions, and if Cassirer is correct, those engaged in the study of values must give credence to his findings. Appropriate symbols may do much to help students identify with particular groups or projects. Rather than use ready-made symbols and emblems, groups may plan and design their own to reflect the beliefs and values they wish to foster and strengthen within their own organizations. Their original designs may, of course, incorporate many of the traditional symbols, but in some respects they should reflect the uniqueness of the group. In this way it becomes *their* symbol. It stands for *their* concerns and *their* hopes and dreams for the future. One group of students in Detroit had fashioned a large penguin with a vivid red heart as the symbol of their club. When asked what the penguin represented, they replied, "We're cool, man, cool, but we have a heart!" In a sense this might also symbolize our work with children in the study of values. We must recognize that there are important feelings reflected in the values we seek to clarify, but we must also keep our "cool". We cannot let our examination of values degenerate into insipid sentimentality.

[24]Ernst Cassirer, *The Philosophy of Symbolic Forms* (translated by Ralph Manheim). New Haven: Yale University Press, 1953.

Chapter VII

DEVELOPING PUPIL SKILLS
IN SOCIAL STUDIES

(With a List of Seventy-eight Activities which May Stimulate Reading Interests
and Strengthen Library Study and Critical Thinking Skills)

Virtually all the skills and understandings in social studies relate to the efficient location, use and communication of ideas. Children secure information from a wide variety of sources — through carefully planned or casual observations of their surroundings, through graphic, pictorial, and printed references, and through oral communications. The teaching of these skills must necessarily be one of the central purposes of social studies education from kindergarten through college. The precise level of refinement at which any skill is taught will depend on the needs and maturity of the learners. To help the student develop skill proficiency as he deals with social studies content, a list of practical activities has been included at the end of this chapter.

SKILL DEVELOPMENT

Recent changes in the area of skill development have not been on the skills which are needed in the social studies program, but in the methods of teaching these skills. Because of rapid changes both in the structure and amount of knowledge, more stress will be required in the identification and analysis of problems, as well as in the reconstruction of present knowledge and the production of new solutions to problems. The skills emphasis will be on *where* the child may find facts and *how* to use the materials which provide these facts.

Skills in social studies fall largely in the cognitive category. They are very complex and when effectively developed result in highly organized and integrated patterns of behavior. They encompass the language arts areas of listening, speaking, reading, and writing with specific application to the social studies as well as new skills such as those relating to the use of maps, globes, time, and chronology.

In planning the social studies curriculum a sequential program of skill development should be followed. In addition, there should be provision for reteaching, practice, and refinement of techniques learned earlier. While it is not realistic to identify all the specific skills to be acquired or particular levels of proficiency to be attained at any grade level, it is clear that the skills emphasized should be useful in understanding the basic principles pervading the social science disciplines.

Many factors, such as ability, training, background, and interest of pupils, the training and enthusiasm of the teacher, as well as the availability of materials, will influence progress in the area of skill development. Guidelines for development are goals toward which the social studies teacher strives.

When setting up a skills development program, there are several factors that should be considered. Among these are:

1. Skills are learned most effectively when a definite need exists.
2. Direct teaching is required for mastery of these skills.
3. Practice in different situations is essential to attain proficiency.

4. The development of each specific skill should be gradual and continuous.
5. Provision should be made for individual pupil needs and interests.

In general, contemporary methods show a trend toward an approach which is logical, analytical, conceptual, and scholarly. Emphasis is focused on:

1. Inquiry and discovery.
2. Problem-solving.
3. Inductive approaches.
4. Formation of concepts.
5. Development of generalizations.
6. Use of comparative methods.
7. Critical appraisal of knowledge.
8. Research methods of disciplines.
9. Use of primary source material.
10. Application of critical thinking.

These trends in the social studies are a reflection of the general movement in contemporary education toward the development of intellectual capabilities (cognitive skills). The stress is no longer on facts alone, since in many instances they have little merit in and of themselves. Instead, the emphasis is upon the development of skills which enable the learner (1) to *locate* information; (2) to *assess* this material intelligently; (3) to *apply* it to a specific situation.

Searching is fun for those who know how to use the resources of the library.

Inductive approaches

The broad term *inductive approaches* is used by many social scientists to include inquiry, discovery, and the making of hypotheses, generalizations, and inferences. The word *inductive* refers to the process of making a general statement based on several specific instances. While the process of induction can be carried out in more depth and with more success in junior and senior high school, some aspects of this skill are suitable, in varying forms, at all levels.

The processes of inquiry and discovery are personal journeys into an exciting land of learning. Basically they utilize the three R's: reading, research, and reporting. Actually, they require ability to select pertinent material, organize the findings into a coherent whole, and to state the conclusions of the inquiry and the results of the discovery in a meaningful way.

In the discovery method the teacher assumes the role of a consultant rather than a director. However, for the elementary grades he has to be ready to furnish "clues." These may consist of eliciting from a student alternate words which are pertinent to the topic; e.g., the student needs more information on wheat, and he hasn't remembered to check grain or cereal, or farming. Perhaps the late primary or early intermediate youngster has just learned to use an encyclopedia and has to be reminded that he still must use other books as well.

The majority of elementary children will need considerable help in the reporting area. Whether the report is oral or written, it must communicate adequately, be composed of summary statements that can be supported by reference to verifiable facts, have sequential organization and pertinent information. The teacher will necessarily assume a more active role in the early stages of developing "discoveries."

As teachers become competent in the use of this method and confident of their own ability to handle a research problem, they will find that it has great advantages. For one thing the student takes an active, thinking role in his education. Additionally, the process becomes sequential as each child masters one skill and proceeds to enlarge his abilities to use materials.

Problem solving, according to Russell, is the process by which the child goes from the task or problem as he sees it to a solution which, for him, meets the demands of the problem.[1] The term "problem solving" is deceptive. It may suggest a relatively simple, unitary skill; in reality it involves a host of competencies which take years to crystalize.

WHAT SKILLS ARE INVOLVED?

In practice, the various areas of skill development are not discrete, yet their component elements must be singled out in order to promote mastery of the whole. There is no single format or method of categorizing these processes. They will be considered here under five headings.

   I. Dictionary and reference skills.
  II. Skills directly related to social studies such as map — globe, time — chronological, and graphic representations.
 III. Critical thinking skills.
 IV. Group participation skills.
  V. Personal growth and independence.

[1]David Russell,*Children's Thinking.* Boston: Ginn & Co., 1956, p. 25.

Each of the five areas should receive appropriate attention at all levels of the student's formal education.

The skills related to the use of the dictionary and reference materials are not unique to social studies; some aspects will require special attention because their application to social studies will be a little different from that in other areas such as language arts or science. Their development will occur as situations arise which require their use.

In dealing with social studies material, children encounter new words. Some words or terms are explained as they occur in texts; others have either been dealt with in easier material, or it is presumed that the word will already be a part of the child's vocabulary. Frequently the youngster will be able to pronounce the words; he may even be able to give a meaning; but he may *not* know that this meaning will not fit the particular situation with which he is confronted. Social studies offers unparalled opportunities to broaden word knowledge while refining thinking and acquiring the background necessary for social interpretations and learnings.

To be able to discover these new meanings, a child must master many basic skills. He must:

1. Know how to find the entry word. (In social studies, practice in alphabetizing may make use of a group of social studies words as "map," "chart," "bay," "lake," "history," etc.)
2. Be able to use guide words to facilitate the location of a word.
3. Understand and apply the pronunciation symbols so that the word can become a part of his speaking vocabulary.
4. Understand references to parts of speech to aid in fitting the word to the context in which he is working.
5. Be able to read well enough to say and *understand* the words that explain the new word.
6. Have enough experience and judgment to pick out the particular meaning which is applicable.
7. Understand the method of showing plurals of nouns, tenses of verbs and degrees of comparison of adjectives in order to select the correct form when he is reporting orally or writing a summary.
8. Be able to pick out key words in phrases in order to find the special meanings which combinations of words may have.
9. Be aware of the kind of information that is available in the dictionary with regard to technical terms, place names, abbreviations, etc.

Seldom will a child be able to compile his information on a topic through the use of only *one* book or *one* device. He will need to have knowledge of many kinds of source materials, understand how each may be used, and know what contributions each type of aid can make to the total. This will involve an intimate acquaintance with both his resource center and the public library.

To use these areas of learning effectively the following skills and understandings are important:

1. An acquaintance with the parts of a book and their use including:
   a. Title page.
      Title, author, publisher, and publication date.
   b. Table of contents.
      Arrangement, purpose, and occasions for use.

    c. Index.
Arrangement — alphabetical order like dictionary headings and subheadings; kind — vertical, horizontal, subject, author, etc; use of key words.

    d. Body.
Arrangement including chapters, headings, subheadings, etc.

    e. Appendices.
Purpose and placement.

    f. Bibliographies.
By chapter and for the entire book.

2. An understanding of encyclopedias including:
    a. Use of the letters on the spine as guides to the selection of the proper volume.
    b. Alphabetizing of proper names and subjects with more than one word.
    c. Use of key words in topic selection.
    d. Ability to classify or categorize information in locating material; e.g., looking for "camel" under "animal" to find further information.
    e. Ability to relate and further extend the range of material; e.g., to look also under desert for camel.
    f. Understanding of cross references as used in encyclopedias.
    g. Understanding of types of encyclopedias — children's, general, those relating to specific subjects such as the encyclopedia of geography, the encyclopedia of furniture, etc.

3. Other types of books and their special contributions to the entire social studies area:
    a. Almanacs.
    b. Atlases, including gazeteers.
    c. *Dictionary of Biography* and *Junior Book of Authors.*
    d. *Georgraphic Index.*
    e. Manuals and directories.

4. Periodicals.
    a. Acquaintance with types of magazines and their general contents.
    b. *Readers Guide to Periodical Literature.*
Instruction in method of indexing of periodicals and synthesizing.

5. Organizing information.
    a. Defining the topic.
        (1) Within competency of writer.
        (2) Within manageable dimension — neither too narrow nor too broad.
    b. Note-taking.
    c. Outlining.
    d. Footnoting.
    e. Making of bibliographies.

6. Using the facilities of the library.
    a. Card catalogue.
Outside letter guides on drawers.
Inside guides.
Author, subject, and title cards.
Kinds of information listed on cards.

    b. Shelf arrangement.
Fiction and nonfiction classifications.
Familiarity with Dewey Decimal and Library of Congress.

Classification systems.
Bibliographies.
c. Vertical file.
d. Acquaintance with references that deal primarily with social studies.
e. Knowledge of method of becoming alerted to new materials in general and also in specific situations.

WHAT PERCENTAGE OF FOURTH AND SIXTH GRADE CHILDREN CAN USE LIBRARY RESOURCES EFFECTIVELY?

During a three-year period from 1965 through 1967 all fourth and sixth grade children enrolled in a metropolitan elementary school with full library services were tested in their use of library resources. The assessment was jointly sponsored by the Knapp School Libraries Project, Ball State University, and the local school system. The testing and assessment of skills and understandings included an appraisal of the children's knowledge of the arrangement and classifications of materials within the library, their ability to understand the organization and function of the important parts of a book (title page, table of contents, index), and their skills in locating and using basic references, including the catalog cards, unabridged dictionary, encyclopedia, and National Geographic Index. A special reading test was constructed with the help and counsel of reading specialists to measure children's abilities in specific reading-study skills, and individual interviews were conducted to assess the children's use of the library, and their ability to express their ideas concerning their readings effectively.

Results of this comprehensive testing program are shown in the table below:

	Fourth Graders	Sixth Graders
1. Percentage of children that could quickly and easily point out the location of materials and references (maps, filmstrips, recordings, magazines, etc.).	85	91
2. Percentage of children that could correctly identify author, title, and subject cards.	85	95
3. Percentage of children that could correctly identify and use information recorded on the catalog cards.	85	95
4. Percentage of children that could locate shelved books using catalog cards.	68	91
5. Percentage of children that could use the table of contents in finding information within a book.	92	100
6. Percentage of children that could use an index within a book to find information.	80	98
7. Percentage of children that could use diacritical markings in pronouncing unfamiliar and unphonetic words.	59	75

8. Percentage of children that could find information within encyclopedias when given topics containing two or more key words.	91	97
9. Percentage of children that could use the National Geographic Index in locating information.	78	84
10. Percentage of children that could form clear, personal judgments about information they read.	45	52
11. Percentage of children that could easily distinguish between printed statements of facts and opinions.	50	78
12. Percentage of children that could skim quickly through printed materials to find information.	58	59
13. Percentage of children that could select books correctly in building a bibliography for a given topic.	41	59
14. Percentage of children that could construct an outline from clearly organized written materials.	80	82
15. Percentage of children that could take abbreviated but useful notes during oral presentations.	70	83
16. Percentage of children that could distinguish between significant information and less important data in written selections.	39	49
17. Percentage of children reading in three or more interest areas (folklore, biography, adventure, science, history, etc.).	78	85
18. Percentage of children who could express their ideas effectively in discussing the books they have read.	82	89

It seems apparent from these findings that most upper grade students should be able to use library materials with varying degrees of effectiveness.

Among the essential skills more common to social studies than those mentioned above are the ones related to maps and globes. These will include:

1. Directions.
   Cardinal or primary and intermediate.
2. Divisions and designations of parts of globe.
   a. Poles.
   b. Hemispheres.
   c. Latitude and Longitude.
   d. Tropics.
   e. Circles.
   f. Equator.
   g. Grids.
3. Scales.
   a. Use of scale of miles.
   b. Comparisons of maps of same area drawn to different scales.
   c. Measurement of elevation or altitude.

4. Symbols.
  a. Landforms.
     Continents, islands, peninsulas, deltas.
     Coasts and coastlines.
     Mountains, ranges, plateaus.
     Valleys and plains.
  b. Water forms.
     Oceans and seas.
     Rivers, creeks, tributaries, channels, sounds, straits, isthmuses.
     Lakes and ponds.
     Bays, inlets, and harbors.
  c. Man-made forms of features.
     Cities, towns, capitals, county seats.
     Highways, streets, and roads.
     Boundaries.
     Railroads, airports, and canals.
     Bridges, dams, and tunnels.
  d. Legends.

5. Special maps depicting climate, rainfall, population distribution.

The skillful use of maps and other graphic materials is one of the basic competencies developed in social studies. It requires careful, systematic teaching. Reading maps, charts, graphs, diagrams, or time lines can be extremely puzzling to a child who sees these graphic representations for the first time. The symbols, the legends, and the vocabulary are but a few of the elements which may contribute to confusion if some attempt is not made to guide children in the intelligent use of these materials.

There is little reason for the many difficulties and misconceptions associated with map reading. If early precautions are taken in teaching children to understand maps and other graphic materials, they should not encounter severe difficulties. Children entering third or fourth grade undoubtedly have been exposed to maps both in and out of school, but it is the responsibility of the teacher at these and subsequent levels to introduce the various purposes of maps and the best ways of interpreting them. This is a gradual process achieved through the use of simple illustrations, demonstrations, and experiences in the actual use of maps.

When the children are first introduced to a map of the world or a globe, attention should be drawn to the projection which has been used. Comparisons should be made with other types of projections. Comparisons should be made with the globe, for this will contribute to a basic understanding of the idea of global projections. A hollow rubber ball may be used to illustrate what happens when we attempt to represent a surface of a sphere on a flat surface. The ball should have an outline drawn on it, both at the center and at both "poles." The ball is then cut from each "pole" toward the "equator" into several segments until it can be flattened against a board.

In the early stages of discovery the teacher may locate a variety of maps in reference books. A marker in each will help children locate the maps quickly. Each should then be encouraged to discover the special type of information offered by each map. In this collection there may be maps showing political boundaries, ship routes, air routes, rainfall, population, natural regions, and products. A list may be made of children's findings. As a result, the children will begin to realize that each map must be selected and used for specific purposes.

Legends which appear on maps are, of course, important tools to understanding. The word "legend" may be familiar to the child because he associates it with the stories he has heard or read. Through discussion a transition in meaning may be made, so the child understands that the legend helps tell the story of the map. Some teachers begin with maps of their own classrooms. Here the children can easily see the entire area that is represented and make legends to fit the area. The bathroom area may be shaded with lines or colors, for example, to set it off from other parts of the room.

The development of maps and globe skills is essential to an understanding of our world.

The crucial understandings related to the use of scales, directions, diagrams, graphs, and time lines may also be developed inductively. In each case the teacher may begin with something that is close at hand and easily understood. A scale drawing of the playground, directions related to streets in the neighborhood, graphs showing some of the characteristics of children within the room (number of boys and girls, those over four and a half feet, and those who stand less than four and a half feet tall, etc.). When we develop concepts and generalizations inductively, children are more likely to grasp the rationale for their use and the functions they serve.

In addition to maps and globes, there are:

1. Pictures
2. Drawings and posters
3. Photographs
4. Filmstrips and slides
5. Films
6. Cartoons
7. Charts
8. Diagrams
9. Graphs — line, bar and circle
10. Dioramas and models
11. Scale models and mockups
12. Learning kits
13. Games
14. Records
15. Tapes and transparencies
16. Realia

As suggested earlier in the chapter concerning the task of the social studies teacher, critical thinking often involves the extensive use of resources. Like other human competencies, critical thinking is not a simple composite of skills; it involves many interrelated competencies with subtle shadings. In the listing below, activities are not mutually exclusive, nor do they appear evenly throughout the elementary grades. Furthermore, varying degrees of precision will be reflected in the problem-solving activities of children at each grade level.

Critical thinking skills in elementary social studies will relate to the following activities.

1. Analyzing.
   a. Definition of terms.
      Are these definitions:
      Clear.
      Complete.
   b. Determination of sequence and trends.
   c. Recognition of problems and aspects of problems.
   d. Ability to recognize valid and invalid reasoning.
2. Weighing the evidence.
   a. Selection of *criteria* necessary to determine if statements are facts, principles, opinions, etc.
   b. Relating facts to one another.
   c. Placement of material in proper classifications and categories.
   d. Comparison of ideas to determine whether they are identical, similar, parallel, inconsistent, unrelated or contradictory.
   e. Ability to distinguish cause and effect relationships.
   f. Formulation and testing of hypotheses.
   g. Decision as to whether the facts support specific generalizations.
   h. The drawing of inferences.
   i. Formulation of judgments.
3. Determining reliability.
   a. Sources of information.
      Adequacy.
      Primary or secondary.
      Verifiable or unverifiable.
      Relevant or irrelevant.
      Fact or opinion.
      Objective or subjective.
   b. Author's qualifications.
   c. Consistency of statements.
      Ambiguity.
      Vagueness.
      Equivocation.
   d. Other relevant factors.
      Slanting of material.
      Use of emotional language.
      Connotation and metaphor.
      Bias of author or publisher.
      Recognition of sterotypes and cliches.
      Propaganda.

4. Assessing validity.
   a. Internal consistency of material — point of view, sequence, logic.
   b. Warranted conclusions; i.e., do the conclusions follow from the premises.
   c. External and internal aspects.
   Authenticity (external).
   Meaning and accuracy of contents (internal).
5. Participating in many types of thinking activity.
   a. Convergent thinking.
   Using many specific examples to arrive at generalizations.
   b. Divergent thinking.
   Using many possibilities to discover several useful modes of expression or hypotheses.
   c. Creative thinking.
   Posing solutions that are not necessarily or only partially based on previously accepted proofs.
   Suggesting entirely new approaches.

Another area of pupil skills relates to human relationships within groups. Frequently this aspect of social studies education has been neglected, but increasingly, social studies educators recognize that specific instruction in this area is necessary if our attempts to develop the full potentialities of each individual are to have any meaning. Some attitudes and skills that are essential to satisfactory group work are:

1. The development of a sensitivity to the needs and feelings of other people.
2. A point of view which is open and flexible enough to change when circumstances warrant.
3. The possession of a self-concept sufficiently mature to allow for interaction with others.
4. Enough maturity and experience to withhold judgments until all evidence is presented.
5. A reasonable balance between emotional and intellectual factors.
6. An ability to both lead and follow.
7. A willingness to assume some responsibility in discussions.
8. Readiness to cooperate with both younger and older people.
9. Enough maturity to expect to help others as well as to be helped.
10. The emotional maturity to practice self-control and self-direction.
11. Willingness to abide by the decision of the majority.
12. Some ability to relate points of view and sources of information.
13. The judgment to choose leaders wisely.
14. A sufficiently developed time sense to allot portions of the work efficiently.
15. An ability to plan alternate courses of action when original plans do not materialize.
16. Experience in cooperative planning.

If, after covering skills such as those outlined above, the individual still is not able to evaluate the outcomes of his efforts, his growth will be limited. Frequently, evaluation is thought to be the sole prerogative of the teacher. Unfortunately, the intent seems to relate more closely to discovering if the teacher is "doing his job" than to whether or not the student is acquiring the basic skills and tools necessary to his continued progress. Evaluation must, of necessity, involve both the teacher and the learner. It is a preliminary, ongoing, and final process and should include elements such as the following:

1. Is the student (or group) ready (intellectually, emotionally, etc.) for the proposed problem?
2. Is motivation sufficient to carry through the project?
3. What skills, attitudes, and values are being or have been acquired, developed, or changed?
4. Do the learnings or problem-solving skills have carry-over after the class session is finished?
5. Is the student or group relating this experience to previous experiences? Can he or they intelligently discuss these relationships?
6. Is the experience a satisfying one? Why or why not?
7. Is there evidence of permanent learning in intellectual, social, and emotional development, as well as in the acquisition of further skills and facts?
8. Do the learning tasks have use-value in terms of the child's perceptions of self and his environment?

The ability to assess all aspects of the problem, whether it be the more mechanical activities or those on the level of critical thinking, is crucial to continued growth in social studies.

ACTIVITIES WHICH MAY STIMULATE READING INTERESTS AND STRENGTHEN LIBRARY STUDY AND CRITICAL THINKING SKILLS

1. Traveling far and near. Make a list of the different cities children choose to visit on an imaginary trip. Appoint ticket agents to represent each city. Each agent is provided with a number of questions which the children must answer before they can board the train or boat and leave the city. They find their answers in library books.
2. Make a tape of your class's sharing periods involving the discussion of stories at the beginning of the year so that you can compare a tape made later in the year with your beginning attempts.
3. In order to interest slower pupils in reading, the teacher may develop a collection of good short stories from children's magazines. Each story may be bound separately in an attractive cover. Short interesting stories require shorter attention spans than full-length books.
4. After studying a number of historical characters, such as Alexander the Great, Columbus, Marco Polo, Daniel Boone, and others, classes may act out a short program entitled "Who Am I?" They may use pantomime.
5. Children from the class may be selected to present a topic of current interest to the class each week. This group has the responsibility of advising the class of the topic chosen, dividing the chosen topic into different areas for presentation, and recommending sources of information.
6. With paper, wire, and scraps of cloth, make book characters. Near them, place descriptions of the people they represent.
7. Libraries often use a picture-completion device, such as adding a part to a comical figure as each new book is read.
8. Children may make overlays for use with the overhead projector to illustrate the development of a story or the major points in a report.

9. The library corner may be made more interesting by adding a number of files. The filing cards may be very large for lower-graders and labeled with interesting questions: (1) What do we know about animals? (2) Where is the sun's family? (3) Where do our clothes come from? etc.

10. Use clay, soap, wood, or plaster to make models of characters or animals from the stories read.

11. Have the students design their own book jackets for the stories they have read. These may be shaped or designed to further illustrate the theme of the book.

12. Create a colorful class mural of historical characters on the blackboard or wrapping-paper.

13. Once a year, have all the oral reports emphasize the setting of the story and its influence on the main character.

14. Provide a small table on which children can place push-out or cut-out scenes from famous books.

15. Help children think through their reactions to books. Stating real reasons for liking or disliking a book requires critical thinking.

16. Occasionally find a musical accompaniment to go with the telling of a good story.

17. Help children learn to compare or contrast books which are similar in content.

18. Have a child think through a story he has read and suggest changes which he feels would improve the story.

19. As a class, think up new adventures or incidents to add to the beginning, to the end, or to the body of a book.

20. Use scenic wallpaper with an early American or Spanish theme as a background for books on these topics.

21. A book featuring unusual incidents in history may lend itself to the making of a colorful map of literary characters and places.

22. Encourage several children to choose their favorite authors. Each may give a brief biography and tell about a few of their author's better-known books.

23. Invite children who have read the same book to each write a set of questions which they think readers should be able to answer after completing the story.

24. Order a film which has been adapted from one of the books which the children have read.

25. Encourage those who have read "how-to-make" books to give a step-by-step demonstration of techniques they have learned.

26. Discuss with the children what they would like to be when they grow up. Encourage each to find a book in the library about someone in his particular field of interest, or about the profession itself, and report to the group on it.

27. Elect volunteers to serve as library news reporters to give reports to the class on new and interesting additions to the library, to help those who have particular interests but cannot find the books they like, to find additional information for the class relating to units the class is studying, etc.

28. Ask children to identify their favorite President, athlete, hero or animal after a study of United States history and organize information on the topic.

29. A general agreement may be worked out whereby each week a different room (or grade) may make book posters for the library on a class-selected theme. Charts may call attention to new reference books, new stories, or non-print materials.

30. The library may feature a particular theme each week — books about Lincoln around the time of his birthday, or insects during a warm month when children may be collecting them. Countries which are commonly studied in social studies may be featured also.

31. The teacher may type children's stories and form them into a book. A table of contents may be made and the book may be catalogued in the library.

32. Develop a small catalog of sketches of authors. Add letters to and from the authors when possible.

When students know how to use the library correctly they are able to work independently and to search for their own information. Some activities which are helpful in . . . .

Developing Locational Competencies to Strengthen Specific Library Skills

33. Classification Game. Each pupil is given a slip of paper bearing a call number. He then arranges himself with the rest of the class according to his call number. Blocks of wood decorated with call numbers and bright paint to resemble a book may also be used. The pupils arrange them in order.

34. Classification Game. Children chosen from groups at different library tables are assigned classification numbers. Each child is directed to see how quickly he can find a book bearing his number and return to his place. As each searcher returns, he is asked to tell the class his number and the subject of the book he has found. This arouses interest in numbers and gives an opportunity to explain the Dewey Decimal System in its most elementary form.

35. Alphabetical Antics Games. This activity is similar to the familiar game of "Hot or Cold." One child is given the name of an author to find on the shelves, and the others tell him his approximate "temperature" as he approaches or misses it. This has the advantage of fixing the attention of the entire group on the shelf arranged while individuals take turns hunting.

36. The teacher may ask the children to print their names on the board neatly. Each child may then copy them in alphabetical order. This is a simple and effective way of introducing alphabetizing.

37. Make a list of words related to library materials (atlas, encyclopedia, vertical file, biography) and play "I'm thinking of a word." Give a short clue and ask the children to guess the term. Library words may also be used on spelling tests.

38. Children may be encouraged to write stories about their favorite place in the library. "If I were a book, I'd like to be in____!" (bio., fict., ref., etc.)

39. Introduce children to the organization of materials contained in the library. Which is the quickest to find? What are the advantages of using particular sources?

40. On paper or cards give a book title, author's name, or subject. Have children see who can get the complete information and find it in a given amount of time. Children may start together after they have found the correct drawer. They check out when finished.

41. Have an unprocessed book from each area of the library on a table in the room. See how many children can match the item with its "home" area in the library. Later, cards may be substituted for books.

42. Ask the class to compile a list of their favorite things (football, puppets, eating, dolls, ice-cream cones, horses, etc.) Then have them complete the assignment by finding as many books as they can that have something to do with their topic. Hopefully, they will want to read some of the books they have found.

43. Ask children to make a list of all the *kinds* of non-printed materials the library contains. Some children may want to demonstrate or explain particular materials for the class.

44. Check yourself to see that you have introduced the class to the following basic resources:

    1. *Famous First Facts*
    2. *The Statesman's Yearbook*
    3. *Who's Who in America*
    4. *Facts About the Presidents*
    5. *Animals of the World*
    6. *Webster's Geographical Dictionary*
    7. *Index to Children's Poetry*
    8. *Roget's International Thesaurus*
    9. *Handbook of Nature Study*
    10. *Bartlett's Familiar Quotations*

45. A copy of a library card may be drawn on the blackboard representing a book with which the children are familiar. The book will be listed under the author's name. Questions relating to the information on the card may be asked. The teacher may then point out that when we don't know the author's name, we can look up the book under its title. She may then draw a copy of the title card for the same book. The same procedure may be used in introducing the subject card.

46. Using the dictionary. After the children have used the dictionary for some time, the teacher and the group may summarize the types of information it offers. This information varies somewhat from dictionary to dictionary, but a chart like the following may be constructed:

Uses of Our Dictionary

1. It gives the correct spelling or spellings of words.
2. It gives the correct pronunciation or pronunciations for words.
3. It may give several meanings for the same word.
4. It shows changes in the form of a word.
5. It sometimes illustrates the meaning of the word.
6. It helps with some abbreviations.
7. It has two or three special lists of words, usually at the back of the dictionary.

47. Knowing Reference Materials. Depending on what reference books are available, the teacher and children may make a chart of the information to be found in various types of references. This may include:

1. What an encyclopedia tells us.
2. What an atlas is.
3. What the almanac tells us.
4. What the *Statesman's Yearbook* tells us.
5. What the dictionary tells us.

After this information has been collected, the children may answer questions such as these:

1. To look up the meaning of *aviation* I will use_____.
2. To look up the history or development of *aviation* I will use_____.
3. To look up modern maps for our study of *aviation* I will use_____.

48. The teacher may pass out 8½ x 11 paper which the children can divide into twelve squares. She may then provide the children with duplicates of cards from the card catalog and ask the pupils to enter the call numbers in the squares in the order they would appear in the card file.

49. The teacher may draw a floor plan of the library on the chalkboard. Have children fasten titles of books or little book jackets on the board with magnetic fasteners. The titles or jackets should correspond to their correct location in the library.

50. A bulletin board may be constructed (either temporary or permanent) with topics in one column and reference sources in another. Children may be asked to match topics with the most likely sources.

51. A treasure hunt may be arranged. The child may be asked to find an encyclopedia article on a particular topic. Within the article a particular person is mentioned most frequently. The children then secure the biography of this person which mentions his home town. When they locate a description of his home town, they find a note that tells them that they have won.

52. Identify a topic for the entire class and see how much information the library has on that particular topic. Explore *all* types of materials.

53. List on the board each week one basic reference (such as the almanac or Lincoln Library) and ask the class to find out what it can be used for.

54. Ask the class where they would look for information on a particular topic. For example:

1. A map of Asia
2. Appendix of a book
3. Glossary
4. Table of contents of a book
5. Index of a book
6. *Famous First Facts*

55. Provide children with individual topics which should be researched, using at least three sources (a book, an encyclopedia, and a magazine, for example).

56. After visiting the Library, kindergarten children may write an experience story (with the teacher), explaining what the librarian does and all the things visitors may do in the library.

57. A chart may be constructed to illustrate five or six steps in finding and using books:

1. We look for a good book	2. We look to see if the book is right for us
3. We fill out the library card	4. We stamp the book at the desk
5. We enjoy the book at home	6. We return the book on time

Developing Comprehension Skills

58. The teacher may want to keep in mind the various levels of discussion:

1. What happened?
   remembering
   recounting
   relating

2. How did you feel?
   deepening awareness of personal reaction

3. Could this really happen?
   checking reality
   bringing incidents from real life to bear on the story

4. What would you have done?
   problem solving

5. What have we learned?
   conceptualizing
   generalizing
   finding the principle
   reapplication of understanding

59. Children may be helped to understand various purposes for reading:

1. Reading for central thought
   Children read a paragraph and give the main idea.
   Children choose an appropriate title for the selection.
   Children give original titles for a selection.

2. Reading to follow sequence of events or ideas.
   The teacher lists a sequence of events and the children arrange the events in the right order.
   The children answer specific questions, such as "What happened when the fox smelled fire?"
   The children supply endings to selections or stories.

3. Reading to note details
   The children give the facts or ideas of a selection, orally or in writing.
   The children answer specific questions.

4. Reading to follow directions
The children actually carry out written directions.
The children answer specific questions about directions.

5. Reading to discover cause and effect
The children answer specific questions about a selection.
Children analyze reasons for, or causes of, major events.

60. Underlying important ideas. The children may be given a short paragraph to read and instructed to underline the word or words indicating the central thought of the passage. Example:

> People who lived *long ago* used *simple tools.* They used some of these tools to hunt or prepare food. Some tools were used for preparing skins; other tools were used for making simple household items.

61. Organizing information. Ask the group to help make a cooperative outline of a familiar story. For example, the story of George Washington could start as follows:

1. George Washington's early life
   a.
   b.
2. Washington's trip West
   a.
   b.
3. Washington's service in the Revolutionary War
   a.
   b.

62. The teacher may discuss the difference between true stories and stories in which imagined events take place. The teacher should then give an example of a very short story of each type. One or two sentences will do. Then the children are asked to tell which story is make-believe and which is true. When the children are familiar with the difference between the two types, a child may volunteer to tell a story. The story may be of some imaginary event or of something which could really happen. The storyteller then asks another child, "Make-believe or true?"

63. The teacher may read short simple stories and ask the children to make up a title for each story. In selecting a title, the children are really identifying the main theme or idea of the story.

64. The teacher may read a short story and ask the pupils to retell the plot in one sentence. The children may need considerable help in making a good summary. Use stories which are on the reading level of the group. At first, the teacher may need to help the children decide which is the best of several summaries.

65. Sometimes it is helpful to read a story to a group of slow readers, have them review the main points, and write what they say on the chalkboard. They are frequently helped by seeing the story written on their own vocabulary level. If a story is a favorite, it may be recorded more permanently on a chart, and a member of the group may occasionally read the simple version to others in the group.

66. If children are unfamiliar with methods of outlining and organizing, it may be well to take several topics and expand them together on the board, using the outline form.

67. Some teachers have found it valuable to identify topics that individual children are pursuing and have the entire class assist in underlining the key words which may be used in locating information on these topics.

68. Middle-grade teachers have sometimes used specimen encyclopedia articles (abbreviated) which lend themselves to outlining and summarizing to teach these skills.

69. It may be helpful to ask children to preview films or filmstrips that are scheduled for class use and prepare guide questions for the class. These same children may introduce new words used in the film.

70. The indexes of books have sometimes been used for a type of detective game. The index may be used to find a map (in the book) which in turn gives further clues to the mystery question.

71. With more advanced pupils, a teacher may ask, "What information would an author need about Canada in order to develop an interesting story with a setting in that country?"

72. As a guide to students, the teacher may have a chart outlining the various steps in simple research:

    1. check question (not too narrow or too broad)
    2. check out the usefulness of particular sources
    3. read and take notes
    4. outline or summarize notes
    5. write a rough draft
    6. rewrite and proof-read
    7. make a bibliography.

73. A TV quiz program may be arranged in which contestants read statements and determine which are facts and which are fancy. When a child answers "fact" or "fancy" correctly, he may keep his card. The child with the greatest number of cards at the end of the contest may be declared the winner. Examples of statements:

    1. Nylon is made from coal (fact)
    2. The flying horse carried the gypsy home (fancy)

74. Authors usually write for one or more of three reasons: to inform, to entertain, to offer social criticism. Pupils may be taught to identify the author's purpose of writing.

75. Stories of historical events usually involve a character, a setting, and a series of events (the plot). Children may learn to weigh the relative importance of these.

76. The teacher may prepare six or eight sample reports of differing quality and ask the class to judge their completeness and accuracy.

77. A teacher may identify a typical problem in social studies and list many statements of information on the board. The children may then be asked to judge the relevancy of the information in the light of the problem identified.

78. Hazy, ill-defined topics may be listed on the board. The teacher may then challenge the class to rewrite them in a form that would allow a student to pursue the topics with profit.

Chapter VIII

FOSTERING CREATIVITY IN SOCIAL STUDIES

"Imagination is more important than knowledge,"
Albert Einstein

THE NATURE OF CREATIVITY

Creativity is a rather elusive factor in human affairs, for in a very real sense it represents the ability to think of *what is not.* Torrance defines it as "The process of sensing problems or gaps in information, forming ideas or hypotheses, testing and modifying these hypotheses, and communicating the results."[1] This process may lead to any one of several kinds of products — verbal or nonverbal, concrete or abstract. It appears that the creative act is a deliberate process involving new combinations or patternings of materials, movements, words, symbols, or ideas.

The word "creative" is not new. According to Bently[2], it came into use in the late twenties when educators chose it as a label to describe child-centered teaching. According to the pedagogues of the twenties, "creative" teaching departed from traditional patterns by fostering unique and original expression in children's writing, art, drama, dance, and music. Today it refers to a new concept of instruction in all areas of the curriculum. The production of something new or original is included in almost all definitions of creativity. It is often contrasted with imitativeness and conformity. Creativity may be thought of as a successful step into the unknown, divergence or deviation from the norm, or breaking out of the mold.

There is some disagreement regarding the extent to which an act must be unique in order to qualify as "creative". According to Thurstone[3] it makes no difference whether society regards the idea as new as long as the individual reaches a solution that implies some novelty for him. Stewart[4] also contends that an idea may be "creative" even though it may have been produced by someone else at an earlier time. Stein[5], however, insists that creativity must be defined in terms of the culture in which it appears. For Stein, "novelty" or "newness" suggests that the creative product did not exist previously in the same form. Although it may contain existing materials and knowledge, it must also contain new elements. At the elementary school level we can hardly expect children to match their imaginative efforts against those of society. It seems more realistic to suggest that "creative" ideas for the elementary child are new combinations of ideas, movements, and materials which he has produced in a form which he and his classmates have not seen before.

---

[1] E. Paul Torrance, *Creativity and Academic Achievement," Journal of Educational Research,* 59:269-271; February, 1966.

[2] Joseph Bently, "Creativity and Academic Achievement," *Journal of Educational Research,* 59:269-271; February, 1966.

[3] L. L. Thurstone, *Applications of Psychology,* New York: Harper and Row Publishers, 1952.

[4] G. W. Stewart, "Can Productive Thinking Be Taught?" *Journal of Higher Education,* 21:411-414, 1950.

[5] M. I. Stein, "Creativity and Culture." *Journal of Psychology,* 36:311-322; 1953.

Intelligence and creativity are not synonymous, but above average intelligence appears to be important to truly creative expression. According to Torrance[6], about seventy percent of the students scoring in the upper twenty percent on measures of creativity would also score in the upper twenty percent on intelligence tests. Standardized tests of creativity have been extremely difficult to devise. The term "creativity" itself suggests a divergence from common standards. Some of the tests that have been developed make use of: (1) inkblots; (2) picture construction from incomplete figures, geometric figures, dots and shades of colored paper; (3) verbalizations while painting; (4) ideas for product improvement; and (5) constructing images from sounds.

Fortunately, a teacher need not rely entirely upon prepared tests in identifying creative behavior. Creative students appear to have some characteristics in common. They tend to enjoy experimentation and often pursue ideas with a tenacity and perseverance unusual for their age group. Their preoccupation with ideas will frequently take the form of day dreams. They often detect relationships that escape the notice of others, and contribute more than their share of provocative and penetrating questions to classroom discussions. They are likely to have an abundance of curiosity and inquisitiveness as well as personal independence and self-assurance. Their originality and individualistic attitudes are, however, frequently interpreted as "social irresponsibility," "incompetence," or "inability to follow directions." Isaac Newton, Winston Churchill, and Thomas Edison were all considered rather dull during their early years of schooling, and even Albert Enstein escaped the notice of his teachers until he was well into manhood. Creative people frequently do not wish to dwell on what they know; they are far more interested in thinking and talking about what they do not yet know.

Research relating to the stages of creative development reveals that most of the creative thinking abilities develop with a relatively high degree of consistency up through the third grade. There is a drop at the fourth grade level, with a corresponding drop in reading efficiency. The earlier trend then continues on uninterrupted through the fifth and sixth grade levels. Educators and psychologists have been unable to explain the fourth grade slump. It appears to be a cultural phenomenon rather than an innate predisposition on the part of students.

CLASSROOM CLIMATES WHICH ENCOURAGE CREATIVITY

Our growing social conformity, our penchant for convention, and our invention of machines to help with problem solving has spawned a profound need for creativity at all levels. We are on the edge of a thoroughly standardized society — one in which our lives are cut to pattern and preplanned like the ingredients in packaged cake mixes. Unfortunately, our homes and schools have contributed as much to the homogenization of our society as other major institutions. Biber[7] contends that individuality among children has been lost under the impact of socializing pressures in child rearing and the realities of teaching children in the classroom. Education has imposed a structure of didactic instruction, right-wrong criteria, and dominance of logical reasoning over the inituitive-subjective so early in the child's life that his creative potential is often inhibited.

[6]*op. cit.*, p. 7.

[7]Barbara Biber, "Premature Structuring as a Deterrant to Creativity." *American Journal of Orthopsychiatry*, 29:280-290, 1959.

Halek[8] suggests that the most important elements within a creative classroom atmosphere are those that relate to the basic factor-complexes influencing perceptions, feelings, and behavior. A creative atmosphere deals with intangibles: attitudes, reactions, and feeling tones. It strengthens mutual confidence and trust, builds courage to venture, and fosters a hope for change. It takes courage to be creative, to break away from the old patterns of reward through conformity. Most children have been taught that "thoughtful," "dependable," "responsible" helpers make the best classroom citizens. They are the ones to whom we point with pride. In any free exchange of ideas there is always the fear that "others" will not be pleased. When a child has to produce to please others, some portion of himself must be withheld.

Children have a natural urge to explore.

One key notion underlying many of the current investigations of creativity is that a high degree of definiteness or focus of attention decreases the likelihood of new insights. Dispersed attention may provide a better setting for creative thought. Toying with ideas or vague wondering may, on occasion, produce better results. It is important to get out on the periphery where problems may be seen from a very different perspective. So long as men focused their attentions on the improvement of the gas lamp we could not have the electric light.

While the classroom atmosphere is the single most important influence on the child in school, the environment of the whole school is also important in supporting the efforts of the classroom teacher. An administration that is interested in progress and change,

---

[8]Loretta Halek, "Atmosphere for Creativity." *Delta Kappa Gamma Bulletin,* 31:10-14, Summer, 1965.

creative teaching, and imaginative programs will challenge teachers to experiment and search for new ideas. And it will also accept the confusion and chaos that frequently accompany such ventures. Whenever old patterns are broken there are loose ends, frustrations, and elements of fear, hesitancy, and ambivalence.

ROLE OF THE TEACHER

A creative teacher is likely to be a secure individual who enjoys probing and analyzing baffling problems, creating and synthesizing ideas. He is comfortable with uncertainty. He has a curious, questioning mind and an acute appreciation of new ideas. He is likely to view learning as a process of social invention, and children as moving, developing personalities rather than inert vessels to be filled with knowledge. In a sense he performs the role of stage manager-producer in a production that encompasses all of human experience. He provides the setting, the props, the supporting cast, and generous applause for those who are willing to play out their interpretations of life.

The teacher's role in stimulating creativity is, in part, like that of all good teaching. Careful planning and timing, the imaginative use of human and material resources, and effective methods of evaluation are basic ingredients found in all of our best educational programs. The *creative* teacher, however, must have acute sensitivity and a feeling of genuine urgency in her efforts to draw out the latent expressions of inquisitiveness, curiosity, and invention within children. All too frequently, creative expression is smothered under a cloak of efficiency and business-like management. Lowenfeld and Brittain[9] believe that what a teacher does in stimulating creativity depends on three factors: (1) his own personality, of which his own creativeness, degree of sensitivity, and flexibility in relation to environment are an important part; (2) his ability to put himself into the place of others; and (3) his understanding and knowledge of the needs of those whom he seeks to teach.

Many teachers possess the qualities and skills needed to perform at the creative level, but they frequently brand themselves as "uncreative" because they do not fully understand what creativity is or how it can be developed. In addition, they usually work under conditions which do not solicit or place a high priority on the release of their own creative powers. An investigation by Williams[10] revealed that the elementary teachers he studied did not understand what was meant by creativity in education and had considerable difficulty recognizing creative talent in their students. Eberle[11] repeated the study in 1966 and again found that elementary teachers were unable to identify creative pupils. However, a subsequent study by Williams[12] suggests that when teachers are given in-service training in creativity, particulary in the understanding of the creative process and its expression in children's work, a significant improvement in teacher recognition of creative students results.

[9]Viktor Lowenfeld and W. Lambert Brittain, *Creative and Mental Growth,* New York: Macmillan Company, 1967, 412 pages.

[10]Frank Williams, "Reinforcement of Originality," in *Reinforcement in Classroom Learning,* Washington, D. C.: U. S. Dept. of Health, Education and Welfare, 1964.

[11]R. F. Eberle, *Teaching for Creative Productive Thinking Through Subject Matter Content,* Edwardsville, Illinois: Edwardsville Community Schools, 1966.

[12]Frank Williams, "Training Children to be Creative May Have Little Effect on Original Classroom Performance — Unless the Traits of Creative Thinking are Taught within a Structure of Knowledge." *California Journal of Educational Research,* XVII (2), (1966), 73-79.

It is not enough for teachers to know that creativity is possible; they must be shown how subject matter can be treated at various conceptual levels in ways which encourage students to value novelty, develop fluidity of associations and flexibility in thinking patterns, as well as to develop an interest in probing new dimensions of knowledge. Student creativity demands both ample opportunity for its exercise and challenging instruction in a classroom atmosphere characterized by encouragement and approval. And teachers themselves must be given freedom and encouragement to experiment with different ways of handling subject matters. Creative teaching takes responsibility for stimulating, guiding, and provoking children in the search for new ideas. Creativity is seldom the product of passive teaching.

It is important to distinguish between excitement and anxiety in the creative classroom. Excitement normally heightens enjoyment and contributes to constructive working relationships; anxiety often has the opposite effect. According to Guenther,[13] anxiety: (1) has a definite tendency to interfere with the cognitive processes; (2) usually produces an interfering effect upon complex learning; and (3) appears to inhibit creative thinking.

STRATEGIES FOR DEVELOPING CREATIVE THINKING

There is no magic formula or approach to creative teaching that will assure success. Creative action, regardless of the end product or the maturity of the children involved, is made up of skills related to comprehension, application, analysis, synthesis and evaluation of information. Williams[14] believes that there are twenty or more dimensions of teaching and learning that often promote creative thinking:

1. Using paradoxes.
2. Using analogies.
3. Sensing deficiencies (unknown knowledge).
4. Thinking about possibilities; formulating hypotheses.
5. Asking provocative questions (inquiry).
6. Listing attributes of things.
7. Exploring the mystery of things.
8. Encouraging original behavior.
9. Learning to expect and accept change.
10. Teaching about rigidity, functional fixation, habit.
11. Teaching skills of search — historical, descriptive, controlled observations.
12. Building a tolerance for ambiguity (setting purposeful blocks).
13. Providing opportunities for intuitive expression.
14. Teaching the processes of invention and innovation.
15. Capitalizing on failures, mistakes, and accidents.
16. Analyzing traits of creative individuals.
17. Encouraging new thinking based on stored knowledge.
18. Teaching for cause and effect relationships.
19. Developing receptivity to unexpected responses, ideas, and solutions.
20. Developing skills in reading creatively.

[13]Richard Guenther, "Anxiety and Its Relation to Cognitive Processes." *Child Study Center Bulletin,* 2:75-84, 1966.

[14]Frank Williams, "Teach for...Creative Thinking", *The Instructor,* 76:88-89; May, 1967.

The things we create are, in reality, extensions of our own personalities.

Sensory awareness is a particularly important part of creative activity. Civilized man may have less sensory awareness than his primitive forbearers, for it is less essential to his survival. We have learned to selectively tune out offensive noises, odors, and irritations in our attempts to adjust to an increasingly complex world. Our sensory awareness has become one of the casualties of modern civilization. The sensory awareness of the child often needs to be sharpened and refined in order to develop and maintain an adequate response to the environment. This is part of being a fully alive and sensitive individual. The creative teacher seeks to keep this dimension of human experience alive and active through intimate contacts with the world around us.

Smith[15] summarizes some of the dimensions of creative teaching as follows:

1. In creative teaching, something new, different or unique results.
2. In creative teaching, divergent thinking processes are stressed.
3. In creative teaching, motivational tensions are a prerequisite to the creative process. The process serves as a tension-relieving agent.
4. In creative teaching, open-ended situations are utilized.
5. In creative teaching, there comes a time when the teacher withdraws and children face the unknown themselves.
6. In creative teaching, the outcomes are unpredictable.
7. In creative teaching, conditions are set which make possible preconscious thinking.
8. Creative teaching means that students are encouraged to generate and develop their own ideas.
9. In creative teaching, differences, uniqueness, individuality, originality are stressed and rewarded.
10. In creative teaching, the process is as important as the product.
11. In creative teaching, certain conditions must be set to permit creativity to appear.
12. Creative teaching is success-rather than failure-oriented.
13. In creative teaching, provision is made to learn many knowledges and skills, but provision is also made to apply these knowledges and skills in new problem-solving situations.
14. In creative teaching, self-initiated learning is encouraged.
15. In creative teaching, skill of constructive criticism and evaluation skills are developed.
16. In creative teaching, ideas and objects are manipulated and explored.
17. Creative teaching employs democratic processes.
18. In creative teaching, methods are used which are unique to the development of creativity.

We may also discuss strategies in the light of specific teaching practices which inhibit creativity. Limiting areas of investigation, so that children must study predetermined topics, or designating highly restrictive time limits for the completion of work will tend to hinder creative effort. Likewise, prescribing the approach, form or style of projects works against pupil creativity. Some teachers focus far too much attention on the mechanics of planning and writing and stifle sparks of imagination and inquisitiveness before the child really gets underway. Studies by Bruner and Caron[16] suggest that early over-achievers in school are likely to be seekers after the "right way to do it," and their capacity to transform their learning into viable thought structures tends to be lower than that of children merely achieving at levels predicted by intelligence tests. Unhappily, teachers are often poor listeners, and good listeners are needed for creative work. If we expect children to generate ideas, we must be willing to listen and react. A creative child without an audience will normally quit producing.

[15] James Smith, *Creative Teaching of the Language Arts in the Elementary School.* Boston: Allyn and Bacon, Inc., 1967.

[16] J. S. Bruner and A. J. Caron, "Cognition, Anxiety, and Achievements in the Preadolescent," *Journal of Educational Psychology,* Vol. 54, (June 1963), p. 197-209.

CREATIVITY IN SOCIAL STUDIES

Creativity in social studies has often been viewed as the imaginative use of student writing, art, music, and drama to illustrate patterns of living, historical events, economic activities and man's artistic accomplishments. Many of these activities are very useful, but they represent correlations with other subject areas rather than the use of creative thinking in the search for understandings and solutions to basic human problems. There has been a recent shift from creative art projects in social studies to a greater emphasis on creative and critical thinking. Divergent thinking is a particularly important element in creativity. Massialas and Zevin describe the dimensions of divergent thinking as follows:

> Divergent thinking ... involves a variety of responses to a problem which is not well defined and which has no established way of solving it. [sic] Divergent thinking involves such attributes as fluency, flexibility and elaboration.[17]

It is important to recognize that the discovery or framing of solutions to problems, particularly complex social problems, does not normally result from sheer happenstance. Discovery favors the well-prepared mind — the mind with knowledge and information, with expectancies that there will be relationships or regularities in the environment, and with some understanding of the heuristics of discovery. Bruner[18] seems to suggest that we do not yet have a formula or strategy that can be taught to children and used in a wide variety of problematic situations. But he concedes that children *do* learn something of the methods of inquiry and the heuristics of discovery through first-hand experiences with problem-centered projects and studies.

Projects are ideas expressed in three dimensions.

[17]Byron Massialas and Jack Zevin, *Creative Encounters in the Classroom: Teaching and Learning Through Discovery,* New York: John Wiley and Sons, Inc., (1967) p. 13.

[18]Jerome Bruner, "The Act of Discovery," *Harvard Educational Review* XXXI (Winter, 1961), p. 21-32.

The creative process is a problem-solving process. If there were no problem, no need or expectation, creative effort would be of little value. In social studies, as in other areas of human endeavor, the creative process is made up of a series of experiences or part processes, each of which continues what has gone on before. One experience leads directly into other experiences so that there is a continuous merging of the whole. Each of these experiences is a problem solving situation in itself, and each contributes to the final creative solution.

Many believe that the creative act is made up of four generalized stages. There is first a period of intense, rather routine work, characterized by trial and error thinking. It is during this time that the problem is examined, and relevant information is collected. An incubation period normally follows the initial frenzy of collecting and analyzing information. It is during this phase that the investigator quietly mulls the problem over in his mind, digesting its basic ingredients and sizing up its major dimensions. The third stage is marked by insight. During this phase the investigator identifies relationships which, in turn, reveal basic patterns and may even bring the fundamental structure of the total problem into focus. It is this understanding of the basic elements and their relationships within problems that makes it possible for the creative mind to construct or "discover" solutions to problems. The fourth stage involves verification, elaboration, revision and refinement. The investigator cannot claim that his hunch is valid until it "proves out." Large, grandiose theories or solutions may take decades, even centuries, to corroborate; those proposed by elementary children will naturally be quite limited in both design and duration.

In conclusion, it may be useful to review seven of the basic considerations in creative learning:

1. Learning experiences which foster creativity, like learning experiences which eventuate in other types of behaviors, must offer the learner tasks which are commensurate with his abilities and in forms that provide him with personal satisfactions.

2. At the elementary level, children should be given opportunities to solve a variety of problems — intellectual, interpersonal, and practical — in a variety of settings — group discussions, individual, and group investigations.

3. Creativity should be viewed as more than simple analysis. It involves originality, invention, and unique expression. At two points, during the formulation and the testing of hypotheses, teachers and pupils have unusual opportunities to stretch their imaginations and search for new ideas.

4. Since basic insights into problematic situations are achieved only after learners have sufficient background information and are able to see fundamental relationships, the teacher needs to see that these conditions are met. She needs to encourage individual initiative and perseverance and, above all, she needs to help children build new skills when they are needed.

5. As mentioned in Chapter V, provocative, open-ended questions often serve as pivotal points of discussions. The teacher needs to learn to use questions that will require children to interpret, apply, analyze, sythesize and evaluate effectively.

6. In our quest for greater creativity we must make certain that children have opportunities to formulate *their own* interpretations and generalizations. The teacher may, of course, offer additional information, raise questions and point out discrepancies, but it is the child's task to refine the final product.

7. Elementary teachers should constantly remind themselves that it takes courage to be creative, courage on the part of both the teacher and the student. It is not likely that truly creative effort can develop and be sustained without large doses of encouragement and recognition.

Chapter IX

PROVIDING FOR FASTER
AND SLOWER LEARNING CHILDREN

SLOWER LEARNING CHILDREN

A child who cannot succeed in school but must attend is not unlike a prison inmate who has been sentenced to seventeen years at hard labor. Each school day serves to remind him that he is inadequate and of less importance than others. Such a child may be culturally disadvantaged, of low intellectual potential, immature, or emotionally disturbed. He may also exhibit various combinations of these four conditions. Most teachers will have some children in their classrooms who should be assigned to special education classes, for few states have provided special learning programs for more than half of their students that need specialized educational opportunities.

Whether the class is predominately slow learners or primarily average or above-average pupils, the social studies emphasis should be essentially the same. All children will eventually become a part of our adult society and, therefore, need similar opportunities to develop basic social understandings. Methods, procedures, and specific assignments will vary, but the purposes should remain essentially the same for all learners in a classroom. This does not suggest that we should not give special attention to the needs of slower learning children. Edwin Fenton believes that far too many curriculum projects concentrate on the development of material for the able student while slighting the needs of the less favored audience (those below the median in achievement).[1]

ORGANIZING FOR LEARNING

Children are often divided into groups or committees to work on a unit of study. This usually results in a high, a middle, and a low group. These groups may be stable in membership and function as a unit throughout the study. Such an organization lends itself to three-level preplanning. Frequently, this type of approach is advantageous to the slower learner. If he does not profit from one activity there are other creative outlets for him to pursue. Seldom should he find himself left out. If his reading skills are limited, he may engage in activities which are closely planned and involve the step by step use of printed materials. If he cannot relate information, he may participate in a group that is using group experience story reporting. A stable group may give him needed security. Often the teacher will be able to devote a majority of the social studies period to the slower learners. If one group is in the library or working on reference materials, the second one may be answering written questions or perhaps writing reports. During this time specialized help is available for those who need it most.

---

[1]Fenton, Edwin. *The New Social Studies.* Holt, Rinehart, & Winston, Inc., (1967), p. 123.

Ideas are refined through give and take discussions.

Whole-group periods, when the slower learner may profit from the questions and contributions of his faster teammates, are often beneficial. If his peers find the material interesting and valuable, the slower learner may be influenced by their enthusiasm and swayed by their judgments. A one-to-one working relationship with a faster classmate may also prove to be helpful to the slower child. He can receive immediate reinforcement and be helped to carry the task to completion. The frustrations encountered by the child who is unable to associate the parts of the larger learning experience, or cannot do more than one step without further instruction, can be reduced by this method. Often a few sessions of continuous help over the rough spots will result in a measure of independence.

Team teaching often proves of inestimable value in providing additional specialized help for the slower learner. While one member of a team of three handles work-study or lecture-type activities with middle and upper groups, two teachers may be available to help pupils with learning problems, or those who have been absent and need to catch up. This provides the additional advantage of continued uninterrupted work. In a normal classroom situation the teacher must move frequently from one group to the next.

Even though children may be grouped for social studies instruction, this does not imply homogeneity within the slower-learning group. Children within this group will have as large a range of personality patterns as those of other groups, and they can assist each other with adjustment problems just like children in other groups. The docile child may be able to influence his rebellious colleague by providing him a safe haven as a working partner. The socially inept child may learn to find satisfactions in a small group that would be well outside of his reach in the large group. If the teacher is skillful, members of a slower-learning group socialize and teach each other in some ways that neither the teacher nor the faster-learning children can provide.

READING MATERIALS

Even with the present plethora of materials, reading for the slower learner is a problem. Social studies textbooks contain vocabulary that may be unfamiliar. Concepts developed are not always within the experiential backgrounds of the children. Sentence patterns frequently are unlike those of reading texts. Often only the best readers can cope with these combined problems. Multiple texts do not always take care of the reading difficulties. If, however, the texts are multi-level, by the same authors, and aimed at the same age-group, they may be quite suitable. Even the better readers often benefit by reading material that is in simpler form.

Texts that cover a general area or treat various geographical regions may or may not be suitable for readers who have not learned to assess material. For example, a book which is devoted to the United States with a few added pages about neighboring countries would not have the same focus on Mexico as one which treats the countries of North America. The first might relate a few facts about Mexican-American relations, while the second would probably treat Mexico much more fully. Slower students, even those who read fairly well, would have great difficulty sorting out the information in these kinds of materials. Materials on the reading level of a child who is reading two to three years behind his classmates would probably be of little value for information purposes. A sixth grader trying to learn about Mexican children his age but reading on a third grade level could become quite frustrated. His information would relate to children three or four years younger than he.

Suitable reading material may often be created in the form of experience charts. These should be in the language of the children using them. There is a real danger, however, of making them either too primary or too stilted to arouse interest. Other students in the class may also create summaries which adequately serve as reading materials for less able readers.

OTHER TEACHING MATERIALS

Often children who do not read will learn readily from audio-visual materials. Filmstrips and slides may prove to be more helpful than films because the material can be shown at a suitable pace. Slower children may follow up a filmstrip by dictating their own reading material from information acquired. The filmstrip may form the basis for a vocabulary list of pertinent terms. These words may be looked up in the dictionary. They may be used to create sentences relating to the unit. These sentences can be oral, written on the blackboard, or used on a summary chart.

Pictures, too, furnish ideas and vocabulary. If the child's background is meager, he may need help in interpreting pictorial information. When a series of pictures is available, the child may match words with pictures, or he may arrange the pictures in sequence, as when they relate to a process or development. For example, he might arrange pictures to show the steps involved in converting raw materials to finished products or in getting the product to its destination and into the hands of the consumer. Pictures are generally less abstract than words and hence more meaningful to the slower learner.

Realia are helpful, if not essential, in making inferences, drawing conclusions, forming generalizations, and clarifying concepts. Most slower learners cannot cope with these abstract associations without the aid of three-dimensional objects. This is an area in which a materials center is of inestimable value. It is impractical, as well as impossible, for any one teacher to have in her personal possession a wide variety of materials related to all the topics that will be studied during a given year.

Graphic materials such as diagrams, charts, and graphs are often difficult to interpret for the child lacking in imagination and the ability to perceive relationships. These children can probably be taught to read simple graphs, but comparisons among sources of information are often beyond their level of comprehension. They have difficulty interpolating and generally are unable to perceive developmental patterns or trends.

SPECIAL TECHNIQUES FOR SLOWER LEARNERS

Material covered by the slower group needs to be reviewed frequently. Unfamiliar words should be pronounced several times when first encountered, then reviewed regularly. A written list or a folder containing terms should be available for review and for varied exercises. After the words or terms have been pronounced and their meanings discussed, they may be reviewed through the use of sentences, finding the word in context, multiple-choice or matching, and crossword-puzzle-type exercises. It is exceedingly important to vary review procedures.

If suitable reading material is available to slow readers, the portion of the social studies period devoted to this group may be used for improving reading and study techniques while acquiring important information about the topic under study. Once the specialized vocabulary is introduced and understood, the children can read to answer specific questions. Until these children gain skills and confidence, they cannot be expected to find and write answers independently; nor can they compose their own answers to questions. Reading aloud the sentence which answers the questions may be the only way to establish these associations between reading and experience. Often the question must be phrased in words that are exactly the same as they appear in the written passage because the child cannot locate the words from a page containing so many statements and at the same time sense the relationship between similar phrases. This procedure may be necessary even when the child can perform similar exercises in regular reading classes. Social studies materials not only contain new vocabulary and sentence patterns but also differ markedly from fictional writings.

If this process of finding answers is difficult for slow-learning children, it may be reinforced by writing almost identical questions on the chalkboard and requesting written answers. Questions may need to be read aloud by the group before they are written. It cannot be assumed that because the child has heard the question, he can read it, or that if he can say the words, they mean the same thing when read silently as they did when read aloud.

Skimming may be a frustrating experience for an insecure learner unless it is tightly structured. First experiences in skimming for information should include a word with a capital letter or a date so that the part to be located stands out on the page. Initial training may require the group to state whether or not the word or date is on the first line. If it is not, the children look at the second line, etc. They are immediately reinforced by a "yes" or "no". After several successful experiences with this locational skill, it may be explained that the required word or phrase is in a specific paragraph. Again, it is likely that the slower learning child's skimming skills in reading stories will not carry over to social studies materials.

Skills in perceiving main ideas is a crucial competency in social studies and may require much preparation. Often slower learning children who have only a hazy notion of the topic of study are unable to crystalize their thoughts because they have no context within which they may operate. Additionally, they are handicapped in stating major ideas because of their limited vocabularies and/or their inability to weigh ideas. These difficulties may often be alleviated by using pictures with captions. The child may state what he thinks the picture illustrates and then check the label which is attached to the picture. (Pictures with labels on the back are helpful for this purpose.) Further experience with unlabeled pictures may be acquired in a variety of ways. Two of three children may provide captions and then compare answers. The class may take turns in providing labels.

Pictures are also useful in teaching children to locate supporting details within written passages. After children have become reasonably adept at stating the subject and purpose of the picture, they may note parts of the picture that support their conclusions. For example, if the picture is of a forest, the size and spacing of the trees may be noted, as well as the size of the trunks and kinds of bark. The presence or absence of leaves on a deciduous tree will give clues to the season of the year, etc.

Filmstrips and transparencies may also be used to teach main ideas and supporting details. When the slower children have become familiar with these techniques, they may try them with social studies reading materials that are within their ability range. Simplified outlining and note-taking skills may be introduced only if the material is commensurate with the reading competencies of the child.

Other study skills, such as those used in locating materials, are more mechanical and thus more easily learned. Slower learning children can learn to use the card catalog, encyclopedia, and other reference books, and locate materials on library shelves more readily than they can assimilate the material once it is found. Much practice in alphabetizing is required. This can be introduced when new vocabulary words are studied. Words listed alphabetically in personal notebooks can naturally be found much more quickly. As soon as the child can match the word he is seeking with the one in the reference book or on the catalog card and at the same time understand the alphabetical system, he can locate specific materials.

To locate alternate sources or to become proficient in the use of alternate listings requires the ability to categorize and to relate materials. Slower children must have considerable practice in each area in which they work. It is not easy for these children to conceive of relationships in hierarchies. A listing such as continent, country, state, county, and city means little to them. Thus it is difficult, if not impossible, for them to perceive that while one might find material on Maine in a book about the United States it is not equally possible to find information about the United States in a book about Maine. Translating the concept into concrete terms, one might use boxes of graduated sizes. The smallest could then be labeled city, the next to smallest box could be county, and so on. These same boxes could be relabeled to show other hierarchies stressed in social studies.

Slower learning children are often unable to find similarities and differences because the objects, pictures, or ideas are too far removed from their own conceptual backgrounds. If two pictures have only one aspect in common out of ten or twelve possible dimensions which may be used for comparison, it is difficult to find a starting point. For example, if in two scenes the child recognizes grass in one and sky in another, but nothing else in either, there is little to be said. He will not only need to identify the remaining parts of the pictures; he will also need to have some experience with the elements within the pictures which are represented. Recognizing a dog in one picture and a bear in another will allow him to state that both are animals; but he will need a more refined concept of a dog, such as acquaintance with the appearance of several breeds, in order to say with certainty that each picture contains an animal, but one is a dog and another is a bear. Similarly, social studies concepts require careful clarification and delimitation before they are useful to the slower-learning child.

Following directions and recognizing sequence may be baffling to the slower learning student. Both of these skills may be approached through the use of a very small number of items. In making a report the child may choose a subject and look for material. He may later read the material and write down one or two parts that he feels are important. He may learn to develop a series of related steps by identifying two steps at a time and later combining these paired steps. After these become thoroughly familiar, others may be added singly or in pairs. If he is trying to grasp the idea of sequence, he may progress from simple counting and alphabetization to dates, to groupings of familiar words such as "morning," "noon," "afternoon," and "night" or "Monday," "Wednesday," and "Saturday," then progress to the more complicated sequences of events within simple stories. When the teacher has ascertained that the child can handle sequential patterns in words and stories with which he is familiar, social studies concepts such as sea level, plain, plateau, and mountain (to show gradations in height) may be attempted. Pointing out sequence words as "first," "then later," etc. is also very helpful to those who have difficulties in this area.

Report-making, panel discussions, and other activities of this nature are best left to more able children. The slower learning child below the junior-high age levels generally has not been able to master all the intricate skills required for these activities. Further, he often feels embarrassed about making a poor showing in front of more able classmates. Since he does need to make a beginning in this skills area, current events often present an easier approach. The child has opportunities to hear news events over television, on the radio, in discussions at home and elsewhere, as well as in newspapers, and possibly one designed for his reading level. Current events may also be useful in learning to relate and compare happenings, particularly if the event described has occurred locally.

Critical thinking is difficult for the child who has a limited experiential background and little skill in reading or study techniques. He may benefit from listening to evaluations and discussions, if he has previously been able to develop some foundation for the particular area in which his more adept classmates perform the complicated skills which lead to critical thinking.

The making of pictures, murals, bulletin boards, and three-dimensional displays may be used as a motivational technique with those who have not yet learned to appreciate and use other approaches to learning. Results are concrete and often provide recognition for the child. Successful displays and meaningful representations require close attention to details, and thus learnings that might otherwise be uninteresting in an abstract form take on importance.

Trips may be helpful to slow learners, but results will not be worth the effort unless the scope of the trip, and the time devoted to it, is limited. Too many new experiences make assimilation difficult and simply add to the child's frustration. Careful preparation is especially important for those children who do not welcome new experiences and cannot meet them with enthusiasm and self-assurance. They must have a very clear understanding of the things they are to observe during each excursion.

Role-playing and dramatics often prove to be of value. As in other activities for the slower learner, careful preparation is essential if the activity is to yield important learnings. Pretending to play the role of a congressman will be of limited value if it stresses only one aspect of the congressman's job. Playing the role so that various phases of his work are portrayed may lead to some worthwhile learnings. If necessary, the same role may be taken by several children, each presenting a different aspect of the congressman's work. This may lead to a more sympathetic understanding of the many responsibilities a national representative may have in Congress.

Dramatics may be disappointing if the roles are complicated or the children do not understand this art form. Slower children cannot produce plays in the usual sense of the term, nor can they readily change roles or create lengthy dialogue. Their parts in dramatic productions usually consist of a few short speeches. They can, however, take part in action sequences and learn to be attentive and alert to their responsibilities in a total presentation.

A continuing problem encountered in social studies as well as other subjects is listening. If the child has learned to "tune himself out" because most of what is said is unintelligible to him, he will need basic training in listening skills. But first of all, he must want to listen because what is being said is understandable and of interest to him. The teacher will need to be precise and clear in her explanations and use ample illustrations. The children must also be encouraged to speak distinctly and loudly enough for all to hear.

If these conditions are met, exercises to improve listening may prove helpful. In the area of social studies, listening activities may develop through the use of records which describe historical characters and events or peoples of the earth. (Care must be exercised to eliminate long, complicated discussions which may be valueless and even harmful.) These are most beneficial when questions or directions for listening activities have been prepared in advance. Filmstrips with accompanying sound may also be used. Listening to classmates is more effective if there is involvement, something for each member of the class to complete as the presentation develops, or follow-up activities of special interest.

When possible, slower-learning children should have their social learnings supplemented by experiences in school groups outside the classroom and in social groups outside the school. Patrol duties often provide a sense of accomplishment as well as an opportunity to make judgments, interact with other children, and serve promptly and faithfully. Even housekeeping duties in the classroom help to bridge the gap between deficiencies in standards of performance as compared with others, and, eventually, pride in satisfactory performance. Some of these lessons may then carry over into assignments related to units in social studies.

While it is not the responsibility of the teacher to provide out-of-school experiences, she is, nevertheless, in a good position to at least make known the opportunities that exist in the child's neighborhood. Often a child may live near a Y.M.C.A., Boys Club, recreation or civic center and be unaware of the opportunities that are offered for participation in group living. Teachers can help timid children overcome their reluctance to go to an unfamilar place by taking the class to the center and by encouraging a child who already attends to introduce others to the activities. Often efforts of this kind on the part of the teacher are looked upon with suspicion by parents. On occasion this may be overcome by a bulletin from the school office listing the facilities available to children.

Counseling is another of the techniques that is useful in social studies. Group counseling in particular has given some disturbed youngsters release from their tensions and greater ability to relate sympathetically to others. A child's cognizance of immediate social relations may provide opportunities for the study of the motivations and interests of other peoples. Not infrequently this release from inhibiting factors has made it possible for children to move well beyond their slower-learning colleagues.

Slower-learning children frequently, if not generally, perform at a much slower pace and display more apathy than other children. Thus, when assignments are given (especially with unfamiliar materials) adequate time to complete the assignments must be provided if the child is to be successful. A sense of urgency on the part of the teacher frequently has adverse effects on an already fearful child. The emotional barrier erected precludes successful communication. If the job is only worth a few minutes' time, it may not be worth including at all. The child who has seldom succeeded needs to know that he is achieving, that his efforts are paying dividends, and that his accomplishments are appreciated. Graphs and charts of many kinds can be used to help each child see his own progress and that of others in his group.

THE CULTURALLY DISADVANTAGED CHILD

Ole Sand and Bruce Joyce, in discussing planning for children of varying ability levels note that "A major problem in the teaching of the social studies revolves around children from urban slums. . ."[2] They further state that the social studies, more than any other part of the school program, bring the lower-class slum culture into contact with the school culture. Riessman contends that the disadvantaged child is most interested in learning the fundamentals and shows far less interest in the social studies.[3] Dropouts frequently state that social studies are among the most difficult courses offered in the schools.

[2]Sand, Ole and Joyce, Bruce, "Planning for Children of Varying Ability," *Social Studies in Elementary Schools,* ed. John Michaelis. N.C.S.S., 1962, p. 295.

[3]Riessman, Frank. *The Culturally Deprived Child.* New York: Harper & Row, 1962, p. 32.

The above statements would suggest that careful attention should be given to implementing social studies programs for culturally disadvantaged children. Considerations for training must recognize that the child's intellectual and creative potential may be as great as that of other children. Though the child may not be able to cope with the regular program, he has specific limitations which, if remedied, may allow him to progress naturally. In many cases he will fit well with other groups of slower learners. Reinforcement materials, books containing simple concepts and vocabulary, a variety of media, field trips, concrete illustrative materials, many firsthand experiences and other teaching aids suggested for slower learners will often help in closing the gap.

Proceeding at a slower pace may make assimilation of new behavior patterns different from his own less difficult for the culturally disadvantaged child. Special techniques are often beneficial, if not mandatory, in spanning the cultural gap. Pronunciation patterns of disadvantaged children are often enough at variance with the general speech of the classroom that special assistance is required. Frequently perceptual and listening skills are underdeveloped. At times it will be necessary to train the child in these areas before he can profit from activities of any kind in the social studies. Motivation may be totally lacking and difficult to foster. The child may be confronted with some or all the limitations already mentioned, and in addition, he may be suffering from a faulty diet, unattended physical defects, parental antagonism to education, almost constant mobility, overcrowded living conditions, filth, and other problems. The school will then need to aid the teacher with counseling, medical services, and perhaps free lunches and clothing. If these problems are not alleviated, even the most imaginative efforts in teaching educational skills are likely to fail.

In addition to providing the essential services mentioned above, many other avenues are open to the teacher which may enhance and strengthen social studies experiences for these children. Modifications of teaching arrangements such as ungraded classrooms and team teaching are often useful in establishing programs for disadvantaged students. Other aids include teaching machines, remedial reading instruction, after-school tutoring or enrichment programs, and the special assistance of home-school teachers, teacher aids, and other personnel. Frequently parent education programs, as well as carefully planned and coordinated programs with youth agencies, are of great benefit.

Even with the coordinated assistance of many agencies and special remediation programs in several areas, the culturally disadvantaged child will still require a sympathetic classroom teacher. The alienated child does not relate naturally to adults whom he has learned to distrust. The social studies teacher who works with the disadvantaged must be flexible. He cannot cling rigidly either to middle-class social values or to highly structured imperatives in the curriculum. He must recognize that it is more important for the disadvantaged child to learn first how to live harmoniously and constructively with others. He must decide how much of the content of the program is useful in teaching the basic goals and how much is pertinent to the child's experiential background.

Having set the limits within which the child can comfortably work at any stated time, the social studies teacher must then revise his expectancies so that they are consistent with the child's overall pattern of accomplishment. Goals must be high enough to challenge the student, yet simple enough to ensure some degree of success.

Teaching patterns must emphasize motivation. These are difficult to formulate for children who are accustomed to failure. The disadvantaged child must, through his social studies learnings, acquire habits of persistence and tolerance, skills in communicating with others, pride in his accomplishments, appreciations for learning activities, and other attitudes previously weak in his experiential background. This is a gigantic task.

The disadvantaged child can acquire many of the necessary intellectual skills important in social studies such as the critical evaluation of materials and procedures, but many of these skills may not be as fully developed as they would have been if the child had richer and wider background experiences. Educating the culturally disadvantaged child in social studies is a complex task, yet a rewarding experience for the teacher who is successful. In a very real sense the teacher is introducing him to a whole new pattern of life.

THE CHILD FROM MINORITY GROUPS

Many children from minority groups see themselves as different and out of step with the rest of the students. This can be a result of living within a close-knit ethnic group whose ideas may be stereotyped and perhaps distorted; it can also be fostered by prejudice on the part of other children who may not have learned that "different" does not necessarily mean odd or queer.

Prejudice on the part of the majority group and feelings of inadequacy on the part of children from minority groups can be partially countered by a social studies program which highlights contributions from various ethnic groups. It can be implemented by trips to particular areas within large cities and, in both large and small communities, by visits of the children to each other's homes. Further understanding may result from observations of classrooms whose major racial constituency is different from that of the visiting group and also from talks and demonstrations by persons from various races. Sometimes a letter writing program involving persons of different ethnic groups is helpful.

Some children from minority groups are further handicapped by language problems, either because of regional variations in English, the use of a foreign language in the home, or a severely limited vocabulary. If the child has little or no training in English, special attention will be required in the acquisition of a basic vocabulary before he can make substantial progress in social studies.

Children from minority groups are often ashamed of their parents. The culture of the home may vary considerably from that of the school. The child's loyalties are divided. He may become rebellious, and further learning may be difficult if not impossible. Counseling by adults and talks with peers who may have faced the same problems can be helpful. The child from a minority group is faced not only with a double set of standards but a double learning task. He must become acquainted with the varying ways of behaving in particular situations and then distinguish clearly between those appropriate to one situation and those required in other social settings. Flexibility and understanding on the part of the social studies teacher and the peer group may help him to accomplish this difficult task.

Because the minority group member is usually culturally disadvantaged, he probably will also be classed as a slow learner. Social studies for him must be a combination of all the techniques applicable to his situation. As in the case of other handicapped learners, goals and outcomes must normally be adjusted.

THE MIGRANT CHILD

The problems of children of migrant workers resemble those of other culturally disadvantaged groups. These children are also generally members of minority groups. They are further burdened by constant moving and the necessity of working in the fields.

If these pupils could somehow be helped in perceiving and interpreting their many varied experiences, they could capitalize on their extensive travels. Unfortunately, the workaday problems of moving and caring for basic necessities usually monopolize their time and energies. If they are taught social studies, it is apt to be nothing more than a hodge-podge of unrelated parts. In most cases only a great effort on the part of teachers will enable the migrant child to catch a meaningful glimpse of the whole spectrum of social studies.

PROVIDING FOR MORE ABLE CHILDREN

The social education of rapid learners in the elementary school has received scant attention in the past. But that, in itself, is hardly surprising since "Exceptional children create exceptional problems in our schools, and no other group has been the *bete noir* of educators like bright children."[4] Overall programs for the gifted usually attempt to accelerate the child's general learning pace. Classroom provisions center around the euphemism labeled *enrichment.* The interpretation and application of the enrichment concept is left to the ingenuity of each teacher.

This is not to say, however, that the individual and his needs have been ignored in social studies instruction. Many articles and books proclaim the necessity of individualizing instruction, and also include suggestions for the accomplishment of this objective. These suggestions usually are general in nature, and thus do not specify procedures fitted especially to faster learning children.

The identification of children who can proceed at a more rapid pace than the average is not always a simple matter of choosing those who excel in performance. Many able children do not respond in accord with their potential. Some are quiet and unaggressive and prefer not to be involved; others have become bored through the lack of challenge and, in some cases, have become accustomed to venting their enthusiasms in other directions. Still others have emotional, personal, or economic problems which interfere with their performance.

Nevertheless, there are guidelines which can aid in the process of selecting those students who should be provided with special opportunities. Superior students tend to read rapidly, comprehend easily, and remember what they read, and they are often imaginative or creative. They assimilate abstract ideas, formulate generalizations quickly, and are generally well-informed in many areas. They tend to enjoy intellectual tasks.

Since bright children are generally adaptable and enjoy meeting new situations, a variety of organizational patterns should be utilized in carrying out the social studies program for them. Groupings which transcend the regular classroom include ability sectionings of classes and even schools where the child works at an accelerated pace in all subjects, track systems where he may work in accelerated groupings in only a few subjects, dual level plans where he works in a regular classroom part of the time and in a faster group the remainder of the time, accelerated grade placement plans which usually contain no special provisions for the particular abilities of the bright child, cross-grade groupings in all or some subjects, and team teaching situations where children are divided into ability sections for specific activities.

The extent to which the child receives differentiated instruction under any of these plans depends on the interest and ingenuity of teachers in using techniques and materials. While none of the above systems is designed specifically for social studies, all could be utilized to afford stimulation and encouragement in social studies for the faster learner.

[4]Ozmon, Howard. *Challenging Ideas in Education.* Minneapolis: Burgess Publishing Company, 1967, p. 97.

Increasing independence of expression is important.

Within the classroom many types of grouping techniques may facilitate an improved program for faster learners. Within the social studies unit itself an unlimited variety of instructional arrangements is possible. Bright children may be used as team leaders and helpers in guiding other children. They may be formed into special subgroups in which they carry out special assignments. Fast learners can participate in extended learning periods in which they work out projects, perhaps in a library or resource center if either of these is available. Pre- or post-school sessions can be provided for special projects or advanced instruction.

Within any of the above grouping plans, many techniques may be employed to challenge the fast learner. None of these ways of working will appeal to all fast learners. However, variety is necessary to foster critical thinking and to keep the child with an active mind both happy and busy.

Some general techniques that are helpful in providing for able learners include the use of broad and diversified reading experiences, training in critical thinking, attention to uniqueness and precision of expression, wide acquaintance with study aids, broad first-hand experiences, extended opportunities for creative expression, and training in evaluation and self-analysis. Each of these is discussed below with suggestions for implementation.

Reading materials in social studies for able elementary children at all levels should include multiple texts representing several authors and publishers. If possible multi-level texts should also be available. For intermediate-age children other sources such as high school texts, magazines, daily papers, advanced encyclopedias and other reference books should be provided.

Reading experiences must be guided so that children become acquainted with as many of the above-mentioned sources as possible. Recommendations to the child frequently need to be specific as to article or page numbers, since he normally has not yet had an opportunity to develop careful judgments relating to these various sources. Items should be chosen, at least part of the time, with a view toward sharpening, deepening, and broadening insight. For example, the child's reading may include many points of view on a topic.

Training in critical thinking at the elementary level will encompass much practical study work as well as creative projects and simulated experiences. Bright primary students may discuss main ideas which they have gleaned from reading various books; e.g., all people have some kind of housing. Supplementary statements which appear in various sources may also be cited; e.g., housing fits the kind of place in which you live, people with more money have better houses, etc. They may then discuss which books about housing gives facts and which might be fanciful or represent the opinions of the author. Able children may work out classifications of homes according to climate, population density, or some other criteria. These children may be asked to recommend particular books for the subject under study — a book for facts, one of high interest, one for unusual information, etc.

Students on the intermediate level may be encouraged to identify relationships of many kinds — comparisons, sequences, principles and their applications, relevant and non-relevant information. If the topic of interest is rivers, we may ask which is longer, wider, or deeper? Which is navigable the greatest distance? Bright intermediate-age students can be expected to list reasons, to state cause-effect relationships; e.g. Why is a particular river so little known? How does this affect the people and the economy of the country? Children of this age may be taught to judge the reliability of material by being provided with criteria against which to check each source. Providing assignments which require the exercise of higher-level mental processes will assist the bright student in acquiring an intelligent grasp of social studies generalizations.

Often the fast learner is apt to be careless in his presentation of material. His ability to read and think may be so much faster than his physical speed of writing that the result is incoherent. His interest in the subject and the volume of information he possesses may preclude attention to precision in speech and writing. The teacher can help by requesting outlines and preliminary drafts of written and oral reports. Bright children should also receive further training in sentence improvement and paragraphing as well as direction in the careful and precise use of words.

Able children may expend part of their efforts in the wider use of study aids, both for the purpose of acquiring information and also for use in implementing oral reports. They may be encouraged to check films, filmstrips, slides, transparencies, tapes, records, newspaper and magazine files, as well as vertical files. They may be able to profit from the use of learning kits containing a variety of materials. Children who are bright and have a broad experiential background may profit from trips which have a scope which is too broad for the general group. They may also gain much from lectures or talks given at upper grade levels. They may conduct personal interviews in their search for information.

Creative expression for bright students may include such activities as the making of intricate murals, bulletin boards, booklets — but need not be confined to these activities. Many able children enjoy writing plays, making costumes and scenery, using papier mache to create appropriate realia, writing booklets, composing poetry, and collecting an assortment of illustrative material. Their creative abilities may be channeled toward such activities as listing all the sources from which one might secure information in writing a biography or, perhaps, a book about costumes.

In order to develop their full potential, bright children must learn to use their time and talents wisely. They should be helped to be systematic in their efforts when working on their own. This might mean learning how to prepare an advance schedule and checking themselves by keeping a log detailing the actual expenditure of time. It will mean learning how to prepare checksheets on activities including points such as:

1. Was the topic I chose appropriate?
2. Were materials available?
3. What phase of the study was most difficult?
4. Did I make a carefully planned and well-written report?

Able students who extend their activities and enthusiasms in many directions will be helped to coordinate their efforts and make worthwhile contributions only if they are taught to be careful and thorough in their study habits.

It cannot be said that there are final or definitive answers to the problem of individual differences. These differences are both a strength within our nation and a source of frustration to teachers. The key to the situation remains with the teacher. One who is sympathetic, resourceful, and knowledgeable can help guide most normal children in significant social learnings regardless of the ability levels. The teacher with enthusiasm for social studies and patience with children can and will find ways to circumvent the road-blocks to meaningful social studies experiences for both fast and slower-learning children. Many specific suggestions are noted in the unit, "How Rivers Affect the Lives of People," for both slower and faster learners.

Chapter X

PLANNING, EVALUATING,
AND TEACHING SOCIAL STUDIES UNITS

Unit teaching is probably the most difficult and challenging task faced by elementary teachers. It requires imagination, resourcefulness, unusual organizational ability and a kind of creative persuasiveness that can be easily translated into exciting plans, sustained effort and rewarding outcomes. The social studies or science unit frequently provides the most interesting and stimulating activities of the school day. A good unit, well taught, offers both unity and diversity, continuity and flexibility. It has a focus and a basic structure; yet within this generalized framework there exist many opportunities for individual studies and personalized projects.

The unit is the most satisfactory method of organizing classroom studies because it most nearly reflects what we know about the learning process. It offers opportunities for group planning and close identification, common goals and cooperative effort. Unit work often strengthens the child's sense of belonging and helps satisfy his need to create and communicate with others. It stresses the interrelatedness of subject matter and provides for the functional use of skills. In short, it approximates the goal-directed, inquisitive nature of human effort. Good units provide real and meaningful problems to be solved and genuine opportunities to participate directly in the search for useful solutions.

Effective units of study center around purposeful activities. They offer each child an opportunity to discover and broaden his own special interests and talents and to contribute and share in a common effort. The child is both an individual and a member of a larger group. Each of these identities can and should find expression in unit work. Good units offer a wealth of stimulating ideas, information, and resources upon which the child can draw. When pursued with care and sensitivity, these studies help children refine and clarify ideas, recognize and define problems, evaluate and organize new learnings.

THE STRUCTURE OF UNITS

Teaching units and resource units usually have from five to seven parts. As a bare minimum, they will normally have a statement of objectives or desired outcomes, an outline of content (generalizations, concepts and activities), suggested culminating activities, procedures for evaluation, and a bibliography or listing of learning materials related to the topic of study. Some units also have a statement of purpose or an introduction. They may have a list of suggested initiatory activities as well.

HOW MUCH PREPLANNING?

Educators have not reached complete agreement regarding the preplanning and prestructuring of learning activities. Advocates of an unstructured curriculum believe that any guidelines which circumscribe the scope and sequence of learning activities will necessarily limit teacher-pupil planning and have an adverse effect upon the total educational program. They believe that the curriculum should emerge through the expression of pupil interests and concerns. Most educators, however, appear to believe that some framework or suggested sequence is not only desirable but necessary in avoiding a general hodgepodge of gaps and repetition, loose ends and superficiality within the curriculum.

Despite the fact that a few school systems allow for no flexibility and no pupil-teacher planning of specific units, the trend is toward overarching themes and suggested guidelines rather than prescribed topics. From among several possible topics or subtopics within the suggested area of study the teacher may guide the pupils in choosing a unit that most closely parallels their needs and interests. The teacher will normally know what experiences the children have had previously, their general ability levels, and something of their working relationships. He may even wish to do some preplanning with the teacher who has had the pupils the previous year. He may visit other teachers who are carrying out similar units and gather background information on the topic from a number of basic sources. Constructive planning cannot be carried out in a vacuum. The teacher in particular must know the general dimensions of the topic and several possible avenues of investigation.

TEACHER-PUPIL PLANNING

Planning is difficult for children. Most have not had any real preschool experiences in planning, and it is extremely difficult for them to anticipate all the problems and outcomes associated with even the most simple group activities. It is useful to recognize that both topics and procedures may be planned cooperatively. By oversimplifying this aspect of unit planning nine combinations may be delineated as follows:

Topics	Procedures
1. Topic chosen by teacher.	1. Procedure chosen by teacher.
2. Topic chosen by children from a list of possible choices.	2. Procedure chosen by children from a list of possible procedures.
3. Topic chosen by children with reference to curricular guides.	3. Procedures chosen by children without reference to curricular guides.

If each of the three options in selecting topics is paired with each of the methods in selecting procedures, we have nine possible combinations. In general, young children appear to be more successful in planning topics, for procedures involve the judicious use of time, materials, space, and people. Even seasoned teachers find that they often miscalculate space and time requirements. Differences in working speeds and unforseen hurdles may necessitate drastic changes in plans.

If there are no curriculum guides, the teacher and children may make their judgments concerning topics and procedures with reference to the background experiences of the children, resources available within the community, the intensity of interest shown by the class members, the maturity of the pupils, and the persistent social issues and problems facing the community.

INITIATING THE UNIT

Teachers frequently initiate units by arranging a classroom environment which arouses interest in the topic. Books, pictures, exhibits, models, scientific objects, and even resource persons may be used to stimulate curiosity. If this plan is used, children should be given ample opportunity to explore and study the objects on display. New units may also serve as extensions of previous studies or develop out of questions raised in discussions. Some units grow out of problems broached by teachers. The teacher may simply ask questions about life in other regions of the world, governments, music, art, economic conditions, social problems, and children's judgments about how we can best meet the challenges which face us. She may invite a local judge, lawyer, probation officer, or representative from a state institution to raise issues or questions with the class. On occasion, units develop out of reading. Children may find a character or a setting within a story which stimulates their curiosity and makes them want to know more about the countries or regions of the world in which the story takes place.

OBJECTIVES OF UNITS

The objectives which are established at the outset of each unit give direction and purpose to the study. Some objectives are developed by the teacher. These relate to the behavioral outcomes he hopes will result from the learning experiences which make up the unit. These objectives normally fall into three or four categories: understandings, skills, and appreciations. Some teachers add an additional category: attitudes. Within each of these categories are found specific behaviors that the teacher hopes to develop or strengthen. Under skills, for example, may be listed particular reading and writing competencies, aspects of map reading, and skills related to the use of library materials. The understandings frequently reflect the major generalizations or concepts that the teacher hopes to develop. The appreciations represent the changes in attitude, preferences, and values which he hopes will emerge from the study.

Children may also establish objectives for a unit of study. Their objectives usually relate to rather specific kinds of information they wish to acquire or skills they hope to develop. They seldom suggest goals related to attitudinal changes or new appreciations. These more subtle learnings are generally more apparent to adults. Children may suggest types of information which they want to know about a country or a particular activity within a country. How do the Japanese find pearls? How do miners live under the ground? How do cowboys protect their cattle from coyotes? An alert teacher can build on these relatively simple questions and help children formulate questions that deal with fundamental relationships. Why did pearl farming or ranching or mining develop in these regions of the world? What factors would you take into consideration if you were trying to establish a business in a particular region of the world? Why are some people so very poor while others are relatively wealthy? An effective teacher will help children widen their perspectives and search for basic meanings.

USING LARGE BLOCKS OF TIME

Fragmented schedules have probably caused more problems in education than any other single administrative device. Far too many teachers teach by the clock. They set aside twenty minutes for handwriting, thirty-five for arithmetic, forty minutes for science and an equal amount of time for social studies. They then select activities to fit these time slots. This is, of course, ludicrous. Schedules should be planned and arranged to serve the school program, not vice versa. Children cannot arbitrarily turn their interests on and off or regulate their working speeds to conform to time allotments. Activities should develop naturally and terminate at points where loose ends and confusions are held to a minimum. No one wants to stop while his story is fresh in his mind and write the remaining five sentences tomorrow. It is normally more satisfying to finish a task before turning one's attention to another project or problem.

Teachers have frequently shied away from large blocks of time in teaching because they know that young children have limited attention spans. What they sometimes fail to realize is that the same topic or subject may serve as the focus for a series of interrelated activities which provide variety and change within the broad unit of study. Large blocks of time afford at least four distinct advantages:

1. They help keep the daily preparations of both pupils and teachers within manageable limits. If a teacher must make preparations for three reading groups and two mathematic groups as well as science, social studies, language arts, handwriting, spelling and art each day, it is unlikely that he can devote enough time to his units in science, social studies, and language (children's literature, for example) to make them stimulating, broad, and meaningful experiences. The use of large blocks of time, however, will allow him to concentrate on science for a two to five week period, then leave this subject temporarily and schedule a similar block of time for social studies and, finally, children's literature. This is not meant to imply that language skills and basic understandings in science may not serve as important components of social studies units; it suggests only that these areas of study exist in their own right and deserve special attention during portions of the year. If an average of one and a half hours a day is devoted to social studies during a three week period, this is obviously equal in time to a series of daily half hour periods over a nine week period.

2. Concentrated studies using large blocks of time allow for flexibility. A full two hours may be used for a field trip on one day while the same two hour block of time may be broken up as follows on a succeeding day:

   1:00—1:30 — Presentations by resource persons from the City Council.
   1:30—2.15 — Study period in the materials center to find answers to questions planned previously around the study of government.
   2:15—3:00 — Work on individual and group projects depicting graphically the economic bases of government, powers vested in various offices, influential power blocks, and patterns of change.

3. Large, concentrated studies make possible the optimum use of classroom space. Bulletin board space, display tables, files, and display cases may all be used at the same time for projects and illustrative work centering around the same unit of study.

4. Large studies using large blocks of time help reduce confusion, for the child's focus of attention is not broken into small, often unrelated segments. The children are immersed in a variety of activities which contribute to the same basic understandings in different ways. We know that some children learn more effectively through visual experiences while others learn more efficiently through the use of printed materials or construction experiences. Large unit studies can provide more effectively for these differing avenues of learning.

HELPING CHILDREN DEVELOP CRITERIA FOR USE IN ASSESSING SOCIAL SITUATIONS, PERSONAL AND GROUP ACHIEVEMENTS

Intelligent, thoughtful men have consistently used carefully constructed criteria in judging the objects and events around them. They know why they like a painting or a story, an explanation or a course of action, and they know why they disagree with a particular proposal or conclusion because they have weighed them against their own pre-established guidelines. They may be wrong in their judgments, but their assessments are more likely to be sound and logical if they have used well-planned, clear, concise criteria in reaching their conclusions. Effective criteria help to focus our attention upon the major components or elements in a situation. They cut through the superficial, extraneous facets of a problem and expose the major dimensions for analysis and examination. If we are attempting to judge a story, for example, it may be helpful to use criteria in the form of questions which ask about qualities of plot, characterization, setting, style, and, perhaps, author's purpose, and the degree to which the author appears to have accomplished his purpose. If we are attempting to assess a social studies project, we may raise questions about its general over-all contributions to the unit of study, its relationship to major points of class concern, the expenditure of time and materials, new and old skills developed or reinforced in carrying out the project, the involvement of class members, and personal satisfactions which may have accrued to members of the project group.

Even kindergarteners and first grade children can learn to use sound criteria in making individual and group decisions. They often begin by establishing criteria for judging tangible objects — a picture, a toy, or a pet. They may decide, for example, that a picture should be colorful, exciting, and happy. These are certainly not the guidelines we use in judging great art, but they represent the beginnings of a type of matching strategy which children must learn if they are going to make wise choices. The criteria children use and the complexity of the situations in which they seek to use their criteria will, of course, change radically from one year to the next. The standards of judgment children develop over the years are exceedingly important, but equally important are the patterns of satisfaction and confidence which accompany success in this important area of human thought and reasoning. An alert teacher will make certain that children are aware of their progress, and she will capitalize on opportunities which promise to sharpen and extend children's skills and understanding in developing and using criteria.

STRENGTHENING PUPIL RETENTION IN UNIT STUDIES

If children cannot remember the things that they study, it is discouraging to both them and their teachers. In fact, there is little reason to study any topic if the newly acquired insights, concepts, and conclusions evaporate as soon as the topic has been completed. There are, unfortunately, no simple formulas or plans that may be followed in helping children remember important ideas, but there are guidelines which have proven helpful. Most of these guidelines reflect the basic psychological principle that children must develop some sense of identification with the topic under study and grasp important relationships before any real learning takes place. Before the study begins, it is important to:

1. Urge that the course of study, and indeed the whole curriculum, be organized around large problems and topics.
2. Identify and delineate important concepts, generalizations, skills, and attitudes that will be of most value to the students involved. It is often useful to have a committee of teachers develop such a list, for it is a large and complex task.

During the unit of study, the teacher may:

1. Integrate subject matter so that students will be better able to see important relationships. This will normally necessitate a variety of teaching methods and materials.
2. Wherever possible, involve students in the process of determining and selecting the procedures and materials that may be used in studying a problem or a topic. Proceeding with a lesson or unit of study without any student understanding of what is to be learned can be disastrous.
3. Help each student develop the feeling that he has something of importance to contribute to the topic. This is, of course, especially difficult if the topic of study is totally unfamiliar to the students.
4. Provide opportunities for students to use and apply new ideas and skills soon after they have been learned. Also, vary the situations within which they make their interpretations and applications. A teacher cannot assume that all learners will develop the same understandings from a shared experience.
5. Recognize that the best review is a "new view" of the topic or problem; not a rehash of old material.
6. Help children learn skills in critical thinking and assist them in applying these to all the conclusions they draw from reading, observations, and class discussions. It is important for children to expect and accept only clearly warranted conclusions. Simple repetition of a teacher's verbalizations should not be construed as evidence of real understanding on the part of the learner.
7. Provide opportunities for students to summarize main ideas, key points, major principles, and specific competencies introduced in the lesson. If the lesson has been well-planned and effectively taught, the class should be able to agree on the central ideas and major conclusions.
8. Develop evaluational techniques that stress the assessment of understandings and skills rather than the retention of isolated facts. Though some skills can be evaluated only through direct classroom observations, test items can often focus upon problematic situations which call for the student to analyze information, trace relationships, and draw conclusions.

EVALUATING PUPIL PROGRESS IN UNIT WORK

In all human endeavors evaluation and assessment occupy a central position, for they are vital components of continued progress. If an activity does not develop successfully, the normal reaction is to determine why it failed. In education the improvement and refinement of assessment techniques has monopolized the energies of many psychologists since the turn of the century. Educational evaluation is the process of gathering, interpreting, and reporting evidence relating to changes in pupil behavior. Unfortunately, many elementary teachers have a very restricted view of evaluation. For many it consists of merely testing children over information presented during a unit of study. Few teachers appear to recognize the wide range of approaches available to them. There are at least a dozen evaluational techniques. These include the use of self-rating scales, student diaries, peer ratings, anecdotal records or unrecorded observations by the teacher, teacher rating scales, objective tests, subjective tests, sociometric analyses, teacher-class evaluative discussions, teacher-pupil conferences, and teacher-parent-pupil conferences. When classroom learning is progressing rapidly, effective evaluation is likely to be a part of every major activity.

On the primary level formal testing is inappropriate because of the limited reading and writing proficiency of the children. Teachers at this level must devise tests which avoid these difficulties. Oral tests or tests with pictures and oral directions frequently offer the most promise.

Oral tests may be given to test information, attitudes and, on occasion, skills. These oral tests may be informal and involve the entire class. Questions such as the following may be used:

Who can name some kinds of buildings in which we live? (information)
Why do you think we have apartment buildings in cities? (reasoning)
If all the land in a city becomes filled with stores and places to live, where will people go? (cause-effect, reasoning, inference)
Tell which pairs go together: river — boat — road — car (categorizing)
Why did you put them as you did? (relationthips)

If oral tests are carefully constructed to assess various types of learning, they will often indicate areas in which additional study is needed. Good questioning procedure suggests that most questions be addressed to the entire class. This encourages everyone to listen, for every child knows that he may be asked to respond. If the question is stated, "John, what are the mountains called?", others in the class may feel that they do not need to listen. Teachers should also avoid parroting children's answers. It may be wise to ask a second child to repeat the statement of the first student if reinforcement seems necessary.

If the whole class is involved in the evaluation, but individual assessments are desired, answers may be written out and duplicated. After making certain that the children can read the words, they may be instructed to underline or circle the correct answer in each pair. Questions may be read aloud. If the children are more advanced, the teacher may write the words on the chalk board and ask children to write the correct word from each pair on their papers.

When attitudes or opinions are being evaluated, squares may be provided similar to those below.

	Yes	No
1		
2		
3		

Questions might include the following: 1. Do you think Jimmy was afraid? Find the number one on your paper. Mark an X in the square on the left side if you *do* think Jimmy was afraid. Put an X in the square on the right side if you *don't* think he was afraid. 2. Should all people try to live in the same way? Find number two on your paper. Mark the *yes* or the *no* square to show what you believe.

Another form of assessment may make use of a chart similar to the one below.

	Much	Little	Not at All
1			
2			
3			

Here the child will put an X in the left square if he likes something very much, in the middle one if he has only little liking for it, and at the right if he doesn't like it at all.

Discrimination may be taught through the use of pictures. The child can be asked to put an X on the picture which shows the correct idea or concept. A primary child can also label a simple map by putting an M on the mountains, an R on the river, and an L on the lake. If individual evaluation is desired, the teacher may also have conferences with each child. These should be scheduled as needed.

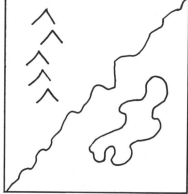

There are few standardized social studies tests available at the primary level. One specifically designated for this aged child is called the Primary Social Studies Test.[1] However, teacher observation and assessment will probably be more useful in tracing growth patterns, a growing awareness of social understandings, and the development of competencies in discussion.

Intermediate children can engage in a wider range of activities. Therefore, evaluations at the upper grade levels are frequently more elaborate. The teacher may find a chart or checklist helpful in assessing the achievements of pupils. An example is shown below.

SOCIAL STUDIES CHECKLIST 11/6 – 11/29

Name	Vocabulary list completed	Written report	Oral report	Class discussion	Panel discussion	Committee work	Helped make chart	Brought in pictures	Brought realia	Worked on mural	Helped others	Did Library work

The chart may be completed by making a check(√) in the proper space or by noting the date that an item was completed. If squares are of a slightly larger size, comments may be

[1] By Ralph C. Preston and Robert V. Duffey. Houghton-Mifflin, 1967.

added. When the unit has been completed, the checklist provides a picture of individual contributions and a summary of the number of children contributing in each category.

Checklists often relate to more than one area of learning. The one below may be used to describe work habits.

WORK HABITS

Area of Growth										
1. Helps make plans										
2. Follows directions promptly										
3. Makes good use of time										
4. Has demonstrated creativity and imagination										
5. Finishes work										
6. Works well with others										
7. Can work without disturbing neighbors										
8. Listens while others are speaking										

The child may receive a simple checkmark in the appropriate spaces, or a series of numbers can be used to indicate varying degrees of capability or participation:

1 — always
2 — generally
3 — sometimes
4 — never

A preponderance of 3's and 4's would alert the teacher to individual need for help.

A similar kind of checklist may be used in assessing children's growth in reading and library skills as shown below.

CHECKLIST ON PROCESSES

1. Can locate materials.
2. Secures materials from more than one source.
3. Can discriminate in choice of materials for various purposes.
4. Can use many reading styles (as skimming, reading slowly for details, lightly for recreation).
5. Can use index and table of contents effectively.
6. Uses maps, globes, graphs, charts, pictures and other aids.
7. Is able to cope with skills such as outlining and notetaking.

8. Can select proper topics for reports.
9. Writes acceptable reports.
10. Is able to give satisfactory oral reports.,

Checklists such as these are not normally used with every unit. They are more likely to be employed intermittently throughout the year.

Evaluation checklists for use with construction projects, such as the making of a map, may prove to be of inestimable help if similar activities are pursued later in the year. Various approaches are possible in identifying and grouping behaviors. For convenience, the evaluation below is divided into three parts: preparation, development of the project, conclusion.

CONSTRUCTION PROJECT EVALUATION

Preparation:

Does he accept his part willingly?
Does he help settle disagreements among committee members amicably?
Can he locate needed materials?
Does he find a space where he can work easily?

Does he think ahead so that he does not waste time running after materials?

Development of the Project:

Is he able to find solutions to problems?
Does he cooperate with his teammates?
Is he patient?
Does he persevere in his work?
Docs he follow helpful suggestions?
Is he careful with tools and materials?
Can he choose the best tool for the job?
Does he take turns?
Does he help others when they need his assistance?

Conclusion:

Does he help put materials away properly?
Does he finish on time?
Does he check to see that his working space is left in a clean and orderly condition?
Can he detect his errors and make suggestions for future improvement?

A tape recorder is valuable in analyzing and evaluating discussions. A tape recording may be kept and compared with children's performances later in the year, or a tape may be analyzed after a discussion when there is time for the recording of major points. The discussion may be played more than once so that different aspects of the discussion may be analyzed. It may also be played later in the school year for the children to evaluate.

The assessment of attitudes is difficult because there are few widely accepted standards against which to judge. Judgments by a teacher are certain to be colored by his own background and attitudes. Yet, gross, relatively accurate, judgments can be made. It is, for example, possible to determine if a child tends to be highly prejudiced in a particular area of human activity.

Values and ideals are frequently translated into symbolic forms and legends.

One of the easiest and best ways to observe children's attitudes is in dramatic play. The possibilities for evaluation here are almost limitless. Dramatic play is perhaps most appropriate at the primary level, while more structured situations may lend themselves to the fuller expression of children in the intermediate grades. Children may write their own plays or set up the scenes and cast of characters, then make up the dialogue as the play proceeds. The teacher may want to make some notes as a reminder of the behaviors and attitudes which can be detected. He may note *what roles the child selects* and whether or not these are consistent from one period to another, thus indicating a dependency, need, or identification with a particular role.

Murals, pictures, trips, bulletin boards, etc. may be evaluated in a manner similar to that already suggested. Each teacher may want to develop his own criteria using areas of evaluation appropriate for the class, unit, and scope of the activity. Points to be used as guidelines may be found in checklists already provided in this chapter.

There are times when an individual progress record is useful. The child may keep his own record for easy reference, or the teacher may prefer to have the records centrally located. Individual folders may include:

1. Copies of written tests corrected and labeled with median class score.
2. Checklists on reports – oral and written.
3. An assessment rating or checklist of reading skills.
4. A checklist of research skills.
5. Samples of maps, graphs, charts, tables, pictures, etc. (dated).
6. An attitude assessment.
7. A rating of social adjustment.

Limited time generally precludes the use of folders assembled and checked entirely by the teacher. The assembling of written tests and reports, plus samples of work as suggested in 5 above (supplemented by the student's own evaluations and an overall checklist by the teacher) may be more practical. It is of value particularly because the child is intimately involved in the evaluation process.

Anecdotal records of each child's progress may be entered on cards as shown below.

Carter, Clyde	
9/28	Excellent choice of sources
10/23	Still needs help in reasoning
11/1	Contributed many suitable objects
11/8	Test score improved
12/14	Wish he could work better with Frank
12/19	Discussions show more sparkle
2/12	Seems to be afraid to give oral reports
3/15	An excellent written report

Teacher-made objective tests are generally used to check the learning of facts, concepts, and generalizations. These tests may be given orally by the teacher with the child writing a one-word answer. They may be written on the chalkboard, or duplicated, using true-false or multiple choice questions. Essay questions are most useful in helping children organize and express their ideas.

Although teacher-made objective tests have been found inadequate in many situations, their value should not be derogated. Children need facts on which to build ideas, concepts, and generalizations. The teacher is in the best position to judge which facts the child could reasonably be expected to learn from a particular unit.

Concepts may be checked through the use of hypothetical, problem-solving situations. The child may be presented with a problem similar to the one below.

> Draw on this map of the world a place where you could grow cotton and rice; where you could go swimming the year round, but have natural skiing conditions close by. Show the natural features of the land; elevations, latitude and longitude, and any other features you consider necessary.

Standardized tests, once the backbone of evaluation programs, now serve in a lesser role. They are most helpful in providing a broad standard of comparison. They also indicate what general facts and understandings within the social studies are considered valuable or important by recognized test-makers. However, a single test is normally not suitable for all situations. If school personnel wish to select their own tests, a list may be found in Buros' *Compilations, The Fifth Mental Measurements Yearbook* and also in *Tests in Print.*[2] If help is desired in determining the suitability of tests for particular school systems, it may be secured from test publishers such as the Educational Testing Service, Princeton, New Jersey.

Evaluation procedures must often be adjusted for slower learning children. Frequently these children do very poorly on written tests, particularly if the answers must be transferred to a coded sheet. The complexity of the operation may be well beyond their comprehension. If a teacher were to rely solely on the number of correct answers these children are able to give on a written test, there would be little or no evidence of progress. The limited reading and writing skills of slower learners often make them appear less able than they really are. A deficiency in either of these areas may contribute to an incorrect assessment of their competencies in dealing with social studies concepts.

Evaluation, like curriculum planning, will need revision in the light of current prevailing conditions. No prescription can be given. The evaluation process itself must be examined regularly to see that it is providing the kind of information that is most useful in helping children achieve at a level commensurate with their abilities.

[2]Oscar K. Buros. *The Fifth Mental Measurements Yearbook.* Highland Park, N. J.: Gryphon Press, 1959. *Tests in Print,* same publisher, 1961.

EXAMPLES OF
SOCIAL STUDIES UNITS

Six sample units are outlined in the following pages. The first, "How Rivers Affect the Lives of People," is a resource unit. It includes virtually all the components which can be incorporated in unit plans, including a justification for the unit, initiatory activities, outline of content, discussions of objectives and planning, direct and related experiences, specific evaluative activities, and extensive bibliographies. No one teacher could use all the suggestions offered; this unit is simply a store house of organized ideas and activities that may be consulted when teachers are contemplating studies in this area. This resource unit emphasizes *ecology,* defined as the interrelationships between living organisms and their environments, in this case man and rivers.

Several brief teaching units follow. These offer examples of plans in other social studies areas. The early primary unit, "Learning to Know Yourself," focuses upon rudimentary aspects of *psychology.* Man's use of *symbols* and *symbolism* is stressed in a short middle grade unit, "How the People of the World Remember." A middle grade unit, "How We Learn About Early Man," stresses aspects of *archeology.* An upper grade unit on "Canada" has a geographical focus, and a second upper grade unit, "Progress in Understanding Each Other," emphasized man's concern for social reform.

All the six units have the following charteristics in common:

1. They are directed toward the development of concepts and understandings, as well as toward the acquisition of skills and knowledge. In most cases, the fundamental generalizations to be developed within each unit form the basic framework around which the other components of the unit are organized.

2. These units emphasize individual and group problem-solving. The activities suggested with each unit include many questions which call for convergent and divergent thinking as well as value judgments, and other aspects of critical reasoning.

3. These units stress the cross-media approach to teaching and learning. Each unit draws upon a wide selection and range of resources. If children are to use problem solving skills effectively, they must have many resources available and a knowledge of their uses.

4. Although each unit has a focus (archeolcgy, psychology, etc.), each is also involved with many areas of knowledge. Virtually all our significant problems deal with broad understandings which cut across the artificial subject barriers established for the "convenience of teaching." The interrelatedness of knowledge is emphasized in each unit.

5. All the units provide for a wide range of experiences, learnings, and activities. Each child learns a little differently from every other child, and each child needs to find those experiences which are most appropriate for him at a given time. He also needs to participate in a variety of experiences which will broaden, as well as deepen, his competencies and understandings.

6. Each unit deals with significant facts and understandings. When there are so many different topics of concern to man, and we can choose only a few, it is important that these be of real significance. In far too many cases, teachers have developed units around relatively unimportant topics. Zoo animals and Eskimos, for example, are not as vital to man's well-being as an understanding of minority groups, economic principles, and the wise use of natural resources.

These units are not offered for direct use in the classroom. As mentioned in the previous chapter, units must be planned with the needs and interests of specific groups of children in mind. (In the resource unit, "How Rivers Affect the Lives of People," older social studies texts, Our Wonderful World, and others, are purposely used as basic references in order to discourage direct use of the unit in a classroom.)

Middle Grade Unit
HOW RIVERS AFFECT THE LIVES OF PEOPLE

TABLE OF CONTENTS

JUSTIFICATION

The children of today are capable and eager to learn. Their heritage is rich and full of events, people, and places which are worthy of study and understanding. These children on the whole have the benefits of modern schools and trained teachers. The problem of what to choose to develop understandings, attitudes, and behaviors becomes that of the teacher and curriculum specialists.

Children need experiences which are primarily designed to aid in the location, evaluation and use of information. The following unit provides experiences in the use of tables of contents, card catalogues, the dictionary, encyclopedias, newspapers, files, and the index. The children will turn to a variety of resources when gathering information and use a variety of recording techniques.

Children must be helped to judge what is appropriate in various situations. And they need generalizations from which they can judge what they read and hear. It is the responsibility of the teacher when teaching this unit to provide such experiences. The unit provides for many creative activities, including the expression of inner feelings through art, music, and dramatizations. This unit also provides experiences in the language arts and science, as well as mathematics.

This unit is one which is in keeping with the needs, interests, and abilities of the group. Children of the intermediate age group are very much interested in a study of the world beyond their immediate community. They are, however, interested in their own community as well. In fact, children of this age group have many interests. At this stage in their development they are able to work at a project or problem for a longer period of time than they were previously. They are also learning how to use the tools of research and are able to form complete, normally accurate, generalizations. They enjoy working in groups.

This unit will give children opportunities for new interests. It is actually a study of how man has interacted with his environment. When the unit is completed the child should have a better understanding of why men settled along rivers as well as an appreciation of the part that our natural environment plays in the lives of all people.

UNDERSTANDINGS

I. Man settled in the valleys of great rivers because they are fertile for agriculture, ideal for transportation and communication, a source of water, and a direct source of food.
II. Man has learned to extend, and in some measure, control rivers as well as make use of the natural gifts which rivers provide. This fact has raised the standard of living which man enjoys.
III. Rivers have been significant in the geographical development of areas because of the properties which enable them to pick up, carry, and deposit soil and because the water nourishes the land.
IV. Rivers are often of deep economic significance to a country or area because of their capacity to carry trade, support the manufacturing of water power, and by means of irrigation, support agriculture.
V. Rivers play an important role in the history of an area. Rivers serve as boundary lines, as routes to the interior of a continent, as arteries along which cities grow, and as part of religious worship in some countries.

ATTITUDES

I. Realization that the valleys of rivers have been, and continue to be, centers of man's civilization because they offer so much that is necessary and desirable for life.
II. Respect for the discoveries and accomplishments which man has made in the area of river transportation, irrigation and flood control.
III. Appreciation for the role that rivers play in the geographical development of an area.
IV. Awareness that the basic human activities of production and distribution are important processes in which man is engaged and that rivers play an important part in these activities.
V. Appreciation for the way in which rivers contribute to the development of a country.

BEHAVIORS

I. Displays interest in why and how people settled our world by reading widely, by asking questions, and by sharing information with other members of his class and family.

II. Endeavors to locate information on the advancements made by man in these fields of study and research: river transportation, irrigation and flood control.

III. Uses maps, diagrams, and tables in attempting to answer problems – thereby taking into consideration the manner in which geographical factors such as rivers influence man and society.

IV. Displays interest in the manner in which all of the basic human activities function, especially those which involve the people of rivers.

V. Demonstrates an understanding of the part that rivers play in the history of man by sharing his facts and understandings with others.

CONTENT OUTLINE

I. Man settled in the valleys of great rivers because they are fertile for agricultural exploitation, ideal for transportation and communication, a source of water, and a direct source of food.

A. Man settled in the valley of rivers because they are well suited to agricultural exploitation.

1. Since man must produce food to provide his family and himself with nourishment, he is in need of certain elements which make farming possible and profitable.

a. The growing season must be of sufficient duration.

b. There must be enough moisture to support the growing of crops.

c. The topography of the land must be such that the farmer can grow crops satisfactorily.

d. The soil must be fertile; it must have sufficient nutrients, oxygen, and organic matter to support the growing of crops.

1'. The fertile soil found in river valleys is, for the most part, carried by the rivers from higher lands into the valleys and deposited.

a' The deposition is rich in nutrients and organic matter.

b' Such deposition forms the top soil on flood plains, natural levees along the banks of rivers, and often deltas at the mouths of rivers.

c' Deposition often hinders transportation.

2. The Mississippi River valley is attractive for agricultural purposes.

a. The valley is extremely fertile due to the flooding of the lowlands and the building up of the silt over long periods of time.

1'. The valley was once an estuary or an extension of the Gulf of Mexico.

2'. The flood plain is extremely flat.

b. The river flows through an area that experiences enough rainfall for the growing of crops without the need of added water.

c. In spite of the danger of floods destroying crops, homes, and even the residents themselves, many people live on these lowlands because the rich soil produces good crops.

B. Improved transportation and communication results in an improved standard of living among men; some rivers serve as water highways of trade and communication.

1. It has been necessary to have a means of transportation and communication because man has made two discoveries.
   a. Men have discovered that by trading they can have a variety of goods and also can dispose of their own surpluses.
   b. Men have also discovered that an exchange of ideas and skills will raise their level of technology and therefore their standard of living.

2. Rivers should have certain physical characteristics in order to be good for transportation.
   a. The river must be free from obstructions such as falls, cataracts, and rapids.
   b. The river must have a relatively constant and even flow.
   c. The river should provide a direct route.
   d. The current of the river should be slow.
   e. The river should have a low gradient and carry little sediment.

3. There are reasons why rivers are and have been used for highways.
   a. Water transportation is a cheap means of hauling heavy, bulky goods over long distances.
   b. In an unexplored land, water transportation is a safer means of getting about.
   c. In a place where there are no roads, water transportation is far easier than cutting a path through the wilderness.
   d. The cost of maintaining waterways is less expensive than other types of transportation routes.

4. There are disadvantages in using water as a means of transportation.
   a. The route is not always a direct one.
   b. Waterways do not always go from the shipping point to the required destination, and another means of transportation often has to be used in conjunction with the waterway.
   c. In higher latitudes, waterways are subject to seasonal use because of ice and snow.

5. The Mississippi River has been used as a means of transportation.
   a. This waterway was extremely important as a route for transporting goods and settlers during the early settlement of the Central States.
      1'. Flatboats could be seen going up and down the river in the earliest part of our history.
      2'. The advent of the steamboat added speed to the traffic of the river.
      3'. With the coming of the railroad, the traffic on the river fell to almost nothing because the rails were faster and could be laid out in any direction; the river, on the other hand, had a predetermined course.
   b. As more people came to the states along the river, industry became more important and more freight had to be hauled; once again the Mississippi was the scene of heavy transportation.

C. Since one of man's basic needs is for water, he makes use of rivers as a direct source of this vital substance.

1. Man must have a supply of pure water for drinking and cleansing purposes. He has learned to purify water for his use.

2. Often man finds it necessary to water his crops in order to obtain enough food to live; this requires great amounts of water, and so man again turns to rivers for a supply.

D. Since a river contains an abundance of plant and animal forms, it often serves as the source of food for man.

  1. Men catch fish from the waters of rivers to use as food.

  2. Men also obtain turtles, frogs, and clams which are eaten for food.

II. Man has learned to extend, and in some measure, control rivers as well as make use of the natural gifts which rivers provide; this fact has raised the standard of living which man enjoys.

A. To help man with his work, he has discovered a means whereby falling water can be harnessed and put to work for him.

  1. A river must possess certain qualities in order to be usable as a source of water power.
    a. The river should be capable of yielding a constant, abundant supply of water.
    b. A precipitous fall is required and the stream should be swift and narrow.

  2. The upper regions of the Mississippi are used for water power generation.

B. To improve the quality of his transportation, man has constructed canals and locks.

  1. By using canals, two waterways can be connected to provide an interlocking transportation system.

  2. By using canals, a route can be made shorter.

  3. By using canals, the waterway can by-pass cateracts and other kinds of obstructions.

  4. Locks are used to go from one water level (such as a river) into a canal which may be higher than the river.

  5. The Mississippi River has many locks and canals in the upper regions.

C. For the purpose of watering his crops in areas of little rainfall, man has developed huge irrigation projects.

  1. Dams have to be built behind which the water level is raised and allowed to flow as needed.

  2. Reservoirs are often needed to store the water until it is needed for the crops.

  3. Miles of irrigation ditches are made to fields.

  4. Many countries, especially the United States, Egypt and India, have extensive programs of irrigation.

D. To keep flood waters off the land man has devised dikes and levees.

  1. Dikes and levees are protections which resemble a wall.

  2. The Mississippi-Ohio Rivers have walls along them in places.

III. Rivers have been significant in the geographical development of an area because of the properties which enable them to pick up, carry, and deposit soil which, in turn, nourishes the land.

  A. The Nile River has changed the geographical development of that area we know as Egypt by flowing through a barren desert and by bringing water and soil to what would otherwise be a wasteland; this development has made it possible for a great civilization to be born along its banks.

    1. Egypt is predominantly desert lands, but one greenstrip can be seen running the full length of the country — this is the land along the Nile.

      The geographical location of the river is fortunate for the people of Egypt.

      1'. The Nile has as its main source Lake Victoria which is located in the interior of the continent of Africa in the Uganda Jungle.

      2'. The river flows down hill and northward through Egypt and empties into the Mediterranean Sea.

        a'. In flowing downhill, a river chooses the path of least resistance; and, by the action of running water, picks up soil and cuts a channel in which it will flow.

        b'. As it flows along, soil is carried in suspension.

        c'. As the current slows, the soil load is dropped to the bottom and near the banks of the river.

          (1) Deltas are often formed at the mouth of rivers. The Nile River has a delta which is extremely fertile.

          (2) Sandbars can become obstructions to the navigation of rivers.

      3'. Before the river reaches Egypt proper, several tributaries empty into the Nile.

      4'. The part of the Nile which is located in Egypt is at a very low altitude and experiences a dry subtropical climate.

        a'. This region is known as a low-latitude desert and is the most nearly rainless region on earth — needing no drainage system.

        b'. The temperature is hot in the day and somewhat cooler in the night.

        c'. The winter is mild.

    2. The fact that the Nile flows through the desert makes it possible for the land to support more people than the area would be able to support without the river.

      a. Desert land has little to offer man in the way of helping to provide his food, shelter, and water.

      b. Deserts are inhabited by nomads who constantly are moving with their herds searching for food and water.

      c. The land along the Nile which has been irrigated is able to support agriculture.

      d. Since the soils are fertile and there is a sufficient amount of water, many people can live along the banks of the river.

  B. On the banks of the Nile, what is probably the oldest civilization known to man gained its foothold; all life was dependent upon the resources of the river, and even today the people there depend upon its gifts.

    1. The geographical location of the river and the river itself served to protect the people from their enemies.

    a. The desert on two sides of the valley served as a barrier to invading enemies.

    b. The lower regions of the Nile were protected by the wide expanse of the Mediterranean Sea.

    c. The Nile at its headwaters appeared to be too treacherous for the primitives from the interior of Africa to invade from that direction.

2. The people who lived along its banks were farmers and depended upon the river to water their crops and make their fields rich with new soil.

    a. Each summer the Nile spread over the lowlands and left a rich deposit of silt on the ground and brought water for the crops; the Egyptians depended upon the annual flood for soil and water.

       1'. The floods were caused by heavy rains occurring in summer from Ethiopian streams.

       2'. The soil which was deposited each year on the floor of the valley was carried by the river from the highlands of Ethiopia.

          a'. The soil was responsible for the rich yields which the Egyptians received.

          b'. The gain of the Egyptian was the loss of the Ethiopian.

          c'. When the flood failed to bring the maximum amount of water, the Egyptians experienced meager crop yields and often were faced with the problem of famine.

    b. The farmers found it necessary to add more water to their crops from time to time and so began irrigating their fields.

       1'. Irrigation ditches were dug from the source of water to the crops.

       2'. For lifting water, simple water-lifting devices were used.

          a'. The shaduf, consisting of little more than a pole and a bucket, was used to raise water to fill the irrigation ditches.

          b'. The saqia was also used to raise water; it consisted of a wheel made of buckets and was powered by an animal.

          c'. The Archimedian screw was also used to raise water.

3. The people made good use of the land along the river and the mud which the river brought them.

    a. Since the land along the Nile is precious, the houses are built close together in villages.

    b. Since the people need something which would keep out the intense rays of the sun, they made their houses out of the best available material —sun-dried brick.

       1'. The roofs were flat because no slant was needed for water run off.

       2'. The floors were hard packed earth, and the walls were either windowless or had long narrow slits for that purpose.

       3'. There was little or no furniture.

    c. Water pots and other vessels were made of clay obtained from the river.

4. The river serves as an artery for trade and communication between peoples.

    a. Cairo, a market city on the Nile delta, depended on the river "for much of its trade and all of its water."

    b. The feluccas, small sailing boats, were used up and down the Nile.

5. The river made it possible for the groups of peoples to become unified into a nation with a government.

    a. The river served as a convenient means of transportation and communication to all parts of the Nile valley.

    b. The people of this area were drawn together by a common need; all were dependent on the gifts from the river, and all needed to work together to realize more benefits from it.

  6. Today, even after centuries have passed, the people of the Nile valley live much as their forefathers did in the past; however, much is being done to improve their standard of living.

    a. The people who live along the Nile are still, for the most part, dependent upon agriculture for their livelihood.

      1'. New and improved tools are being used to farm the land.

      2'. Dams have been constructed to distribute the water more evenly over a period of plantings and harvests.

        a'. It is now possible to raise two and sometimes three crops on one piece of ground a year.

        b'. More land is now under irrigation than ever before.

    b. The people are still building their houses in the same way with little or no concern for sanitation; and on the river feluccas can still be seen going from one part of Egypt to another.

    c. The glory that once was Egypt has now fallen away; now the government is desperately trying to help the common man to enjoy a better way of life. With the completion of the Aswan Dam greater benefits from the Nile are anticipated.

IV. Rivers are often of deep economic significance to a country or area because of their capacity to carry trade, support the manufacturing of waterpower, and by means of irrigation, support agriculture.

  A. The Rhine river is of economic significance to the lives of the people of Germany and the Netherlands, in particular, because it serves as Europe's busiest highway of commerce.

    1. The physical aspects of the Rhine make it ideal for transportation.

      a. The river is located in a climate which has enough rainfall to supply the people and land with water needs.

      b. The Rhine rises in the Alps and flows along the northern edge of Switzerland and serves as the boundary between France and Germany before it flows into Germany proper. From inside Germany it flows into the Netherlands and empties into the North Sea.

      c. The Rhine is navigable for barges from the Swiss port of Basel to the sea.

    2. Germany, a great industrial country, ships many tons of goods each year on the Rhine.

      a. The river flows through the Ruhr, a heavy industrial district.

      b. Germany has no seaport on the Rhine, however, and the Netherland ports are frequented by German ships.

    3. One of the most important German river ports is Duisburg-Ruhrort.

    4. The people of the Netherlands have been skippers for centuries and rely on trade with foreign countries for much of their income.

      a. The Netherlands handles much of the trade of Germany because the Germans lack a river port on the sea.

   b. One of the important Dutch ports on the Rhine is Rotterdam.

B. The water in rivers serves as a source of power which men can put to work to run their machines and light their homes, thus rivers have an indirect economic value.

   1. All over the world men use water for mechanical power. We see water turning mill wheels and lifting water into irrigation ditches.

   2. In highly developed areas, electrical power is generated and used to provide light and power.

C. The Ganges River in India is instrumental in providing the food needs of many people; the major portion of the population is directly dependent on agriculture and they depend on the monsoon rains for moisture.

   1. The climate of India makes it necessary for the people to adjust their lives to its peculiarities.
      a. The climate here is classified as tropical; a wet and dry climate which is characterized by an uneven distribution of precipitation through the year and by having a distinctly wet and dry season.
      b. The precipitation comes in the form of monsoon wind and rain in mid-summer.
         1'. The monsoon season comes during the months of June and September.
         2'. The winds over the cooler ocean pick up the water and carry it over the land which is warmer; this creates a low pressure system over the land while a high pressure zone is over the sea.
         3'. The air flow is from sea to land at this time, and water is dropped on the surface of the land.
      c. The village people are dependent upon the summer monsoon for water for their crops.
      d. Failure of the rain to come would produce famine throughout the land.
      e. The Ganges supplements the water supply provided by the monsoon rains in the valley when the rainfall is irregular and (or) inadequate.
      f. The crops which are grown in India most often go to feed the hungry population, but other crops, such as cotton, are grown for commercial purposes.

D. The Ganges river is of importance in the religion of the people of India.

   1. The Ganges river is looked upon as a gift of God which supplies the people with their needs and is, therefore, worshipped by traditional Hindus. People bathe in its waters and desire to be cremated near its shores.

V. Rivers play an important role in the history of an area. Rivers serve as boundry lines between lands, as routes to the interior of a continent, and as arteries along which cities grow.

A. The Hudson river has played an important role in the history of the United States in that it served as a route to the interior of the continent.

   1. Henry Hudson, searching for a short trade route to China from the Netherlands, sailed up the Hudson to a point where Albany stands today, exploring as he went.
      a. He was disappointed that it was not the way through the land to China.
      b. But he went home saying, "This territory is the finest for cultivation that I ever in my life set foot upon, and the situation is well adapted for shipping."

2. A water route is the best one to follow when entering the interior of a strange, new continent for several reasons.
   a. The dense growth of wilderness makes travel very difficult over land.
   b. Because the wilderness serves as a hiding place for men and animals, journeys are dangerous.
   c. Since no roads or bridges have been built, carrying heavy goods is a problem when traveling over land.

3. Settlers soon came to America from the Netherlands and settled along the river because the land was accessible.
   a. Trading with the Indians to obtain furs was of major interest to the settlers.
   b. Soon they began to farm.the valley floor.
   c. Then a river harbor called New Amsterdam, now New York City, began to grow.

4. Today the Hudson serves as an important economic waterway to the interior of the land.

B. At another period in the history of the Americas, the Hudson river and the settlement of the Dutch served to divide the northern English colonies from those in the south.

1. The British, not liking their colonies to be divided, forced the Dutch to surrender New Amsterdam and changed the name to New York.

2. As the river had divided the colonies before, now under the control of the English, the river served to unify the colonies as it became a trade route.

INITIATION

The initiatory phase is an important part of each unit of work. This is the experience which the teacher has already planned with specific purposes in mind. The initiation serves to stimulate or revive interest, identifies goals and problems to be solved, and supplies the group with a common orientation. This is the phase of the unit during which the teacher must convince the children that this experience will help meet some of their needs and interests. With this in mind, the teacher plans experiences which will generate interest. She includes pupil activity and class discussion. During the period of class discussion, the children identify the problems that they want to solve. The following is a plan of initiation which is believed to be suitable for this particular unit of work.

The type of experience which has been chosen to initiate this unit of work consists of having an arranged environment and viewing carefully selected materials through the use of the opaque projector.

There are many advantages to having an arranged environment and including in it some kind of viewing materials such as films, filmstrips, or opaque materials for the opaque projector. A list of these advantages are listed below:

1. The children are able to take an active part in the initiation.
2. This approach makes use of many senses — seeing, hearing, touching, and sharing experiences through discussion.
3. This method employs a variety of materials which may touch the lives and interests of all the students.
4. Using this method gives the teacher a chance to view the interests and questions of the individuals, often without becoming obvious.

5. This method provides a common experience upon which students can draw during the unit, while participating in group discussions and attempting to answer some of their questions.
6. Such an environment can stimulate children to think critically and sense some of the dimensions of the total study.
7. The opaque projector helps focus attention on one object at a time, getting to the main problems more quickly.
8. This type of initiation is easily adapted to any intermediate grade level in which this unit may be used.

A. It is necessary for the teacher to do a great deal of preliminary planning to insure success.

  1. It will be necessary to collect items that will be used in the arranged environment.
    a. Books may be borrowed from the library.
      1'. *Huckleberry Finn*, Mark Twain
      2'. *Rip Van Winkle* and *The Legend of Sleepy Hollow*, Washington Irving
      3'. *Terry's Ferry*, Marion B. Cook
      4'. *All Around You*, Jeanne Bendick
      5'. *All About Great Rivers of the World*, Anne Terry White
      6'. *The Little Flute Player*, Jean Bothwell
      7'. *The Wind in the Willows*, Kenneth Grahame
      8'. *The Gift of the River*, Enid LaMonte Meadowcroft
      9'. Other books will be added according to the immediate facilities of the library.
    b. Magazine articles and pamphlets may be selected and gathered.
      1'. *National Geographic Magazine* articles will be gathered from a private collection.
      2'. Other sources, such as *Holiday* and *Look* will be obtained from library services.
      3'. Pamphlets will be procured from library services and from free and inexpensive materials sources.
    c. Pictures may be collected. The pictures needed are as follows:
      1'. Dam across a river
      2'. Boats in a canal
      3'. Harbor busy with trade
      4'. Irrigation from rivers
      5'. Harbor with snow on docks and ice in the water
      6'. Boats of general nature on river
      7'. Fishing in river
      8'. Animals along river
      9'. Boys playing along river
      10'. A city using water from a river
      11'. Other suitable and useful pictures which are available (may include art work of children completed previously with no thought of unit in mind)
    d. Maps may be selected.
      1'. Map of the United States
      2'. Map of the world showing where the first four civilizations now known to man were developed
      3'. Map emphasizing population of the river valleys to be studied
    e. Articles may be assembled.
      1'. A world globe

   2′. A model of a felucca

   3′. Some rice, sugar cane, and cotton

   4′. A bottle of river water and silt from a river bottom

   5′. A plant which is healthy and one which is dying

   6′. A small pile of clay and another of straw

  f. Projection materials may be selected.

   1′. A representative area of the Mississippi River valley

   2′. A representative picture of a hot, dry area – Egypt

   3′. A picture of the Rhine Valley

   4′. A picture of an Indian farmer during a monsoon rain season

2. Some articles may have to be made.

 a. Pictures to be used in the opaque projection may need to be mounted.

 b. A map depicting the first four civilizations known to man in their locations in the world will have to be made or located.

3. The materials which are now assembled will have to be arranged attractively and in some kind of relationship one to another.

 a. Bulletin boards will contain maps and pictures.

  1′. The teacher-made map of the early civilizations of the world should occupy a central position on one of the bulletin boards, and pictures that apply may be placed around it.

  2′. Another bulletin board may be attractively arranged with pictures.

 b. Materials may be arranged on tables.

  1′. On one table, the world globe, a model of a felucca, and some rice and sugar cane and cotton may be exhibited.

  2′. On another table, a bottle of river water and some of the river bottom, a dying and a healthy plant, and a small pile of straw and one of clay will be exhibited. Near the bottle of soil a sign may read, "Shake it. What happens?" Near the two plants a sign will be placed which may read, "What makes the difference?" Near the straw and clay a sign will read, "What could be done with these materials?"

 c. The books, pamphlets, and magazines may be placed on the exhibit tables and on the reading table.

4. The procedures which make up the initiation must be carefully planned.

 a. The children will be encouraged to examine the materials which have been placed in the classroom.

 b. After sufficient time has elapsed (about two days), the selected materials to be used in the opaque projector will be shown during and after which the students and teacher may discuss their observations.

B. The pupils must become actively involved in the experience.

 1. The pupils may be allowed time for and may be encouraged to look at the pictures, study the maps, browse through books, and examine the models and other three dimensional objects.

 2. The pupils may view selected projection materials as a group.

 3. The students may take part in a discussion which they direct themselves.

C. The discussion period gives the teacher a chance to stimulate the thinking of the children even further and to find out what knowledge they already have; it also gives children a chance to ask questions and to tell what they think they know.

1. Questions the teacher may ask to find out what the children already know are listed below:
   a. What experiences have you had with rivers?
   b. Have you decided what has caused one plant to die while the other continues to live?
   c. Are you able to show where the river valleys are located by using the globe? By using the flat world map?

2. Questions the teacher may desire to ask to stimulate the thinking of the students are listed below:
   a. Why did I put a dead plant out for all of you to observe?
   b. What one thing do all of the early civilizations have in common?
   c. Why is water more plentiful in some regions than in others?
   d. Why did all of the early civilizations settle along rivers?
   e. What title could we make for our bulletin board?

3. Questions the students may ask during the discussion period are listed below:
   a. Where does the water come from that we see in rivers?
   b. What makes rivers flood?
   c. What can men do to keep the river off their land?
   d. What are the ways a river works for us?
   e. Why do men build canals?
   f. How can a river help a farmer?
   g. How do rivers build land?
   h. Why don't we irrigate from the Mississippi?
   i. Why do people use rivers when trains and trucks are a faster way of moving materials?
   j. How can water make electricity?
   k. Why are some rivers used for irrigation and some not?
   l. Why are rivers important?
   m. How do canals work?
   n. How can a river help a city grow?
   o. Why did those first people build their homes by rivers?
   p. Why do we need to trade with each other?
   q. Why are there no tributaries along the Nile in Egypt?
   r. What does it mean when a river drains a land?
   s. Why do explorers use rivers?
   t. How can rivers make history?
   u. How do rivers change an area?
   v. How do rivers help a country?
   w. Why are some rivers used for transportation and some not?

D. It may be useful for the teacher and the class to analyze the judgments which have been displayed.

   1. The teacher will listen carefully for any misconceptions which the children may have developed.
      a. A misconception children usually have is one concerning the way in which rivers flow.
      b. Another misconception concerns the manner in which electricity is produced.

2. The class may discuss these and other points which come up briefly, or it may be necessary to have several experiences to help clarify these ideas.

3. Each child should be encouraged to express his ideas, opinions, and questions.

4. The children may be led to recognize the values of ideas, opinions, questions, and procedures.

5. The children may be helped to recognize relevant and irrelevant problems and questions.

E. ORGANIZATION OF PROBLEMS FOR STUDY

HOW DO RIVERS AFFECT MAN?

A. What are the ways that rivers work for man?
  1. What does it mean when a river drains a land?
     a. Where does the water come from that we see in a river?
     b. Why are there no tributaries along the Nile in Egypt?
  2. How can a river aid farming?
     a. How can a river build up land?
     b. Why are some rivers used for irrigation and some not?
  3. Why do men use rivers for hauling when trains and trucks are a faster way of hauling materials?
     a. Why are some rivers good for transportation and some not?
     b. Why do explorers use rivers?
     c. Why do we need to trade with each other?
  4. How can a river make a city grow?

B. Why did people build their homes in river valleys?
  1. What did the rivers do for them?
  2. How did they make use of the rivers?

C. What are the ways men control and extend rivers?
  1. What do men do to keep the flood waters off their land?
  2. Why do men build canals?
  3. How can water make electricity?

D. How do rivers add to the prosperity of a country?

E. How can rivers make history?

COOPERATIVE PLANNING

Cooperative planning is basic to the democratic process; it is also a way of planning activities for the group. Below is a list of points at which cooperative planning could be used most successfully during the progress of this unit.

The children may:

1. Plan how to find answers to questions.
2. Plan a starting point.
3. Plan background reading on rivers.

4. Plan how to report findings from reading to the class.
5. Plan standards for listening and reporting.
6. Plan for everyone to keep an individual notebook.
7. Plan for the class to make a class log of activities, etc.
8. Plan to make a water shed area in the sandtable.
9. Plan to make a terrarium.
10. Plan to have an agricultural agent come and talk.
11. Plan to make a flood plain.
12. Plan to talk to community residents about how own community has developed.
13. Plan to make a map of the Nile Valley or some other region.
14. Plan to visit a dam in the area.
15. Plan questions to be asked at the dam.
16. Plan the standards for behavior on the trip.
17. Plan to make a dam on the watershed area.
18. Plan to visit a hydro-electric plant in the area.
19. Plan questions to be asked about the generation of electricity.
20. Plan to make a "Movie" for the culminating activity.
21. Plan to have an exhibit for parents and friends.

EXPERIENCES

The direct and indirect experiences in this unit are designed to develop the understandings, attitudes, and behaviors which have been established as appropriate and desirable for this particular unit of work. Having determined the understandings, attitudes, and behaviors to be developed, the teacher must select the experiences which will best develop them. Time is an important consideration in elementary teaching. Experiences which are planned with no specific purpose in mind will only waste time which could be put to better use. All experiences should be practicable, should contribute to the achievement of the goals of the unit, and should stimulate problem-solving and critical thinking. In addition, they should be varied in materials and in scope, interesting, and realistic. Appropriate materials for each topic may be selected from those suggested.

HOW DO RIVERS AFFECT MAN?

What does it mean when a river drains a land?

SPECIFIC LEARNINGS:	DIRECT EXPERIENCES	RELATED EXPERIENCES	
		SKILLS	CREATIVE
Rivers are the result of water draining from an area and flowing into streams from streamlets and on to becoming rivers.	**AUDIO-VISUAL** Viewing the film "The Making of the River." Viewing filmstrip, "How Rivers Are Formed."	**Writing** 1. Writing a factual summary of the way in which a river is formed for their personal notebooks from information taken from both film and readings.	**Writing** Writing a poem about the beginning of a river.
The beginning of a river is called the source and the area which is drained is called a watershed.	Displaying S.V.E. Picture-story Study Print Sets, S.P. 118, Land Forms of Running Water.	**SCIENCE** Experimenting with water to see where it goes.	**Writing** Writing a creative story or short essay on the formation of a river.
The source of a river is usually a melting glacier or a lake which is fed by springs high in the mountains.	Viewing filmstrip, "The Origin of Rivers."	1. Children use sand in bottle and add water to watch how water soaks the ground.	**MUSIC** Compose music of the sounds which might be heard as a river is forming.
The path that the river cuts is known as a channel and the place where the river junctions with the sea is known as the mouth.	**COMMUNITY EXPERIENCE** Walking in the rain in a hilly field. 1. Seeing how water runs downhill forming small streams which meet larger ones.	2. By adding too much water for the amount of earth, they can see water drainage.	1. Use homemade as well as conventional instruments. 2. Make a tape recording of the music which was created and listen to it.
Rivers always flow from higher to lower land but can either flow north, south, east, or west.	2. Seeing how soil is carried along also.	**SCIENCE** Experimenting on watershed area.	**READING** Reading the poem "Song of the Brook" by Alfred Lord Tennyson.
The water cycle influences the amount of precipitation in an area, and the amount of precipitation influences the volume of water in rivers.	**CONSTRUCTION** Making a watershed area. 1. To see how all elements work together in the formation of a river.	1. Trying to form a small river. Examining Land Form Models. 2. See that river cuts path of least resistance; put up stones in path.	Teacher reading to class Ross' The River, prose of the birth of a river until the day it joins the ocean.
A river usually has several tributaries which join it and add to the volume of water in the river.	2. Watershed area can be made in sand table. Use plastic so water may be added. 3. Reference: Page 298 of Delia Goetz "At Home Around the World."	3. See appendix.	**Music** Listening to "The Brook" by Tennyson, Dolores. 1. This music correlates with the poem by Tennyson so may want to use together.

READING

To gain background information on rivers. Children will be grouped.

1. Better readers will read from "Our Wonderful World," Vol. 10, 414-419; 427-434 and "The World Book Encyclopedia," Volume 15, pages 326-330.

2. Average readers use "Journey Through the Americas," pages 120-122 and "Living Together in The Americas," Cutright, King, Dennis, Potter, pages 282-284.

3. Slower readers read from "At Home Around the World," by Delia Goetz, page 156 and 298.

4. All may read material on watershed which teacher has available in files.

5. Reading Jauss, The River's Journey.

CONSTRUCTION

Constructing a terrarium to observe the water cycle.

1. The children will read to discover the correct way of making it.

2. The planning and building of the terrarium will be a cooperative project.

WRITING

Copying a poem into the individual notebooks.

1. Accurately copying a poem will help in understanding the form of poetry.

2. Use language-arts text for reference.

READING

Reading the section on water and rivers in the book "All Around You," by Jeanne Bendich. (For slow readers)

Reading Naden, Corinne. "The First Book of Rivers."

READING

To learn how to build a terrarium. The basic science text will serve as a reference.

SCIENCE

Observing changes and happenings in the terrarium.

WRITING

Taking day by day notes of what happens in the terrarium for the class log.

WRITING

Making notes on important facts learned from this question.

MUSIC

Singing the song, "The Wondering Stream," page 146 in "New Music Horizons."

ART

Making a composition depicting the beginning of a river. Use any satisfactory available media.

ART

Making a creative composition of what happens as it rains. Use any desired media.

ART

Creating a cover for individual notebooks on rivers.

CONSTRUCTION

Making a diagram of the water cycle for their individual note-books. Colored pencils can be used or any other the child wishes besides chalk.

DISCUSSION

Discussion of the question "Why are there no tributaries along the Nile in Egypt?"

1. Children will study maps together in groups.

2. Using what they already know and information found on these maps, they should be able to draw conclusions and answer this question.

3. Maps needed are as follows: Annual precipitation, climate, terrain.

DISCUSSION

Discussion to share information and learning about the function of river drainage.

1. Each child participates in discussion by contributing from his readings.

2. Summarize learnings.

LANGUAGE ARTS

Making a vocabulary dictionary section to the individual note-books.

1. Include these words - highland, mouth and source of a river, flood plain, tributary, swamp channel.

2. Write out meanings.

Language Arts

Learning to spell commonly used words such as tributary and channel.

How can a river aid farming?

SPECIFIC LEARNINGS:	DIRECT EXPERIENCES	RELATED EXPERIENCES	
		SKILLS	CREATIVE
To make farming possible and profitable a farmer must have fertile soil, moisture, a sufficient growing season, and land that is level enough to be tilled without too much difficulty.

The soil in river valleys is carried from higher land into the valley and deposited.

The river deposits soil when it overflows its banks or when it slows as it does at its mouth. These latter forms of obstruction are known as deltas. | READING

Reading in committees.

To discover what things influence farming. _The World Around Us_, by Zoe A. Thralls, pages 34-40.

COMMUNITY EXPERIENCE

Interviewing the county agricultural agent to find out about the conditions for farming in own area.

A committee will visit the agent with certain questions in mind to be answered. These may be supplied by the class.

CONSTRUCTING

Making a cross-section model of a flood plain and showing its features.

1. To visualize the various features of the flood plain which are brought about by the river.

2. The planning and construction may be in the hands of a committee.

3. See Appendix for ideas and plans.

CONSTRUCTION

Making a diagram of a flood plain for their individual notebooks. | Writing

Recording worthwhile information as they read to later share with the class concerning "How a river aids farming."

Writing

Writing a letter to the county agent requesting permission for an interview. Consult the language arts textbook to find out how to write such a letter.

Writing

Taking notes during the interview. Emphasis will be upon taking only key sentences.

Writing

Writing a thank you to the county agricultural agent thanking him for the information.

REPORTING

Making a report to class about the visit to the agent's office.

1. Discussion of the ways of making reports and being good listeners may take place at this point. | ART

Draw a picture of a farm scene with a stream running through it.

MUSIC

Singing the song "Oh, Lovely Meadows" from page 126 in _Around the World_ (Book Six).

WRITING

Writing a creative story or essay about a farmer and a river. |

MUSIC

Listening to "Mississippi Suite" by Grafe.

---

2. After reports are given, the group can evaluate themselves as reporters and listeners.

Writing

Recording in the class log the information given to the children by the county agent. Reports may be written from report given to class and one may be chosen for the log.

Writing

Writing a paragraph telling how a delta is formed. This is to be a factual account and may be included in their notebooks.

LANGUAGE ARTS

Adding to the vocabulary section of their notebooks.

1. The class may add delta, valley, levees, and silt.

LISTENING

Listening to the book, Huckleberry Finn, by Mark Twain, read by the teacher. This book may be read throughout the unit.

Writing

Recording activities in the class log.

---

1. Colored pencils may be used.
2. The model can be used as the guide for making it.

CONSTRUCTING AND PROCESSING

Making a model of a delta.

1. Adding a delta to the already constructed watershed area.

2. The planning and construction may be in the hands of a committee.

CONSTRUCTION

Making a diagram of a delta for individual notebooks. Again colored pencils are good to use in constructing notebook diagrams.

READING

Reading about Mississippi and Nile Valleys.

1. To see the differences in climate between the Mississippi Valley and the Nile.

2. This reading may be done by a committee and reported to the class.

3. Resource book The World Around Us by Zoe A. Thralls, pages 125-126; 30-34.

Listening to Reports

Listening to learn "why some rivers are used for irrigation and some are not."

The river supplies water to nourish the land in some places; other areas experience enough rainfall to sustain crops.

Just as farmers often have to use fertilizer to make their soils better, often, in lands of little rain, they must add water to their crops.

AUDIO-VISUAL

Viewing film "Understanding our Earth, How Its Surface Changes."

1. Seeing film to learn about the forces which build up and wear away the land.

2. Children may look for the ways water affects own land surface.

Viewing "Guarded Treasure" (Film) 16mm sd 10 min.

WRITING

Taking notes on film "Understanding our Earth, How Its Surface Changes" for their individual notebooks.

READING

Reading Bowman, James C. Mike Fink.

Reading Western Writers of America Rivers to Cross.

Why do men use rivers for hauling
when trains and trucks are a faster way of moving goods?

SPECIFIC LEARNING:	DIRECT EXPERIENCES	RELATED EXPERIENCES	
		SKILLS	CREATIVE
As routes of transportation, rivers have certain advantages and disadvantages. Water transportation is an inexpensive means of hauling heavy, bulky goods over long distances. Water transportation is easier than cutting a path through the wilderness in unexplored territory. Water transportation is safer in unexplored territory. The cost of maintaining waterways is less expensive than other types of transportation. However, the river route is not always a direct one. And, in higher latitudes, waterways are subject to seasonal use because of ice and snow obstructions. To be an ideal route for transportation a river must be free from obstructions, must have a slow current, should have a low gradient, carry little sediment and be a direct route.	READING Children may read in groups to discover advantages and disadvantages of river transportation. 1. Better readers use Our Wonderful World, Vol. 11, 446-449. The World Around Us by Zoe A. Thralls, pages 162, 196, 362, 205. 2. Average and below average readers may read from teacher prepared materials. 3. Reading Ewen, William. Days of the Steamboats. AUDIO-VISUAL Viewing film "Transportation by Water." 1. Children may view the film to learn about water as a means of transportation. 2. Children may look for information about the advantages and disadvantages of river transportation. 3. This film will also help answer the question "How can a river help a city grow?" Viewing filmstrip, "Pathfinders Westward."	LANGUAGE ARTS Reading to find out something about minstrel shows which were so much a part of the early transportation on the river. Emphasis is on research techniques such as use of card catalogue, scanning, indices and table of contents and selection of best information. READING Reading the story of Terry's Ferry by Marion B. Cook. (For slower readers) WRITING Taking notes on the film "Transportation by Water." Notes may be used to write a short summary for notebooks. ARITHMETIC Measuring wood for the model of the flatboat.	MUSIC Singing the song "Travel," page 23, in New Music Horizons. ART Drawing pictures of river travel. MUSIC Listening to records that the class found in their search for minstrel show materials. Music Singing old minstrel tunes. Music Singing the song, "Down the River," page 126 in Music for Young Americans. ARTS Making charts of the advantages and disadvantages of river transportation. 1. Care shall be taken to make letters of correct size. 2. Posterboard and showcard ink may be used.

Men need to engage in trade because:

(1) Men have discovered that by trading they can have a variety of goods and also can dispose of their own surpluses.

(2) Men have discovered that by trading technical skills and ideas, their standard of living may also increase.

AUDIO-VISUAL

Studying pictures of the early river boats to see how they were made.

CONSTRUCTION

Making a model of the flatboat which was used on the Mississippi river extensively.

1. The work of planning and making this model may be the responsibility of a committee.

2. Care should be taken to make it authentic. People and cargo may be placed on board.

READING

Children may read to discover why we trade.

1. Reading may be done by a committee.

2. Reference Our Wonderful World, Vol. 10, page 15.

COMMUNITY EXPERIENCE

Examining articles from home.

1. To see how many come from places outside the United States.

2. To determine which articles must be transported long distances across the United States.

LANGUAGE ARTS

Adding to the vocabulary dictionary section in notebooks. The class may add definitions for these words: falls, rapids, and up and down stream, flatboat.

SCIENCE

Answering the question, "What makes a ship float?"

How can a river help a city grow?

SPECIFIC LEARNING:	DIRECT EXPERIENCES	RELATED EXPERIENCES	
		SKILLS	
Cities developed along rivers because of the opportunity for trade.	READING Children read in groups to find information on background of New Orleans and river trading. 1. Better readers will find information in Our Wonderful World, Vol. 3, pages 453-455 and from files of teacher. 2. Average readers may read from files.	READING Reading poem "Rivers Are Like People" by Jean H. Breig in Moving Ahead. WRITING Writing a short summary to answer this question for their individual notebooks.	GAME Playing the game "Twenty Questions" (see Appendix for description). ART Collecting pictures for individual notebooks.
Cities developed along rivers because of the water power available.	AUDIO-VISUAL Studying maps of Mississippi river to see how many important cities are found along its banks. READING Reading about water wheels that were used on rivers. 1. Reference Our Wonderful World, page 20-21. AUDIO-VISUAL Viewing the film "Mississippi - Upper River." To see development of water power and relation to cities located there.		
Cities developed along rivers because they can be a direct source of water for a large population.	READING Reading about rivers as a direct resource for water by a committee.	REPORTING Making committee reports on using the water from rivers as a direct source for a city's supply.	ART Drawing pictures of how rivers make cities grow.

DRAMATIC PLAY

Enacting what might have happened as men decided to build a fort or a city. Ask children:

1. What things would they consider as they looked at the wilderness country?

2. No properties are actually needed but may be supplied as the children desire.

---

1. Our Wonderful World, pages 138-148 may be used as a reference.

2. Children may try to learn what needs to be done to the water to make it safe.

Reading Bethers Ray, Rivers of Adventure.

Reading Judson, St. Lawrence Seaway.

LISTENING

Listening to reports on using water from rivers as a direct source for a city.

COMMUNITY EXPERIENCE

Asking residents how their community has grown. (If near a river, use immediate community.)

1. To help children gain a better understanding of how cities grow.

2. If community has grown because of a river, further study may be very useful.

COMMUNITY EXPERIENCE

Ask residents about their supply of water for the community. This may help children gain a better understanding of how their community functions.

WHY DID PEOPLE BUILD THEIR HOMES IN RIVER VALLEYS?

What did rivers do for them?

SPECIFIC LEARNING:	DIRECT EXPERIENCES	RELATED EXPERIENCES	
		SKILLS	CREATIVE
The early civilization of Egypt was dependent upon the Nile for its needs.	**READING** Reading background information on "Egypt - Gift of the Nile." Read to find out how they rely on the river. 1. Better readers may read from The Eastern Hemisphere, pages 356-361; Man's Story, pages 44-51 and 67-69; The World Around Us, pages 136-138; and from Our Wonderful World, Vol. 2, pages 92-95, Vol. 5, pages 326-334, 337-339, 342.	**WRITING** Taking notes of important information as background reading is done. 1. Children may use these notes extensively throughout the rest of this section. 2. Emphasis may be placed on simple outlining procedures. 3. Children may want to prepare notes for their notebooks.	**WRITING** Writing a story about the development of the Egyptian civilization. **ART** Creating a mural called "Egypt - Gift of the Nile." 1. The children may all contribute ideas and sketches for the mural. 2. The planning and executing of the mural may be a cooperative project. 3. Materials used may be water colors on paper.
The existence of the Nile made it possible for many more people to live in this area than could otherwise survive there.	2. Average readers may read from Old World Lands, pages 290-296. 3. Below average may read from Homelands of the World, pages 141-148. **AUDIO-VISUAL** Viewing "Life in the Nile Valley." 1. Seeing the film to learn ways in which the people are dependent upon the river for their living.	**ARITHMETIC** Solving problems having to do with the number of people the land would have supported if the land had been desert and compare to the number it will support because of the Nile River. Facts will need to be obtained from population tables.	**MUSIC** Singing the song "The Nile" in The American Singer, page 241. **DRAMATIC PLAY** Enacting an incident which might have happened as people who had been living in the desert, following their birds, stumbled on the valley of the Nile.
The people depended upon the river for a yearly flood which watered their crops and brought quantities of rich soil to the valley.	2. Children may watch for ways in which the people use the river.	**READING** Reading story "Oxen for Anper" which stresses gifts the river gives in Distant Doorways, page 112.	**WRITING** Write a one act play about the coming of the yearly flood.

		ART
Soil was used for making their homes and pottery. Farmers found it necessary to add water to their crops and began irrigating them.	READING Reading information on the Nile from the book "All About Great Rivers of the World" by Anne Terry White to learn more about the Nile River. Reading Adler, Irrigation. Reading Joy, Island in the Desert.	READING Reading the story "The God of the Nile" on page 127 in Distant Doorways. WRITING Writing a paragraph or more for their notebooks using information compiled from reading and viewing experiences. 1. Writing to tell how the river influences the lives of the people of Egypt. 2. Children may use their language arts book as a guide.	Making pinch pots from self-hardening clay.
The river made it possible for groups of people to become unified through common needs, and so government was established. The river even served to protect the people from enemies.	AUDIO-VISUAL Viewing the film "Nile River Valley and the People of the Lower River." 1. Seeing the film to learn about irrigation projects and the delta of the Nile. 2. Children may want to pay particular attention to the facts given about the delta.	REPORTING Giving oral reports on the Nile from the book All About Great Rivers of the World.	
	CONSTRUCTION EXPERIENCE Making a map of the Nile river valley. 1. To gain a visual approach to the concept of the Nile as the giver of life. 2. To emphasize the importance of the Nile, make desert yellow-ish gold and land along river green.	READING Reading story "Nazli Goes to Market" from Distant Door-ways, page 101. (River used for transportation) READING Reading "How the Stars Helped the People of Egypt" in Distant Doorways page 124. SCIENCE Growing plants in a controlled situation.	

CONSTRUCTION
EXPERIENCE

Making a claybrick house out of clay.

1. To gain a better appreciation for the lives most of the people of the Nile must live.

2. Materials needed are simply clay. Self-hardening clay would be best.

3. Bricks must be made individually, then laid.

4. Several houses can be grouped to make a model village.

1. To aid the children's understanding of the importance of water and to let them experiment with plants requiring little moisture.

2. Plants selected may be cacti and any other available house plant requiring daily watering.

3. See Appendix.

SCIENCE

Opening a cacti plant and viewing it through a microscope to see if we can find water stored within the plant.

ARITHMETIC

Measuring for the making of a map of the Nile Valley.

WHAT METHODS HAVE MEN DEVISED TO CONTROL AND EXTEND RIVERS?

What do men do to keep floods off their land?

SPECIFIC LEARNING:	DIRECT EXPERIENCES	RELATED EXPERIENCES	
		SKILLS	CREATIVE
Floods are caused when snows melt in the mountains and surrounding land faster than the river can carry away the runoff.	**AUDIO-VISUAL** Viewing filmstrip: "Water Resources." Viewing film: "The Mighty Columbia River." **READING** Children may read to find background information on floods and the control of them. Children may read in groups. 1. Better readers may read from Our Wonderful World, Vol. 10, pages 420-423. 2. Average readers may read from Moving Ahead, page 103. 3. Below average readers may read from teacher-prepared materials. Reading Taming Asia's Indus River by Charles R. Joy. **COMMUNITY EXPERIENCE** Visiting dams in the area to see how they function. Plan questions to be asked. **CONSTRUCTION** Building a dam on the already constructed watershed area.	**WRITING** Taking notes from reading materials on ways to control flooding of rivers. Notes will be put into individual notebooks. **READING** Reading article in Our Wonderful World called "River, Stay Way from My Door" written by H.S. Pryor; Vol. 10, pages 423-426. To learn how a flood affects people. Reading Water: Riches or Ruin by Bauer. **LANGUAGE ARTS** Adding to the vocabulary dictionary. The words "dam" and "dike" may be added to the class list. **READING** Reading the story "High Water," page 75 in Moving Ahead.	**ART** Making a picture of a flood. **MUSIC** Listening to "The Storm" by Rossini (William Tell Overture).
Men have built dams, levees, and dikes to keep the flood off their lands.			

1. To see how dams are able to prevent floods by regulating the amount of water in the river.

2. Dam can be made of clay with movable draw door of wood or metal.

3. Part of the problem will be to choose the best location for the dam.

4. Reading must be done prior to construction of dam.

COMMUNITY EXPERIENCE

Asking parents and residents of community to relate incidents during previous floods.

READING

Reading to discover best way to represent a dam, to see how they are constructed and to discover the best place to place it in the watershed area.

READING

Reading story "Stocky's Race with the River," page 116 in Moving Ahead.

LANGUAGE ARTS

Clipping articles about floods and flood control in the newspapers and magazines.

LANGUAGE ARTS

Giving individual oral reports on memories of floods by members of the community.

WRITING

Writing a factual account of the best experience which was related about floods for their notebooks.

WRITING

Writing stories into which they project themselves as participants during a flood.

LISTENING

Listening to the singing of "The Flood of Shawnee Town" written by Gene B. Fields. (Copy of words in Appendix)

Why do men build canals?

SPECIFIC LEARNING:	DIRECT EXPERIENCES	RELATED EXPERIENCES	
		SKILLS	CREATIVE
Men build canals for the purpose of improving water transportation.	READING	Writing	MUSIC
By building canals, two waterways can be connected, providing a longer route.	Reading for background information on canals to answer question "why do men build canals?"	Making a list of the ways canals aid in improving water transportation.	Sing song "The Erie Canal," page 194 in The American Singer.
By building canals, a route can be made shorter.	1. Better readers may read from Using Our Earth (Whipple), pages 256-257; Our Wonderful World, Vol. 5, pages 150-152 and Vol. 11, pages 449-456.	This list may be entered in the notebook.	ART
By building canals, traffic can pass cateracts and other obstructions.	2. Average readers may read from Homelands of the Americas, pages 67, 73, 74, 169.	WRITING	Make a table scene depicting the Erie Canal. Might include scenery, boats, people, and town.
	3. Below average readers may read from teacher prepared materials.	Writing a summary paragraph about the uses for canals.	
	Reading The Erie Canal by Ralph Andrist.	LANGUAGE ARTS	
	Reading Building the Suez Canal by S. C. Buchell.	Locating information to be read on canals, such as the Erie Canal.	
	Reading The Land Divided the World United by Paul Rink.	LANGUAGE ARTS	
	AUDIO-VISUAL	Reading about the manner in which boats have been and are moved in canals.	
	Viewing the film "Ohio River Lower Valley."		
	1. To help build an understanding of the purposes canals serve.		
Canals are also built as parts of irrigation systems.	2. Children may look for canals and locks around rapids and also pay close attention to the flood-wall shown.		

Locks are used to lift boats from one water level to another.

Viewing filmstrip, "Canals and Progress."

READING

Reading to discover how locks work. Reading may be done by a special interest group.

A resource which may be used is Our Wonderful World, Vol. 11, pages 456-458.

CONSTRUCTION

Making a workable model of locks.

1. To gain insight into the way locks work.

2. This may be done as a special interest project.

LISTENING

Listening to report given on how a lock works.

LANGUAGE ARTS

Adding to the vocabulary section of their notebooks.

Students may add "canal" and "lock."

SPEAKING

Giving an oral report on the subject "The Way in Which Locks Work." It may be helpful to use visual aids.

MUSIC

Listening to Handel's "Water Music."

How can water make electricity?

SPECIFIC LEARNING:	DIRECT EXPERIENCES	RELATED EXPERIENCES	
		SKILLS	CREATIVE
Water turns the shaft in the generator which rotates between huge magnets causing electricity to be generated in the armature.	AUDIO-VISUAL Viewing the film "Energy in our Rivers." 1. To gain basic information about water power. 2. Children may look for information on the way that water-power is generated. COMMUNITY EXPERIENCE Visiting a hydro-electric plant in the area. READING Reading for information concerning early means of using water-power. Reading may be done by a committee which is responsible for locating information. COMMUNITY EXPERIENCE Having a visitor from a power and light company come give a talk. 1. To illustrate where the electricity is being generated that is used in their homes and at school; and to answer questions and give general information on water-power.	WRITING Recording information from the film by writing paragraphs for individual notebooks. LANGUAGE ARTS Reading a story called "Water's Power," page 69 in Moving Ahead (Hildreth). WRITING Writing thank you notes to the representative from the power and electric company. 1. Everyone may write and one may be selected by a group to be sent. 2. Use language arts book as a reference.	GAME Playing the game "To Be Continued" (see Appendix for description). MUSIC Listening to "Reflections on the Water" by Debussy.

2. Make maps available for illustrative purposes.

Outlining maps: Transparencies.

DISCUSSION

Discussion of the problem "What are the ways men control and extend rivers?"

HOW DO RIVERS ADD TO THE PROSPERITY OF A COUNTRY?

SPECIFIC LEARNING:	DIRECT EXPERIENCES	RELATED EXPERIENCES	
		SKILLS	CREATIVE
Rivers play an important role in the economy of an area because they carry goods and transport people.	READING Reading for background information. 1. To get facts on the transportation system on the Rhine River. 2. Children may read in groups. Better readers will read from Geography of World Peoples, pages 56-57, 62-68, 102-105, 143-144. 3. Average readers may read from Our Big World, pages 55-59. 4. Below average readers may read from teacher prepared materials. Reading The Wonders of Water by James Winchester. AUDIO-VISUAL Viewing the film "The Rhine" to see what significance the river plays in Germany and the Netherlands. Viewing the filmstrip, "Rivers and Rice in Thailand." Viewing the filmstrip, "Factories, Mines and Waterways."	WRITING Taking notes on important information about the transportation on the Rhine. WRITING Writing a paragraph about the importance of the Rhine in Europe.	Writing Writing a story about some aspect of transportation on the Rhine. ART Making a painting of a harbor. DRAMATIC PLAY Dramatizing the happenings when docking with goods to be unloaded. ART Making a 3-dimensional harbor scene. 1. Boxes (wood) may be used. 2. Paint and clay objects may be added.

Rivers are important in the economy of an area because they supply the means whereby waterpower is generated and can be used for industrial purposes.

AUDIO-VISUAL

Studying maps to see where the Rhine river flows, to see how many important cities are built on its banks.

DISCUSSION

Discussing the different jobs which are made available for people due to a river flowing through a city.

READING

Reading is done on subjects of "How does Germany make use of the river?" and "How does the Netherlands make use of the river?"

Reading may be done by two committees and reports made to the class.

LANGUAGE ARTS

Recording important facts brought out in discussions about job opportunities.

SPEAKING AND LISTENING

Reporting on the uses made of the Rhine River in Germany and the Netherlands.

ARITHMETIC

Measuring to make the map of the Rhine river valley.

RHYTHMS

Creating the rhythms which might be heard as men load or unload a ship.

WRITING

Writing a short essay or poem expressing how one feels when they see a big boat. (Useful only with those who have seen a big boat.)

MUSIC

Listening to "Boating" by Debussy.

Rivers are important to the economy of some areas because they provide water for the growing of crops.

CONSTRUCTION

Making a map of the Rhine river valley.

1. To gain a visual and kinesthetic understanding of the course the river follows.

2. This map may contain principal cities, the Rhur, the source, mouth, delta region and countries it flows through.

LANGUAGE ARTS

Reading the book The Little Flute Player by Jean Bothwell. Children that are slower readers will enjoy reading this book.

LANGUAGE ARTS

Taking notes of important concepts during discussion of the monsoon season.

LANGUAGE ARTS

Locating information on rice farming in India.

1. To refine the skills which they have been using in social studies.

2. Emphasis may be placed on scanning, the use of the card catalogue, tables of contents, and indexes.

MUSIC

Listening to "The Sea" by Edward Mac Dowell.

DRAMATIC PLAY

Enacting the happenings at an Indian family farm during the monsoon season.

WRITING

Writing an imaginative story of life in India using factual background.

ART

Making a display or mural depicting the monsoon season in India.

DRAMATIC PLAY

Pretending to be taking a trip to India to study the Ganges River and its effects on the people.

LANGUAGE ARTS

Writing a short summary of rice farming in India.

READING

Reading to gain background information on the country of India whose economy is directly related to the amount of water available for the growing of crops.

1. Children may read in groups: Better readers will read from library and teachers file on India.

Reading Water by Suna Leopold and Kenneth Davis.

Reading A Book To Begin on Rivers by Lee Sebastian.

2. Average readers may read from At Home Around the World, pages 155-184.

3. Below average readers may read from teacher-prepared materials.

DISCUSSION

Discussing the concept of the monsoon season.

1. To gain a better understanding of its nature and the role it plays in shaping the lives of the people of India.

AUDIO-VISUAL

Viewing the film the "Ganges River."

1. To gain a clear impression of the role it plays in the economy of the country.

2. Children may observe particular uses made of the river.

HOW CAN RIVERS MAKE HISTORY?

SPECIFIC LEARNING:	DIRECT EXPERIENCES	RELATED EXPERIENCES	
		SKILLS	CREATIVE
Rivers serve as routes to the interior of a continent.	**READING** Reading about the explorations of Henry Hudson. 1. To see how rivers lead to the interior of a continent during exploration. 2. Obtaining own references may be part of children's responsibility. Reading <u>About Rivers</u> by Dickey. **LISTENING** Listening to reports about the Hudson River. **DISCUSSION** Discussing the role the Hudson river valley settlement played in dividing the English colonies. **CONSTRUCTION** Labeling a map of the eastern part of the United States to show correctly how the Hudson river settlement divided the English.	**LANGUAGE ARTS** Reading the story of the <u>Legend of Sleepy Hollow</u> by Washington Irving to gain an appreciation for the literature that grew up in the Hudson river valley. **LANGUAGE ARTS** Reporting on the explorations of Henry Hudson up the Hudson river. **WRITING** Recording facts heard in reports for individual notebooks. Outline or paragraph form may be used. **READING** Reading about the war between the Dutch and English over the New York territory.	**GAME** Playing the game "Cities, Mountains, or Rivers." (see Appendix for description.) **WRITING** Writing own story to go in a bag of tales about exploration on rivers. Stories might be collected and made into a book. **DRAMATIC PLAY** Dramatizing what might have happened aboard ship as Henry Hudson sailed up the Hudson river in search of China.
Rivers are often barriers and boundaries for areas.			
Sometimes rivers are important in the religious worship of a country.	**READING** Reading about the role of the Ganges River in the religious worship of the people of India.		

1. Children may read in groups. Better readers will read from Eurasia, pages 335-340, 340-349.

2. Average readers may read from At Home Around the World, page 173.

3. Below average readers may read from teacher prepared materials.

CULMINATING EXPERIENCES

The purpose of the culminating experience is to organize and summarize the major concepts, generalizations and understandings from the unit of study. An effective culmination should give the children a feeling of accomplishment. It may also serve as a stepping stone to other problems which the children wish to explore. The culmination should be a logical extension of the experiences which have been pursued during the unit of study. The teacher and the pupils should select the best procedures for summarizing and reviewing the major ideas stressed during the study. These will differ with each unit.

It is not unusual to have displays, dramatizations, exhibits of drawings and objects that have been constructed, debates, formal and informal talks, tape recordings, charts and photographic reviews of various phases of the study. The planning of the culminating activity is an important learning experience for both the children and the teacher. It may be planned at the beginning, the middle or the end of the study. It is an excellent opportunity for the children to learn to discriminate between the more important and the less important phases of the study.

Most teachers find that an interested audience helps assure the success of unit culminations. Other classes in the school, parent or teacher groups frequently serve as willing audiences.

EVALUATION

The evaluation is an important part of any learning experience. By evaluating work habits, processes, finished construction projects, discussion periods, and individual progress; most children are able to see clearly the places where improvements can be made. Children are given standards and goals toward which to work and better knowledge of their strengths and weaknesses. Teachers are given insight into the needs and interests as well as the problems of the children. Through evaluation better group planning and organization can be accomplished. Evaluation is necessary, of course, in making reports about the progress of individual students.

Many problems arise in evaluating students and their work, but many types of evaluations, if used correctly, will help the teacher in planning and reporting. On the following pages are several types of evaluations grouped within three major categories: pupil self-evaluation, pupil-teacher evaluation, and teacher evaluation.

I. Pupils' self-evaluation:

    A. Evaluating the audio-visual experiences (such as seeing films within the unit) by checking themselves on the following questions:

        1. Did I have in mind the purpose for viewing?

    yes (_____-_____) no

        2. Did I have in mind the questions or problems to be solved and know what to look for during viewing?

    yes (_____-_____) no

        3. Did I find the answer to the question (s) or problem presented?

    yes (_____-_____) no

        4. Did I observe the standards set up by the class for viewing audio-visual materials?

    yes (_____) no

B. Evaluating the community experiences (such as the visit of the county agent, the trip to the dam and interviewing residents of the community) by checking the following questions:

   1. Did I understand the purpose for having this community experience?

yes (_____-_____) no

   2. Did I behave according to the standards which the class had made?

yes (_____-_____) no

   3. Was I respectful and polite to the visitors and guides who helped us answer our problem?

yes (_____-_____) no

   4. Did I have in mind the questions that I was responsible for asking?

yes (_____-_____) no

   5. Did I ask the questions that I was supposed to ask and other questions which I felt were worthwhile also?

yes (_____-_____) no

   6. Did I listen for information which would help me or others to solve problems?

yes (_____-_____) no

   7. Did I learn something which was of particular interest to me or to others?

yes (_____-_____) no

   8. Did this experience further my understanding of the problem?

yes (_____-_____) no

C. Evaluating work habits in construction activities such as the constructing of the watershed area in the sandtable, the terrarium, the mural and the "movie".

   1. Did I contribute ideas to the group for consideration?

yes (_____-_____) no

   2. Did I listen while others gave their ideas, too?

yes (_____-_____) no

   3. Did I listen to the directions carefully?

yes (_____-_____) no

   4. Did I make plans and follow them?

yes (_____-_____) no

   5. Did I help others who were in need of assistance?

yes (_____-_____) no

   6. Did I share my materials and tools?

yes (_____-_____) no

   7. Did I do my part for the project?

yes (_____-_____) no

   8. Did I make the best use of my time and materials?

yes (_____-_____) no

   9. Did I put away tools and materials in the proper places?

yes (_____-_____) no

  10. Did I work willingly?

yes (_____-_____) no

D. Evaluating the discussions of the group which arose during the initiation, the experiences, and during cooperative planning by answering the following questions:

1. Was I able to state the topic to be discussed in a clear manner?
   yes (_____-_____) no
2. Did I think about the topic to be discussed before the time for the discussion?
   yes (_____-_____) no
3. Did I try to find some information on the subject to be discussed?
   yes (_____-_____) no
4. Did I contribute relevant, interesting information and ideas to the discussion?
   yes (_____-_____) no
5. Did I present my ideas in clear, meaningful sentences?
   yes (_____-_____) no
6. Did I speak loudly enough for all to hear?
   yes (_____-_____) no
7. Was I courteous to others when it was their turn to speak?
   yes (_____-_____) no
8. Did I ask questions which I was unable to get answered by other means?
   yes (_____-_____) no

E. Evaluating their progress in the unit by answering the following:

   1. Am I finding answers to my questions? yes   no
   2. Am I finding new questions to answer? yes   no   If so, list — _____
      _____
   3. Am I participating actively in groups? yes   no
   4. Am I having trouble locating information or finding answers to questions?
      yes   no
   5. Am I having trouble understanding anything that we have discussed? yes
      no   If so, what — _____
      _____

II. Pupil-teacher evaluation:

   A. Evaluating the selection of various experiences to answer specific questions by using a checklist and perhaps discussing it.

      1. Does this experience provide the answer to the problem?   Y N
      2. Is this experience practical as far as time and effort and money spent
         are concerned?   Y N
      3. Does this experience keep us growing in the ability to observe, listen,
         report, and read for information?   Y N
      4. Does this experience give us all something to learn together and give us
         a chance to plan with each other?   Y N
      5. Is this experience closely related to the problem to be solved?   Y N

   B. Evaluating the audio-visual materials such as films, maps, and models by discussing questions together.

      1. Were we able to answer any of our questions by viewing the film (or other media)?
      2. Was the film the best source of information we could have used to find the answer to our question?
      3. What did we learn about rivers in general from the film?
      4. Was the film easy to understand and enjoyable?
      5. Did the film verify what we already have learned?

C. Evaluating through discussion the group and individual reports given during the unit experiences by having a discussion period.

   1. What did you enjoy most about the report?
   2. Did we get the answer to any of our questions by listening to the report?
   3. Could we offer any suggestions for improvement in the future?
   4. Did we ask relevant questions of the reporters?
   5. Did the reporters answer our questions satisfactorily?
   6. Did we listen considerately?

D. Evaluating the construction experiences such as maps and the watershed area through discussion.

   1. What are the learnings that we have obtained from our construction experiences?
   2. Are there ways in which the activity might be improved?
   3. Does it make sense to others who have not taken part in our experiences?
   4. Was there another way in which we might have obtained this learning?

E. Evaluating through group discussion the progress they have made toward answering their problem.

   1. Have we found the answers to all of our questions?
   2. What questions have we found answers for?
   3. What questions have we not found answers for?
   4. Do our answers represent our best efforts?
   5. How can we finish answering our questions?
   6. Are there any more questions which we might answer?

Every phase of a project offers opportunities for planning and evaluation.

III. Teacher evaluation of children's learnings:

A. Evaluating understandings, attitudes, and behaviors by observing the individual child during discussion, construction, and play periods. (Below is a checklist which will be helpful in observing children's *behavior.*)

Name:_____ Class:_____	
BEHAVIORS to be OBSERVED	DATES
Is sensitive to needs and problems of others	
Helps others meet and solve problems	
Willingly shares ideas and materials	
Accepts suggestions and help	
Makes constructive suggestions	
Supports group plans and decisions	
Works courteously and happily with others	
Gives encouragement to others	
Respects the property of others	
Enjoys group work	
Thanks others for help	
Commends others for contributions	

This test is designed to test the children's skill in using what they already know and the information they are able to interpret from maps to find the answers to questions.

Directions: Below you are given a list of several questions and a map of an island. Using what you know about rivers and what you can see by studying the map, answer the questions by drawing a line under the correct answer.

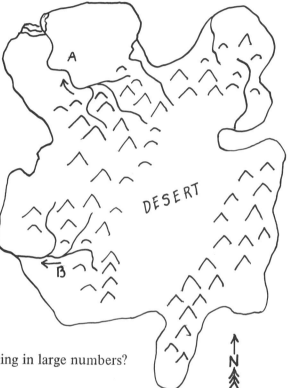

1. The fact that one river is flowing north and another south indicates that:
   a. The map is wrong.
   b. Rivers sometimes flow up hill.
   c. *Rivers may either flow north or south.*

2. The rivers are flowing
   a. From the sea to the land.
   b. *From high land to low land.*
   c. Through the desert.

3. The river marked A is an old river. At its mouth is (are)
   a. A harbor for shipping
   b. A very fast current.
   c. *Large quantities of sediment which is known as a delta.*

4. The desert has no drainage pattern developed in it. Why doesn't it have a river flowing through it?
   a. *Because little rain falls between the mountains so there is no need of draining the land.*
   b. Because the hot sun would dry a river up.

5. Where would you most likely find people living in large numbers?
   a. In the mountains by rivers.
   b. In the desert.
   c. *Along the lower course of rivers.*

6. The river marked B has a number of other rivers joining it. This whole area is drained
   a. By the main river.
   b. *By a river system.*

APPENDIX

CONSTRUCTION

Construction of Floodplain (cross-section)

Materials: container with one side of glass
                           sand, gravel, dirt
                           adhesive tape
                           poster card

Description: Reproduce diagram in the container by using gravel for bedrock, sand for alluvial soil, and dirt in the backswamp and old meander scar. Tin foil can be used for the channel of the river. The parts can be labeled by using adhesive tape on the glass. A standing sign can be made to stand near by.

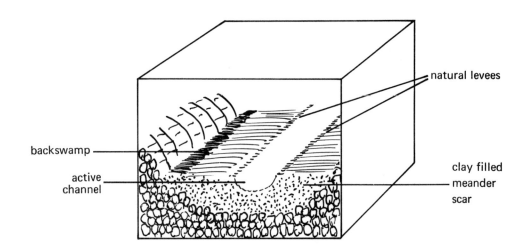

CONSTRUCTION

Construction of "movie"

Materials: Two old broom handles
Box larger than 18″ X 24″
Paper (18″ X 24″)
Water colors
Drawing pencils

Procedure: Having had the dialogue planned, make pictures to correspond with it. A good plan would be to let each individual do a series of pictures instead of one for each aspect of the story. This will keep the artistic qualities of pictures more harmonious.

After the pictures are completed and in proper order, fasten them together with extra paper (see diagram below) and glue. Lap edges ½ inch and glue. Add extra pieces of paper on back by gluing. Make a title page and put a blank page at each end to be left on the roller each time. When the pictures are all together, the film is ready.

The box is the stage and screen and will need to be decorated. Paper can be used or fabric depending on the wishes of the group.

The film is attached to the rollers by tacking. (See figure two.) The rollers are placed in the box as seen in figure three by cutting two holes in the sides at the bottom. A slot is cut in the top into which the full roller may be placed. Once the rollers are in place the movie is ready to begin.

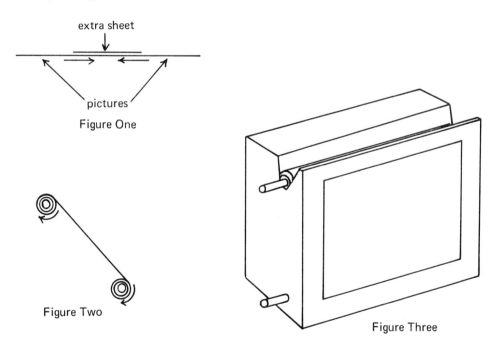

extra sheet

pictures

Figure One

Figure Two

Figure Three

EXPERIMENTS

Experiment One:	Where does rain-water go?
Materials:	large jar sand and gravel to fill jar pitcher of water
Procedure:	1. Fill jar with gravel at bottom. 2. Cover to 3/4 level with sand. 3. Slowly pour water on top. 4. Observe what happens. (Water should permeate the entire jar.) 5. Stop pouring when water reaches two inches below the top of the sand.
Experiment Two:	How is a river formed?
Materials:	previously constructed watershed area on sandtable can of water
Procedure:	1. Pour slowly (do not sprinkle) on the side of a "hill." 2. Observe what happens. (Water should run down hill seeking the lowest level.) 3. Put stones or similar blocks in the path of the river. If the water leaps over the obstruction, a waterfall can be said to have formed. 4. Observe what happens.

GAMES

CITIES, MOUNTAINS, OR RIVERS

Equipment needed: none

Explanation of activity: With players in a circle, "IT" points to a player and says either "city", "mountain", or "river". The player must respond with the name of whatever was called in as short a time as is possible. The play would go like this: "River!...."Nile!" If the player succeeds he gets to be the new "IT".

Teaching suggestions or variations: This game may get very noisy, and so it is a wise idea to caution against this before the game begins.

Source: adapted from game called "Beast, Bird, or Fish", taken from *A Pocket Guide for Games and Rhythms* by Marjorie Latchaw and published by Prentice-Hall, Inc., New York, 1959.

Place played: classroom

Group involved: good for intermediate grade children and older, any number but best in groups of 8-12, both sexes

TO BE CONTINUED

Equipment needed: none

Explanation of activity: Players sit in a circle; one starts to tell a story. When he is ready to stop, he says that it is to be continued. The next person picks it up and passes it on. The only object is exciting listening.

Source: *Recreation Leader's Handbook* by Richard Kraus, New York, 1955

Place played: indoors in classroom

Group involved: ages upwards from 8, both sexes, small groups are better than large ones.

TWENTY QUESTIONS

Equipment needed: none

Explanation of activity: One person (or a panel may be used) is set aside to guess. The rest are observers and a spokesman is chosen. The spokesman chooses a person, place, or thing and records it for future reference. The person(s) who is going to guess is told that it is either animal, vegetable, or mineral and is given twenty questions in which to determine the object. The questions are answered either "Yes", "No", or "I don't know".

Teaching suggestions or variations: Restrict the object to things concerning the river study such as canal, delta, etc.

Source: *The Complete Book of Games* by Clement Wood and Gloria Goddard, published by Garden City Publishing Co., Inc., New York, 1940.

Place played: classroom

Group involved: good for elementary pupils and upwards, both sexes. Small groups are better than large ones.

SONG

FLOOD OF SHAWNEETOWN

G. B. Fields

In the town of Shawneetown as the evening shades came down,
On a quiet Sabbath evening cold and gray,
While the people walked the street or in dear communion sweet,
Sat within their peaceful homes at close of day,

All at once the bells were ringing with a wild and awful din
While the fearful fact breaks over one and all,
That the fateful levees broke pale the lips of those who spoke,
While the roaring, crashing awful flood comes in.

On it came with mighty force spoiling all within its course,
Wrecking homes and snatching loved ones from their friends,
While they found a wat'ry grave 'neath the cold and silent wave,
To be covered over by the drifting sands.

Tongue nor pen can ne'er describe the hopeless anguish and despair
Of the poor survivors of that awful flood,
And they'll ne'er forget the day Shawneetown was washed away
Till they rest beneath the cold and silent sod.

BIBLIOGRAPHY

I. **References for teacher use:**

A. Books for the teacher

Bardoch, John E., *Downstream: A Natrual History of the River,* Harper & Row, New York, 1964.

Finch, Venor C., et al, *Elements of Geography,* McGraw-Hill Book Company, Inc., New York, 1957.
An excellent basic reference for the cultural and physical aspects of geography.

Gresswell, R. Kay, *Standard Encyclopedia of the World's Rivers and Lakes,* Putnam, New York, 1965.

Hart, Henry C., *New India's Rivers,* Orient Langmans, Bombay, 1956.
This provides a good look at what the Indians are doing to improve their rivers.

Kitson, Edward, *Bookbinding,* Dover Publications, Inc., New York, 1954.
A comprehensive study of the skills, materials and methods used in bookbinding.

Kohn, Clyde F., Editor, *Geographic Approaches to Social Education,* (Nineteenth Yearbook of the National Council for the Social Studies), The National Council for the Social Studies, Washington, D. C., 1948.
Among the topics discussed were: goals and philosophy and objectives, tools and implications for the elementary curriculum.

Kraus,Richard, *Recreation Leader's Handbook,* New York, 1955.
Good for games, dancing, singing, and drama.

Latchaw, Marjorie, *A Pocket Guide for Games and Rhythms,* Prentice-Hall, Inc., New Jersey, 1959.
Handy reference for games according to age and grade levels.

Ludwig, Emil, *The Nile,* The Viking Press, New York, 1937.
This is a "huge" volume containing vivid descriptions of the Nile from its source to the sea.

Michaelis, John U., *Social Studies for Children in a Democracy,* Prentice-Hall, Inc., New York, 1950.
A basic reference for teaching social studies.

Popescu, Julian, *Rivers of the World,* Walck, 1962, 2 vol. I-A.
Separate chapters on the great rivers of the world, giving history, course and effect on the region through which each flows. Contents. – v. 1. Danube, Amazon, Ganges, Niger, – v 2. Rhine, Murray, Nile, St. Lawrence.

Ross, George Maxion, *The River,* Dutton, 1967, P–I.
The adventure of a small river from its birth until the day it joined the ocean, told in lilting prose.

Schreiber, Otto L., *The River of Renown,* Greenwich Book Publishers, New York 17, New York, 1959.
This is an interesting and informative book on the Hudson River. Its valley, cities, some of its famous people and legends, and the role it played in the history of the United States is included in the book.

Tiegs, Ernest W. and Adams, Fay, *Teaching the Social Studies,* Ginn and Company, New York, 1959.
A basic reference for the teacher of social studies.

Childcraft, volume 11, "Ways of Learning", Field Enterprises, Inc., Chicago, 1949.
The book contains several valuable concepts which will aid the parent in becoming more understanding of the role which the school and the home play in the development of

children. Parents may be interested in the topics "Emotional Factors in Children's Learning" page 10, and "Learning Through Social Studies" page 143. A help for the teacher when interpreting the program to parents.

B. Community resources

II. References for children's use:

Barrows, Harlan H., et al, *Our Big World,* Silver Burdett Company, Chicago, 1959. 1964, ed. pp. same.
> *A general text with information on the importance of the Rhine in the Netherlands on pages 55-59.*

Old World Lands, Silver Burdett Company, Chicago, 1959. 1964, ed. pp. same.
> *A general text at sixth grade level with information on Egypt on pages 290-296.*

Cutright, Prudence, et al, *Living Together in the Americas,* The MacMillan Company, New York, 1955, pages 282-284, 1961 ed. add pp. 20, 282-284.
> *Contains information on the Mississippi, Ohio and Hudson Rivers.*

Dederick, Nelle, and Mackenzie, Josephine, *Your People and Mine,* (Revised Edition), Ginn and Company, Boston, 1960. 1966 ed.
> *Social studies content covers the United States and is particularly good for the Mississippi river and delta.*

Glendriming, Robert M., *Eurasia,* Ginn and Company, New York, 1958, pages 335-340, 346-349. 1961 ed. pp. same.
> *A basic text which considers critical thinking of the reader within the context. Significance of the Ganges River in the lives of the Indians is described.*

McConnell, W. R., *Geography of World Peoples,* Rand McNally and Company, New York, 1952.
> *An older book but some pertinent material on Rhine on pages 56-57, 62-68, 102-105, 143-144.*

Sorenson, Clarence Woodrow, *A World View,* (Book in the series "Man in His World"), Silver Burdett Company, New York, 1954. 1964 ed. pp. 200-208.

Stull, DeForest, and Hatch, Roy W., *The Eastern Hemisphere,* Allyn and Bacon, Inc., New York, 1956, pages 356-361.
> *Describes the role of the Nile River in the country of Egypt. Does not include new data.*

Thralls, Zoe A., *The World Around Us,* Harcourt, Brace and Company, New York, 1956. 1965 ed. pp.
> *Information on the lands of four seasons on pages 30-40.*
> *Information on the dry lands on pages 125-126.*
> *Information on river transportation on pages 162, 196, 362, 205. 1965 ed. p. 356.*
> *Information on the Nile River on pages 136-138. pp. 159-164 in new ed.*

Thurston, Ernest L., and Hankins, Grace C., *Homelands of the World,* Iroquois Publishing Company, Inc., New York, 1958. 1964 ed.
> *Pages 141-148 discuss Egypt – a country dependent on a river. Old but useful.*

Thurston, Ernest L., and Hankins, Grace C., *Homelands of the Americas,* Iroquois Publishing Company, Inc., New York, 1958. *Our Homelands and The World,* 1960 ed.
> *Pages 67, 73-74, and 169 have information on the Hudson river and canals.*

Compton's Pictured Enclopedia (1960 Edition), F. E. Compton and Company, Chicago 1960.
> *Egypt – The Land of the Nile in volume E pages 318 325.*
> *India – Farming and irrigation volume I pages 70-75.*

Wallbank, T. Walter, *Man's Story,* Scott, Foresman and Company, Chicago, 1951. 1956 ed.
> *Excellent source for better readers. Material includes history of the world with special*

reference to its geographical setting. Information on the early civilizations and why they settled in the valleys of rivers. Pages 44-51 and 67-69 concern the Nile specifically.

Our Wonderful World, (Young People's Encyclopedic Anthology), Spencer Press, Inc., New York, 1956. *Old but useful information.*

Volume 2 pages 92-95 on the Nile River
Volume 3 page 159 on the Nile River
Volume 3 pages 453-455 on New Orleans
Volume 3 pages 138-148 on water for cities
Volume 4 pages 20-21 on how electricity is generated
Volume 5 pages 356-344, 337-339, 342, on the Nile River
Volume 10 pages 414-419, 427-434 on how a river begins and develops
Volume 10 pages 420-423 on flooding of lands from rivers
Volume 10 pages 423-426 a story: "River Stay 'Way From My Door" by Helen S. Pryor
Volume 10 page 15 on why we trade
Volume 11 pages 449-456 on canals
Volume 11 pages 456-458 "How a Canal Lock Works"
Volume 11 pages 150-152 irrigation
Volume 11 pages 430-432 on how electricity is generated
Volume 11 pages 446-449 on transportation

The World Book Encyclopedia, Field Enterprises Educational Corporation, Merchandise Mart Plaza, Chicago, Illinois, 1966.
General information on rivers on pages 326-330 and in volume 16.

B. Trade books and fiction for children:

Adler, Irvin, *Irrigation,* Day, 1964, P–I.
From thousands of years ago in Europe up to present day in our country and in Mediterranean area, the story is told of how man has worked to water the desert.

Andrist, Ralph, *The Erie Canal.* American Heritage Publishing Co., New York, 1964.
Describes how the canal works, was developed, and has affected the life around it.

Bauer, Helen, *Water: Riches or Ruin,* Doubleday Co., Garden City, 1959.

Bendick, Jeanne, *All Around You,* McGraw-Hill Book Company, 1951.
This book answers questions and stimulates them also. Best for slower readers.

Bethers, Ray, *Rivers of Adventure,* Hastings House, New York, 1960.
Describes the way rivers have evolved and includes brief descriptions of the major rivers as well as the life along them.

Bothwell, Jean, *The Little Flute Player,* William Morrow and Company, New York 1949.
Ten-year-old Teka Rom, player of the flute, keeps his family from starving during a famine in Northern India. Recommended for slower readers.

Bowman, James C., *Mike Fink,* Little Brown & Co., Boston, 1957.
This is a fictionalized biography of Mike Fink's legendary life on the river.

Buchell, S. C., *Building the Suez Canal,* American Heritage Publishing Co., New York, 1966.
Discusses the background and building of the canal. It also includes a discussion of the effects on the peoples of the world.

Cook, Marion B., *Terry's Ferry,* E. P. Dutton and Company, Inc., Publishers, New York, 1957.
Story of a boy who was kept busy taking people across a river in his boat trying to catch enough fish to pay the price of a ticket to the circus.

Dickey, Albert, *About Rivers,* Melmont Pubs., 1959, P–I.
Pictures of rivers in the United States show how rivers begin, what happens to them and how they are used.

Even, Williams, *Days of the Steamboats,* Parents Magazine Press, New York, 1967.
> *Discusses the steamboats and how they were used in different areas. It includes many illustrations showing the problems of early travel and transportation on rivers.*

Hildreth, Bertrude, et. al, *Moving Ahead,* John C. Winston Company, Philadelphia, 1953. (A sixth grade reading text.) Old but useful.
> *Water's Power on page 69*
> *High Water on page 75*
> *Water Storage and Floods on page 103*
> *Stocky's Race with the River on page 116*
> *Poem: "Rivers Are Like People" on page 123*

Jauss, Ann Marie, *The River's Journey,* Lippincott, 1957, I.
> *Follow a river from its beginning as a mountain spring until it enters into the sea.*

Joy, Charles R., *Taming Asia's Indus River,* Coward-McCann, 1964. 1964. I-A.
> *This mighty river which drains India and whose mouth is in Pakistan is being tamed for better service to man by a variety of persons and projects. Eventually a better life for the people of these two countries should develop.*

> *Island in the Desert: the Challenge of the Nile,* Coward-McCann, 1959.

Judson, Clara Ingram, *St. Lawrence Seaway,* Follet, 1964, I.
> *The St. Lawrence Seaway opened the Great Lakes to oceangoing vessels. Describes the cooperation of Canada and the United States in this venture, the engineering problems which had to be overcome and what the future holds for the residents of this region.*

Leopold, Suna and Kenneth Davis, (Water) Time, 1966. and editor of Life.
> *This is photographic essay of the story of water and its uses for man.*

Meadowcroft, Enid LaMonte, *The Gift of the River,* Thomas Y. Crowell Company, New York, 1937.
> *A history of ancient Egypt; much information is given about the culture. Old but useful.*

Naden, Corinne, *The First Book of Rivers,* Franklin Watts, New York, 1967.
> *Explains what a river is and how rivers have changed the land.*

Rink, Paul, *The Land Divided the World United,* Julian Messner, New York, 1963.
> *Describes the story of the development of the canal. It includes the story of the people involved and the effects the canal has had.*

Sebastian, Lee, *A Book to Begin on Rivers,* Holt, Rinehart, and Winston, 1966, I.
> *The many different uses of rivers are explained in this introductory book.*

Smith, Nila Banton, *Distant Doorways,* Silver Burdett Company, New Jersey, 1956. (A fourth grade reader)
> *"Nazli Goes to Market" on page 101*
> *"Oxen for Anper" on page 112*
> *"How the Stars helped the people of Egypt" on page 124*
> *"The God of the Nile" on page 127*

Twain, Mark, *Huckleberry Finn,* A Classic
> *Finn has delightful adventures, many of which are on a river.*

Western Writers of America, *Rivers to Cross,* Dodd, New York, 1966.
> *This is a collection of stories centering around rivers.*

White, Anne Terry, *All About Great Rivers of the World.* Random House, New York, 1957.
> *Very interesting and informative, The Nile River is dealt with in great detail.*

Winchester, James H., *The Wonders of Water,* G. P. Putnam's Sons, New York, 1963.
> *This book explains how rivers have figured in the history and development of man. It also shows current uses of the river.*

III. For use by students and teachers

A. Films:

Energy in Our Rivers, ten minutes, sd, color and b&w, #FSC-169 and #FS-169, distributed by Coronet Films.
> *From the water wheel to the modern hydro-electric turbine, this film shows how falling water is harnessed to provide man with power, Dams in the U. S. are shown.*

Ganges River, Seventeen minute, sd, color, #GSC-755, McGraw-Hill.
> *Uses actual photographs to trace river from source to mouth. Cities and people and customs are stressed.*

Guarded Treasure, ten minutes, sd. 16mm.
> *Need for conserving, controlling and redistributing water in California. Emphasis on human efforts to adjust irrigation in natural supply and distribution of water.*

Life in the Nile Valley, eleven minutes, sd, color and b&w, #GSC-575 and #GS-575, distributed by Coronet Films.
> *Glimpses of life along the Nile and describes the influence of the geography of the region upon the environment of the farm family.*

The Making of the River. eleven minutes, sd, color and b&w, #GSC-657 and #GS-657, distributed by Coronet Films.
> *Using musical accompaniment and poetic narrative, the formation of the river from its source in the mountains to the termination of the river at sea is viewed.*

Mississippi – Lower River, sd, color and b&w, #GSC-276 and #GS-276. Academy Films, 15 min.
> *Shows important features of transportation, and agriculture. Also shows the flooding of the lowlands.*

Mississippi – Upper River, 15 min., sd, color and b&w, #GSC-275 and #GS-275. Academy Films.
> *Covered are the following: waterpower, dams, locks, and principal tributaries.*

Nile River Valley and the People of the Lower River, 17 min., sd, color, #GSC-505. Academy Films.
> *Shows how people are influenced by the Nile river. Includes scenes of irrigation projects and delta section.*

Ohio River – Lower Valley, 11 min., sd, color, #GSC-434, Academy.
> *A look at the Ohio from Cincinnati to the Mississippi junction. Canals, locks and a floodwall are shown.*

The Mighty Columbia River, eleven minutes, sd, color, Coronet Films.
> *Shows shipping, salmon fishing, hydroelectricity and irrigation. Grand Coulee and Bonneville Dams.*

The Rhine: Background for Social Studies, 11 min., color and b&w, distributed by Coronet.
> *The film presents an over-all view of the significant influence of the Rhine River.*

Transportation by Water, 15 min., sd, b&w, #CS-1010, distributed by McGraw-Hill.
> *Describes water as one of the most important means of transportation and also discusses its relation to the growth of cities and industry in the world.*

Understanding Our Earth: How Its Surface Changes, 10 min., sd, color and b&w, #GSC-695 and #GS-695, distributed by Coronet Films.
> *The film acquaints viewers with the forces which build up and wear away land. Includes the influence of water.*

B. Filmstrips

"Canals and Progress"
> *Origin of canals, how they have contributed to progress of man.*

"Earth Science Series: Geomorphology," Wards Natural Science Establishment, 1963, 6 film-strips, color.
> *Partial contents – 2. Streams and rivers.*

"Factories, Mines and Waterways,"
> *Industrial Western Europe. 45 frames: Emphasizes Alsace-Lorraine area.*

"How Rivers are Formed"
> *From source, how grows, flows, delayed. What it does for inhabitants along course. How man uses, abuses, improved waterways, recent developments.*

"Pathfinders Westerward," 1961, 3 filmstrips.
> *Contents – 1. Daniel Boone's Wilderness trial, 2. Rivers and roads to the Mississippi, 3. Lewis and Clark expedition pt. 1.*

"Rivers and Rice in Thailand," Encyclopedia Britanica.
> *Shows how people use rivers and canals for transportation and how rice is grown in river lowland.*

"The Story of Rivers," Encyclopedia Britanica, 1953.
> *Origin and growth of streams, the causes of soil erosion and reasons for changes in characteristics of rivers.*

"Water Resources."
> *Dangers of flood, why rivers flood. Value of control led to provision of water for drinking, irrigating, power dams. How science attempts to reduce flood by systems of dams, reforestation of head waters.*

C. Magazines

The National Geographic Magazine, (to show historical developments).
> "Along the Banks of the Colorful Nile" Vol. L, pages 322-399, September 1926.
> "Along the Nile Through Egypt and the Sudan" Vol. XLII, pages 379-410, October 1922.
> "Barrage of the Nile" Vol. XXI, pages 175-184, 1910.
> "Daily Life in Ancient Egypt" Vol. LXXX, October 1941.

D. Songs

Beattie, John W. and others, *The American Singer,* American Book Company, New York, 1955.
> "The Erie Canal" page 16
> "The Nile" page 220

Berg, Richard C., et al, *Music for Young Americans,* American Book Company, Chicago, 1959.
> "Down the River" page 126

Mursell, James L., et al, *Around the World,* Silver Burdett Company, New Jersey, 1956.
> "Ah Lovely Meadows" page 126

New Music Horizons, Silver Burdett Company, New York, 1953.
> "Travel" page 23
> "The Wandering Stream" page 146

E. Maps and Pictures

Land Form Models, Hubbard Scientific Company, Northbrook, Illinois.

S.V.E. Picture–Story Study Print, SP118, *Land Forms of Running Water,* Society for Visual Education, Inc., Chicago, Illinois.

Outline maps: boundaries, and rivers (Transparency), Western Publ. Ed. Ser., 1965.
> *Includes, Africa, Asia, Australia and New Zealand, Canada, Carribean, Europe, Mexico, North America, South America, U.S., U. S. Eastern, U. S. Western, West Indies, Western Hemisphere, World mercator's flat spread, World mercator's Western Hemisphere Centered.*

EARLY PRIMARY SOCIAL STUDIES UNIT
LEARNING TO KNOW YOURSELF

"...the concept of self takes root and grows in a cultural world of ideas, of persons and of things."

---Robert S. Fleming

"Children who like themselves and know themselves will have a head start in life over those who do not know nor accept themselves so well."

---Richard M. Brandt

BASIC CONCEPTS TO BE DEVELOPED

I. We learn to know who we are by what we look like, by what we learn, and by how we feel about things.
II. We learn to know who we are by being a member of a family.
III. We learn to know who we are by playing and working with friends.

SKILLS TO BE DEVELOPED

1. Identification of oneself.
2. Attainment of emotional maturity appropriate to age level.
3. Discovery and development of individual talents and abilities.
4. Learning to deal constructively with feelings such as anger, fear, resentment, prejudice, etc.
5. Recognition of human similarities and differences.
6. Awareness of the behavior of others and adjustment to it.
7. Realization that one must learn to live harmoniously in all groups, large and small.
8. Understanding of the importance of working together to achieve common goals.
9. Ability to evaluate experiences.
10. Learning simple discussion skills.
11. Ability to make summaries.
12. Ability to develop generalizations.

ATTITUDES TO BE DEVELOPED

1. Acceptance and appreciation of one's body.
2. Respect and confidence in oneself as a worthy person.
3. Respect and confidence in one's rights and feelings.
4. A reasonable sense of personal and social security.
5. Appreciation of human similarities and differences.

6. Respect for individual human personality and appreciation of the dignity and worth of every individual.

Appropriate materials for each topic may be selected from those suggested.

INITIATING THE UNIT

1. In an attractive manner prepare a bulletin board of photographs of individual pupils. Include a large picture of the total group, if possible.
2. Arrange on the reading table a display of appropriate books selected from the children's bibliography.
3. View film, "The Toymaker," in which two puppets play together until they discover differences in their appearance. These surface differences lead to conflict, until the two puppets realize what they have in common.

I. We learn to know who we are by what we look like, by what we learn, and by how we feel about things.

Understandings

No two people are exactly the same physically.

We look alike in many ways, yet we have differences.

Activities

Discuss pictures of pupils that were previously arranged on the bulletin board. Point out obvious similarities and differences.

List ways in which people are alike in physical appearance. List ways in which people are different.

Provide opportunity for each pupil to stand in front of a full-length mirror. Ask him to describe what he sees.

Play "Guess Who" game.

Have each pupil lie down on a large sheet of paper and another pupil trace his outline, with each one drawing in his own features.

Read *All Except Sammy* by Gladys Y. Cretan.

Play singing games for identification of individuals and parts of body.
 "Inside Our Circle," p. 41,
 Growing With Music
 "Sing and Do", p. 92,
 Growing With Music
 "Mary Wore Her Red Dress,"
 p. 19, *This is Music.*

Read poems, "Growing Up" and "My Other Name", pp. 32 and 34 in *Whispers and Other Poems.*

Provide opportunity for creating original songs and poetry about oneself.

No two persons learn exactly the same things nor have exactly the same interests.

There are certain things we especially like to do, and there are certain things we especially like to learn.

Draw a picture of self, show and describe to class how pupil perceives himself. This can be the first page in a picture story booklet, "All About Me."

Discuss what pupils enjoy doing — listening to stories and records, playing house, outdoor activities, games etc.

How does each activity help us?

Should we all like the same things? Why or why not?

Provide for a selection of activities — exploring, manipulating, playing with toys, blocks, tools and other equipment. Have a "choosing time."

Learn songs, "Things I like to Do,"
p. 57, *Meeting Music* and "I like to Pretend," p. 11, *Growing With Music.*

Pantomime game: What each pupil likes best to do.

Draw a picture of something one especially likes to do when he can choose.

Draw a picture showing one thing he does not like to do.

Arrange both sets on bulletin board.

Discuss pictures and make generalizations about them, such as

Many of us like to read.

Some of us like to paint.

Different children like to do different things.

All of us don't like to do the same things.

Add pictures to "All About Me" booklet.

Read *What Mary Jo Shared,* by Janice M. Udry.

Read *Is It Hard? Is It Easy?*
by Mary M. Green.

Discuss: What would happen if we never did anything we did not like?

Why is it exciting to learn new things — riding a bicycle, skipping, foods, reading etc.

Conclude by drawing and discussing "What's hard for you? and "What's easy for you?" Add to "All About Me" booklet.

Display a picture of a child. Let the children tell all the things this child might do for fun by himself.

Read poem, "I Am What I Do,"
p. 6 in *The Life I Live.*

Discuss meaning of poem.

No two persons have exactly the same things happen to them, nor

Provide for emotional outlet and creative expression through use of various media — finger paint-

do they feel the same way about things.

We can know ourselves by what happens to us and by the feelings we have about things.

ing, clay or dough, paper tearing, collages, musical instruments, etc.

Pupils may tell and illustrate something pleasant that happened to them. Discuss how pupil felt, differences in various experiences, etc.

Read *Sam* by Ann Herbert Scott.

Make a chart of different kinds of feelings, under "pleasant" and "unpleasant" categories.
Find magazine pictures showing these feelings and attach to chart.

Sing song, "If You're Happy,"
> p. 16 in *This is Music* or compose an original song about happiness.

Read *I Should Have Stayed in Bed* by Joan Lexan.

Draw pictures of something pupils would like to have happen.
Discuss whether they are in the realm of possibility, make-believe, etc. Add to "All About Me" booklet.

Read *Someday* by Charlotte Zolotow.

Tell stories on "When I Am Angry" or "What Makes Me Angry." Discuss.

Provide for pupils to express themselves creatively to music through dancing or use of various art media.
> Example: Sherzo in B Flat
> by Franz Schubert.

Show film, *What to do About Upset Feelings,* 11 min. color, b&w, Coronet Films, Chicago.

Show film, *Ways to Settle Disputes,* 11 min. color, b&w, Coronet Films, Chicago.

Each individual is unique. It is important to know this in understanding oneself.

Everyone is a very important person. It is a good thing that each person is special.

Read *The Smallest Boy in the Class* by Jerrold Beim or *The Important Book* by Margaret Wise Brown, to give children a feeling of importance.

Discuss again the differences among pupils — physical appearance, interests, happenings, feelings, etc.
> Why is this better than if we were all the same?

Each pupil may dictate a story about what he likes about himself. Add to "All About Me" booklet.

View film, *Just Like Me,* which dramatizes why it is good that all people are not just alike. It shows what things would be like if everyone were exactly alike.

Allow each pupil to use the tape recorder to tell about himself. Play back if he so desires.

Read poem, "Me, Myself and I," for identification of self. One always remains "me."

Provide opportunity for original poetry, songs, dance, etc. with the theme, "you're the only one in this whole wide world that is *you.*"

Read *Tom in the Middle* by Berthe Amass.

II. We learn to know who we are by being a member of a family.

As part of a family, we are important and our families are important to us.

Plan and arrange a housekeeping corner.
Read *A Baby Sister for Frances* by Russell Hoban.

Bring baby pictures from home.
Arrange on bulletin board, titled "When We Were Babies."
Discuss how parents probably felt when child was born.

Read *Family* by Margaret Meade and Ken Heyman.

Bring pictures of pupils' families. Point out family likenesses and differences — facial features, body build, etc.

Show film, *Allen is My Brother,* Churchill Films.

Make clothespin or paper bag puppets. Write a simple script for a puppet show centering around family living.

View film, *Date With Your Family,* showing how family ties are strengthened by simple courtesies.

Display and discuss "Feeding Her Birds" or "First Steps" by Jean-Francois Millet.
How are love and concern shown in the picture?

Show film, *Your Family* Coronet Films.

Read *The Littlest One in the Family* by Lois Duncan or *Home is a Very Special Place* by Eva Evans. Develop generalizations.

Show film *Appreciating Our Parents,* Coronet Films.

Draw pictures of family members. Add to "All About Me" booklets.

Read *Welcome Child* by Pearl Buck,

We have rules which help us live together.

Read poems, "My Mother Tells Me" and "My Daddy Scolds Me," pp. 16 and 17, *The Life I Live.* Discuss pupils' experiences which are similar.

Read *Peter's Chair* by Ezra Jack Keats.

View film, *A Happy Family.*

View film, *Families Have Fun,* Society for Visual Education.

Read *Daddy is Home* by David Blomquist.

Discuss:
> Why do parents teach their children to behave in certain ways?
> What would happen if everyone did just as he pleased?

Draw or paint a picture illustrating one way in which the pupil obeys his parents. Add to "All About Me" booklet.

Read *Middle Matilda* by Winifred Bromhall.

Discuss:
> Should parents always say "yes" to the things children ask for?
> Why or why not?

Each member shares in family living.

Provide opportunity for role playing in housekeeping corner.

View filmstrip, *Brothers and Sisters*
or *Our Family Works Together.*

Read *Lucky, Lucky White Horse* by Beryl Epstein.

Dramatize stories about home life that emphasize helping others, working together, etc.
> Roles of various family members
> How to do various tasks

Read *Daddies* by Lonnie Carton.

Read *Here Comes the Band* by Frances Horwich or "Daddy Helps" in *I Live With Others,* pp. 40-44, emphasizing that when we all help we can do many things.

Read *Giving Away Suzanne* by Lois Duncan.

Observe ways in which mother, father, brothers and sisters work together at home.
Report to class.

Read *My Sister and I* by Helen E. Buckley.

Bring magazine pictures showing members of families working together, gardening, cleaning the yard, shopping, baking, etc.
After discussing, arrange attractively on bulletin board.

View filmstrip, *Family Members Work,* Society for Visual Education.

View film, *Family Teamwork* or *Patty Garman, Little Helper.* Conclude with generalizations.

Discuss home activities and responsibilities of pupils.

How does helping make one feel?
Why should each person do his share?
What would happen if he didn't?

Make chart or illustration on "How I Help at Home." Add to "All About Me" booklet.

Make generalizations about the various activities for which pupils are responsible in their homes.

Families have many different ways of having good times together.

Provide opportunities for pupils to tell about happy times they have had with their families — holidays, birthdays, visits of relatives, travel, etc.

How did these times make you feel?
Why did you feel this way?

Draw pictures of family's favorite activities.
Categorize the various activities, making a group list.
Add pictures to "All About Me" booklet.

Experiment: Each pupil tries to make his family happy by helping with a certain task or doing something special.
Report to class.

What was attempted?
Was it successful?
How did the others and you feel?

Summarize and make conclusions.

Read "Company", pp. 45-47 in *I Live with Others,* emphasizing that company is fun and we can have a good time with them.

III. We learn to know who we are by playing and working with friends.

By having friends, we find out that we are important to them and that they are important to us

Read *Contrary Woodrow* by Sue Felt, in which a boy discovers how nice it is to have friends.

Dramatize doing something with a friend (in teams of two).

View film, *Fun of Making Friends.*

View filmstrip, *Little Things That Count,* Eye Gate House, 1966.

Listen to record, *Little Things That Count,* Eye Gate House, 1966.

Discuss:
How does it make one feel to be with friends?
Is it more fun when one is playing with friends?
Why or why not?

Read *Two On An Island* by Bianca Bradbury.

Draw pictures of self and friends in a favorite activity. Add to "All About Me" booklet.

Read *My Friend Mac* by May McNeer.

Doing things with friends helps us feel useful to others.

Plan and execute cooperative games and activities. Example: The whole group may attempt to get a given score by throwing bean bags or to pick up jacks until a given number has been reached.

Read *Next Door to Laura Linda* by Janice Udry.
Discuss:
Is Your room at school a good place to work and play?
Why or Why not?
How can we make it a good place to work and play?

Read *Look Who's Talking* by Ylla, pseud.

Organize committees and work groups for projects and/or housekeeping tasks. Discuss how jobs should be assigned and carried out.

Read *Time for Gym* by Jerrold Beim.
Discuss:
How can you help others?
How can others help you?

Show film, *The Fun of Making Friends,* 11 min. color, b&w, Coronet Films, Chicago.

Read *The Three Funny Friends* by Charlotte Zolotow.

Some ways in which we act help us to make and keep friends. There are other ways that make it difficult for us to play and work with others.

View film, *Courtesy for Beginners,* or *Kindness to Others,* which demonstrate that how one says things can affect the way others feel.

Discuss things that make one feel "good" in his relations with others.

Discuss those things that make one feel "less than good".

Provide opportunity for role playing demonstrating simple manners and courtesies.

Write a chart story about first grade pupils working and playing together. Include harmonious acts and acts of conflict. Illustrate with cut-outs. Encourage pupils to tell how they would feel about the various acts.

Read *Evan's Corner* by Elizabeth Starr Hile.

View filmstrip, *Playing Fair* or *Sharing with Others.*

Conclude by making generalizations.

View film, *Fairness for Beginners,* 11 min, color, b&w, Coronet Films, Chicago.

View film, *Beginning Responsibility: Other People's Things,* 11 min, color, b&w, Coronet Films, Chicago.

View film, *Let's Share With Others,* 11 min, color, b&w, Coronet Films, Chicago.

View film, *Kindness to Others,* 11 min, color, b&w, Coronet Films, Chicago.

View film, *Playing Community Helpers,* Encyclopedia Brittanica Films, Inc., 1960.

CULMINATING ACTIVITIES

1. Plan a party in which every pupil has a definite responsibility. Be sure to keep committees small.
2. Invite parents and younger brothers and sisters.
3. Present an informal program, including the puppet dramatization of family living and/or getting along with friends. Include original songs and poetry.
4. Play a simple game in which the total group (familes and pupils) participates.
5. Display "All About Me" booklets.
6. Serve simple refreshments of cookies and milk or juice.

EVALUATION

Evaluation should include:
1. To what extent is each child improving his own living?
2. Is he gaining in self-confidence?
3. To what extent is he better able to adjust himself to people and to situations?
4. To what extent is he cooperating with others?
5. Does he complete worthwhile tasks once begun?
6. To what extent is he developing skill in work habits?
7. Is he volunteering to assume special tasks or duties?

TEACHER'S BIBLIOGRAPHY

Alpenfels, Ethel "Culture Shapes Self." *Childhood Education* 33: 295, March, 1957.

Ambrose, Edna and Alice Miel. *Children's Social Learning.* Washington, D. C.: Association for Supervision and Curriculum Development, 1958.

Bandura, Albert and Richard H. Walters. *Social Learning and Personality Development.* New York: Holt, Rinehart and Winston, Inc., 1963.

Baruch, Dorothy Walter. *New Ways in Discipline.* New York: McGraw-Hill Book Co., Inc., 1956.

Baxter, Bernice, "Eye Level of Children." *Childhood Education* 33: 310-313; March, 1957.

Brandt, Richard M. "Children Who Know and Like Themselves." *Childhood Education* 33: 299-303; March, 1957.

Ellsworth, S. G. "Building the Child's Self-Concept," *NEA Journal,* Vol. 56 (February 1967) 54-56.

Fleming, Robert S. "Discovering Self." *Childhood Education* 33: 290-291; March, 1957.

Gesell, Arnold and Ilg, Frances L. *The Child from Five to Ten.* New York: Harper and Bros., 1946.

Hamalainen, Arthur E. "How a Child Grows," *Childhood Education,* Vol. 43 (February 1967), 351-352.

Havighurst, R. J., Robinson, and Dorr. "The Development of the Ideal Self in Childhood and Adolescence." *Journal of Educational Research* 40: 241-257; 1946.

Iscoe, Ira, ed. *Personality Development in Children.* Austin: University of Texas Press, 1960.

Levine, Louis Samuel. *The Psychology of Effective Behavior, Personal and Social Development.* New York: Rinehart and Winston, 1963.

Limbacher, Walter J. "An Approach to Elementary Training in Mental Health," *Journal of School Psychology,* Vol. 5, No. 3 (Spring 1967) 225-234.

McIntire, Alta *Exploring with Friends* Chicago; Jollett, 1964.

Marburg, Francis W. "Studying the Child's Social World." *The Journal of Educational Sociology* 21: 535-543; May, 1948.

Miel, Alice and Peggy Brogan. *More Than Social Studies,* a view of social learning in the elementary school. Englewood Cliffs, N.J.: Prentice-Hall, Inc., 1957.

Moustakas, Clark. *The Authentic Teacher: Sensitiveness and Awareness in the Classroom.* Cambridge: Howard A. Doyle Printing, 1967.
The Teacher and the Child, Personal Interaction in the Classroom. New York McGraw-Hill Book Co., 1956.

Munkres, Alberta *Personality Studies of Six-Year-Old Children in Classroom Situationss.* New York: Teachers College, Columbia University, 1936.

Mussen, Paul Henry, John J. Conger, and Jerome Kagan. *Child Development and Personality.* New York: Harper & Row, 1963.

Ojemann, Ralph H. "Incorporating Psychological Concepts in the School Curriculum." *Journal of School Psychology.* Vol. 5, No. 3 (Spring 1967) 195-204.

Pearce, Jane Edwin and Saul Newton. *The Conditions of Human Growth.* New York: Citadel Press, 1963.

Peck, Robert F. "Why Should We Teach Elementary School Children About the Principles of Human Behavior?" *Journal of School Psychology,* Vol. 5 No. 3 (Spring 1967),235-236.

Phillips, B. N. "Anxiety in Elementary School Children," *Childhood Education* (July 1968) Vol. 44, 340-342.

Roen, Sheldon R. "Teaching the Behavorial Sciences in the Elementary Grades," *Journal of School Psychology,* Vol. 5, No. 3 (Spring 1967), 205-216.

Roy, Mary M. *Spark,* A Handbook for Teachers of Elementary Social Studies. Benton Harbor, Michigan: Educational Services, 1965.

Samford, Clarence *You & the Neighborhood* Chicago: Benefic Press, 1963.

Shane, H. "Social Experiences and Selfhood." *Childhood Education* 33: 297-303; March, 1957.

Strang, Ruth. "How the Child's Identity Grows: with a Study-Discussion Program." *PTA Magazine* Vol. 60 (October 1965), 28-30.

Thomas, Alexander. *Behavioral Individuality in Early Childhood.* New York: New York University Press, 1963.

Witherspoon, R. L. "Teacher, Know Thyself." *Childhood Education* 35: 56-59; October, 1958.

Music

Growing With Music, Grade One.
   Englewood Cliffs, N. J.: Prentice-Hall, Inc., 1966.
Meeting Music, Grade One, Music for Young Americans Series.
   New York: American Book Company, 1966.
This is Music, Grade One.
   Boston: Allyn and Bacon, Inc., 1967.

Films and Filmstrips

"Children Who Draw Pictures." Brandon color; 38 min.
"Families Have Fun". Society for Visual Education, 1967.
"Family Members Work". Society for Visual Education., 1967.
"From Sociable Six to Noisy Nine." One of the Ages and Stages Series. (McGraw-Hill) color; 22 min.
"Little Things That Count". Eye Gate House., 1966.
"Playing Community Helpers". Encyclopedia Britannica Films, Inc., 1960.
"Emotion Takes Form." Art Council Aids. 50 Slides.
   Teaching Materials Service, Ball State University Library, Muncie, Ind.
"Know Your Children." New York Metropolitan School Study Council.

TAPES

Beauchamp, Mary. "Learning to Understand Boys and Girls."
   Muncie, Ind.: Teaching Materials Service, Ball State University Library, 1958.
Cattell, Psyche. "Behavior Limits and Feelings of Security."
   Cincinnati, Ohio: Sound Seminars.

CHILDREN'S BIBLIOGRAPHY

Amoss, Berthe. *Tom in the Middle.* New York: Harper, 1968.
Anglund, Joan Walsh. *A Friend is Someone Who Likes You.* New York: Harcourt, Brace and Company, 1961.
_____. *Love is a Special Way of Feeling.* New York: Harcourt, Brace and Company, 1960.
Annett, Cora. *The Dog Who Thought He Was a Boy.* Boston: Houghton Mifflin Company, 1965.
Averill, Esther Holden. *The Fire Cat.* New York: Harper and Brothers, 1960.
_____. *Jenny's Adopted Brothers.* New York: Harper and Brothers, 1952.
_____. *Jenny's First Party.* New York: Harper and Brothers, 1948.
Bannon, Laura. *Baby Roo.* Geneva, Ill.: Houghton Mifflin Co., 1947.
_____. *Big Brother.* Chicago: Albert Whitman and Company.
Beim, Jerrold. *Country School.* New York: Wm. Morrow and Co., 1955.
_____. *Kid Brother.* New York: Wm. Morrow and Co., 1952.
_____. *The Smallest Boy in the Class.* New York: Wm. Morrow and Co., 1949.
_____. *The Taming of Toby.* New York: Em. Morrow and Co., 1953.
_____. *Time for Gym.* New York: Wm. Morrow and Co., 1957.
_____. *Too Many Sisters.* New York: Wm. Morrow and Co., 1956.
Beim, Jerrold and Lorraine Beim. *Two is a Team.* New York: Harcourt, Brace and Company, 1945.
_____. *Who's Who in Your Family.* New York: Franklin Watts, Inc. 1954.
Belmont, Evelyn. *Playground Fun.* New York: Hastings House.

Bennett, Rainey. *The Secret Hiding Place.* Cleveland: World Publishing Co., 1960.

Bethell, Jean. *Hooray for Henry.* New York: Grosset & Dunlap, 1966.

Blomquist, David *Daddy is Home.* New York: Holt, Rinehart, 1963.

Bonsall, Crosby Newell. *Who's a Pest?* New York: Harper & Row, 1962.

Boutwell, Edna. *Red Rooster.* New York: Aladdin Books, 1950.

Bradbury, Bianca *Two on an Island.* Boston: Houghton, 1965.

Bromhall, Winifred. *Belinda's New Shoes.* New York: A. A. Knopf. 1945.

_____. *Middle Matilda* Knopf, 1962.

Brown, Margaret Wise. *The Important Book.* New York: Harper and Brothers, 1949.

Buck, Pearl. *Welcome Child.* John Day Co., 1963.

Buckley, Helen. *Grandfather and I.* New York: Lothrop, Lee and Shepard, 1959.

_____. *My Sister and I,* Lothrop, Lee and Shepard, 1963.

Burton, Virginia Lee. *The Little House.* Geneva, Ill.; Houghton Mifflin Co.

Carton, Lonnie. *Daddies* New York: Random House, 1963.

Caudill, Rebecca. *Happy Little Family.* Chicago: Winston, 1947.

Clark, Ann N. *In My Mother's House.* New York: Viking, 1941.

Clymer, Eleanor L. *A Yard for John.* New York: Dodd, Mead and Co.

Cretan, Gladys Yessagan. *All Except Sammy.* Boston: Little, 1966.

Cutler, Lin. *Peg-aLeg, the Cobbler of Dunsoon.* New York: A. A. Knopf, 1948.

Daugherty, James Henry. *The Picnic.* New York: Viking, 1958.

Dennison, Carol. *What Every Young Rabbit Should Know.* New York: Dodd, 1948.

Diska, Pat. *Andy Says Bonjour!* New York: Vanguard Press, 1954.

Dudley, Ruth. *Good Citizens, Good Neighbors.* Los Angeles: Melmont Publishers, 1957.

Duncan Lois. *Giving Away Suzanne.* New York: Dodd, Mead, 1960.

_____. *The Littlest One in the Family.* New York: Dodd, Mead, 1960.

Duvoisin, Roger Antoine. *Petunia, Beware!* New York: A. A. Knopf, 1958.

Epstein, Beryl. *Lucky, Lucky White Horse.* New York: Harper & Row, 1965.

Ets, Marie Hall. *Little Old Automobile. New York: Viking, 1948.*

Evans, Eva. *Home is a Very Special Place.* New York: Capitol Publishing Co. 1961.

Felt, Sue. *Contrary Woodrow.* Garden City, N. Y.: Doubleday, 1958.

_____. *Rosa Too Little.* New York: Doubleday and Co., 1958.

Fischer, Hans, Pitschi, *The Kitten Who Always Wanted to be Something Else.* New York: Harcourt, Brace and Co., 1953.

Garrett, Helen. *Angelo, the Naughty One.* New York: Viking, 1948.

Gilbert, Helen Earle. *Dr. Trotter and His Big Gold Watch.* New York: Abingdon-Cokesbury Press, 1948.

Green, Mary McBurney. *Is it Hard? Is It Easy?* New York: William R. Scott, Inc., 1948.

Harris, Isobel. *Little Boy Brown.* Philadelphia: J. B. Lippincott, 1949.

Haywood, Carolyn. *Two and Two are Four.* New York: Harcourt, Brace and World, 1940.

Hill, Elizabeth Starr. *Evan's Corner.* New York: Holt, 1967.

Hoban, Russell. *A Baby Sister for Frances.* New York: Harper, 1964.

Hoffman, Elaine and Jane Hefflefinger. *Family Helpers.* Chicago: Children's Press, 1964.

Horwich, Dr. Frances R. *Here Comes the Band.* Chicago: Rand McNally and Co., 1956.

Hunnicutt, C. W. and Jean D. Grambs. *We Live With Others,* 2nd Edition. Chicago: L. W. Singer Co., Inc., 1963.

_____. *We Play.* Chicago: L. W. Singer Co., Inc., 1963.

Hurd, Edith and Clement Hurd. *Nino and His Fish.* New York: Lothrop, Lee and Shepard Co., 1954.

Johnston, Johanna. *Sugarplum.* New York: A. A. Knopf, 1955.

Kahl, Virginia. *Away Went Wolfgang.* New York: Scirbner's, 1954.

Keats, Ezra Jack. *Peter's Chair.* New York: Harper, 1967.

Krasilovsky, Phyllis. *The Man Who Didn't Wash His Dishes.* New York: Doubleday and Co., 1950.

_____. *The Very Little Boy.* New York: Doubleday and Co., 1962.

_____. *The Very Little Girl.* New York: Doubleday and Co., 1953.

Krauss, Ruth. *A Very Special House.* New York: Harper, 1953.

Lenski, Lois. *The Life I Live.* New York: Henry Z. Walck. 1965.

Lexau, Joan M. *I Should Have Stayed in Bed!* New York: Harper & Row, Publishers 1965.

MacDonald, Golden, *Little Lost Lamb.* New York: Doubleday, 1945.

_____. *The Little Island.* New York: Doubleday, 1946.

MacGregor, Ellen. *Theodore Turtle.* New York: Whittlesey House, 1955.

McGinley, Phyllis. *Lucy McLockett.* Philadelphia: Lippincott, 1959.

McNeer, May. *My Friend Mac.* Boston: Houghton, 1960.

Mead, Margaret and Ken Heyman. *Family.* New York: Macmillan, 1965.

Merrill, Jean. *The Travels of Marco.* New York: A. A. Knopf, 1956.

Miles, Betty. *A House for Everyone.* New York: A. A. Knopf, 1958.

Newberry, Claire. *T-Bone, the Baby Sitter.* New York: Harper, 1950.

Nicole. *The Happy Family.* New York: Golden Press, Inc.

Oftedal, Laura and Nina Jacob. *My First Dictionary: The Beginner's Picture Word Book.* New York: Grosset & Dunlap, 1948.

Pickard, Vera. *Mr. Hobbs Can Fix It.* New York: Abingdon-Cokesbury.

Quigley, Lillian. *The Blind Men and the Elephant.* New York: Scribner's, 1959.

Rand, Ann and Paul Rand. *Sparkle and Spin: A Book About Words.* New York: Harcourt, Brace and Company, 1957.

Rey, Margaret Elisabeth and Hans Augusto Rey. *Billy's Picture.* New York: Harper, 1948.

Rowand, Phyllis. *George.* Boston: Little, Brown and Co., 1956.

Rukeyser, Muriel. *Come Back, Paul.* New York: Harper, 1955.

Savage, Joan. *Hurray for Bobo.* Chicago: Children's Press, 1947.

Schneider, Nina. *While Susie Sleeps.* New York: Wm. R. Scott, 1948.

Schlein, Miriam. *Laurie's New Brother.* New York: Abelard-Schuman, 1961.

Scott, Ann Herbert. *Sam.* New York: McGraw, 1967.

Scott, Sally. *Jenny & the Wonderful Jeep.* Harcourt, 1963.

Seuss, Dr. (Theodor Seuss Geisel). *Horton Hears a Who!* New York: Random House, 1954.

Tresselt, Alvin. *A Day with Daddy.* New York: Lothrop, Lee and Shepard Co., 1953.

Udry, Janice May. *Let's Be Enemies.* New York: Harper & Brothers, 1961.

_____. *Next Door to Laura Linda.* Chicago: Whitman, 1965.

_____. *The Moon Jumpers.* New York: Harper & Bros., 1959.

_____. *What Mary Jo Shared.* Chicago: Whitman, 1966.

Weil, Lisle. *The Busiest Boy in Holland.* Boston: Houghton Mifflin, 1959.

Will and Nicolas. *Chaga.* New York: Harcourt, Brace and Co., 1955.

Witte, Eva Knox. *People Are Important.* Irvington-on-Hudson, N. Y.: Capital Publishing Co., 1951.

Wright Ethel Belle. *Saturday Walk.* New York: Wm. R. Scott, 1954.

Yella, psued. *Look Who's Talking.* New York: Harper, 1962.

Zolotov, Charlotte. *Big Brother.* New York: Harper & Bros., 1960.

_____. *The Three Funny Friends.* New York: Harper, 1961.

_____. *Someday.* New York: Harper, 1965.

POETRY

Arbuthnot, May Hill, ed., *The Arbuthnot Anthology of Children's Literature.* Chicago: Scott, Foresman, 1952.

Association for Childhood Education. *Sung Under the Silver Umbrella.* New York: Macmillan and Company, 1952.

Livingston, Myra Cohn. *Whispers and Other Poems.* New York: Harcourt, Brace & Company, 1957.

FILMS

"Allen is My Brother". 11 min., color. Churchill Films, Los Angeles, California.
"Appreciating Our Parents." 11 min., color, b&w. Coronet Films, Chicago.
"Beginning Responsibility: Being on Time." 11 min., color, b&w. Coronet Films, Chicago.
"Beginning Responsibility: Books and Their Care." 11 min., color, b&w. Coronet Films, Chicago.
"Beginning Responsibility: Doing Things for Ourselves in School." 11 min., color, b&w. Coronet Films, Chicago, Ill.
"Beginning Responsibility: Lunchroom Manners." 11 min., color, b&w. Coronet Films, Chicago.
"Beginning Responsibility: Other People's Things." 11 min., color, b&w. Coronet Films, Chicago.
"Beginning Responsibility: Rules at School." 11 min., color, b&w. Coronet Films, Chicago.
"Beginning Responsibility: Taking Care of Things." 11 min., color, b&w. Coronet Films, Chicago.
"Caring for your Toys." 11 min., b&w. McGraw-Hill.
"Children Growing Up with Other People." 30 min., b&w. Contemporary Films, San Francisco.
"Courtesy for Beginners." 2nd Edition. 11 min., color, b&w. Coronet Films, Chicago, 1967.
"Date with Your Family." 10 min., color. Encyclopedia Britannica Films, Wilmette, Ill., 1950.
"Fun of Making Friends." 11 min., color, b&w. Coronet Films, Chicago.
"Happy Family, A." 13 min., color, b&w. Classroom Film Distributors, Inc., Los Angeles, 1960.
"Just Like Me." 8 min., color. Karl Lohmann, Jr.
"Kindness to Others." 11 min., color. Coronet Films, Chicago.
"Let's Share With Others." 11 min., color, b&w. Coronet Films, Chicago.
"Our Class Works Together." 11 min., color, b&w. Coronet Films, Chicago.
"Our Family Works Together." 11 min., color, b&w. Coronet Films, Chicago, 1958.
"Patty Garman, Little Helper." 11 min., color. Frith Films, Los Angeles, 1946.
"Taking care of Myself." 12 min., color. Educational Horrizons, Los Angeles, 1957.
"The Toymaker." 15 min., color, b&w. Athena Films, Inc., New York, 1952.
"Ways to Good Habits." 11 min., color, b&w. Coronet Films, Chicago.
"Ways to Settle Disputes." 11 min., color, b&w. Coronet Films, Chicago.
"We go to School." 11 min., color, b&w. Coronet Films, Chicago.
"We Play and Share Together." 10 min., b&w. Bailey Films, Inc., Los Angeles, 1951.
"What to Do About Upset Feelings." 11 min., color, b&w. Coronet Films, Chicago.
"Your Family." 11 min., color, b&w. Coronet Films, Chicago.

FILMSTRIPS

"Alan Mends His Manners." #305, Adventures in Personality Development Series. Creative Education, 1958.
"Brothers and Sisters." Encyclopedia Brittanica.
"Michael Finds a Better Way." #303, Adventures in Personality Development Series. Creative Education, 1958.
"Sharing With Others." #8491, Guidance Stories. Encyclopedia Brittanica Films, Inc.
"Tom Misses a Picnic." #202, Adventures in Character Dimensions Series. Creative Education, 1958.
"Tommy Tries to Help." Adventures in Character Dimensions Series. Creative Education, 1958.

HOW THE PEOPLE
OF THE WORLD REMEMBER
Middle Grade Unit

INTRODUCTION

All the people of the earth, regardless of whatever else they may lack, do not lack holidays. Indeed, the story of all the holidays ever celebrated in the world would serve as a rough outline of what people have found important and desirable throughout their recorded histories on earth. Holidays are tokens of devotion to some person, event, or expectation. They fall into three main categories — family, national, and religious. The most important of the world's holidays are religious in nature. These special days, which are often tangible manifestations of intangible ideas, help to preserve particular ideas and frequently serve as a release from the ordinariness of everyday life. Special foods and rituals are usually associated with holidays and festivals, both here and abroad.

UNDERSTANDINGS

People celebrate three main types of holidays. The most personal celebrations are those which concern our own families.

National celebrations indicate what people in a particular country consider important or desirable.

People of the world celebrate many religious holidays. These generally mark the memory of important historical events in the development of a religious faith.

ATTITUDES

Greater realization of the respect which should be shown toward other people.

Growing understanding and appreciation of the similarities among people everywhere.

Realization that most of the holidays of the world emphasize the hopes and aspirations of mankind.

SKILLS TO BE DEVELOPED

Skill in locating information by using such aids as the table of contents, book index, tables, charts, and card catalogues.

Skill in determining the relevance of information.

Skill in juding the importance of information.

Skill in organizing information by outlining, using sequential steps, and summarizing.

Skill in retaining ideas.

Skill in learning to plan and establish criteria for later evaluation.

Skill in creative expression involving imaginative writing, illustrating, and speaking.

Skill in working in groups.

Appropriate materials for each topic may be selected from those suggested.

INITIATORY ACTIVITIES

Devise a bulletin board with articles, pictures, etc., specifically designed to arouse interest in this study of holidays and festivities.

Have books and other appropriate materials available for browsing so that the child may be stimulated to look further.

View appropriate slides and films, or listen to stimulating records or tapes which will captivate their interest.

Invite a citizen of the community who has a hobby or collection relating to one or more holidays to talk with the class.

PEOPLE CELEBRATE THREE MAIN TYPES OF HOLIDAYS. THE MOST PERSONAL CELEBRATIONS ARE THOSE WHICH CONCERN OUR OWN FAMILIES.

1. Once upon a birthday
   A. No celebration because of inability to mark time

   Why was it difficult for early people to record time?

   Read aloud some of the early Biblical birthday celebrations.

   B. Progression of time and subsequent evolution of special celebrations

   Do you feel that the people were justified in celebrating only the birthdays of important persons?

   Read *Anniversaries and Holidays* by Mary Emogene Hazeltine.

   Read *Days to Remember* by William Lipkind.

2. Birthday customs developed from magical ideas and superstitious beliefs in many lands.
   A. Birthday parties originally given to protect honoree from evil spirits

   Read *In the Middle of the Night* by Aileen Fisher.

   Read *Birthdays* by Lillie Peterson.

   Read *Little Boy and the Birthdays* by Helen Buckley.

   Read *Happy Birthday, Mom!* by James S. Ayars.

   Read *The Happy Birthday Present* by Joan Heilbroner.

   What prompted these people to believe in the existence of evil spirits?

   Why do we believe in them today?

   What if birthday parties were given for this reason today?

   B. Birthday cakes originally baked to serve magical purposes

   Ask children to discuss the birthday cakes they usually have.

   Read *Candle Tales* by Julia Cunningham.

   Encourage children to understand the use of cakes as a means of learning one's fortune.

   Discuss the German belief that candles on a birthday cake have magical qualities.

C. Not to be spanked on one's birthday originally insured bad luck

What evidences are there today in words or phrases that suggest the lasting implications of this belief?

Do you think this belief is still realistic?

If not, why does the custom persist?

Why do you not feel hurt or sad when spanked on your birthday as you do on other days?

D. The birthday song is America's own contribution to the birthday customs

Locate through use of library facilities the composers and history of this song.

Do you think this song is appropriate to the occasion?

How can a song such as this one spread around the world without the aid of publication?

Sing the song in French.

E. Americans owe a "thank you" to many countries for their birthday traditions.

Write "thank-you note" themes to the various other lands which have given us our birthday customs.

Honor with an American birthday party children from other countries who have helped make our birthday celebrations possible.

3. Characteristics of birthdays, name days, or saints' days in Brazil, Germany, India, Italy, and Russia.

A. Brazil

Read *The Saints and Your Name* by Joseph Guadflieg.

Learn the Portuguese phrase for "Happy Birthday!": "Feliz Anniversario."

Initiate a library research project on Brazilian birthdays.

What are the differing features of their celebrations?

Why is the fifteenth birthday considered so important, and how is it similar to an American tradition?

Locate resource persons in the community who can discuss birthday celebrations in other countries.

B. Germany

Continue the library research project, extending it to include birthday celebrations.

Ask a selected group to dramatize a typical German "kinderfest."

Discuss the Germans' unique contribution to our birthday celebration, "Light of Life" candles.

C. Italy

What is the justification for the celebration of two birthdays?

What makes the Italian celebration a more serious, spiritual, and formal affair?

Begin comparison charts by listing for bulletin-board display similarities, differences, and contributions as they relate to birthday celebrations.

D. India

Expand the library research project to include not only Brazil, Germany, and Italy, but also India.

What are the similarities between Italian and Hindu celebrations?

Record information regarding similarities and differences in birthday celebrations on a chart or bulletin board.

E. Russia

Conclude the library project with a study of birthday celebrations in Russia.

What similarities are recognizable between the Brazilian and Russian celebrations?

Introduce the traditional Russian birthday singing game, "The Round Loaf."

What two characteristics of the Russian birthday celebration might be different if the temperament of the people were different?

NATIONAL CELEBRATIONS INDICATE WHAT PEOPLE IN A PARTICULAR COUNTRY CONSIDER IMPORTANT AND DESIRABLE

1. Presidential birthdays
   A. Lincoln's birthday

Read *How We Celebrate Our Fall Holidays* by Marjorie Ann Banks.

Read *How We Celebrate Our Spring Holidays* by Marjorie Ann Banks.

Read *Holidays of Significance For All Americans* by Trevor Nevitt Dupuy.

Read *Just Like Abraham Lincoln* by Bernard Waber.

Read *Lincoln's Birthday* by Clyde Robert Bulla.

Why do we celebrate the birth of Lincoln?

Locate and note the date on a calendar constructed for this purpose.

Do you feel that the nineteen Southern states which do not celebrate this holiday are justified in feeling this way?

Review the life of Abraham Lincoln and discover why these attitudes exist.

Film: *Happy Holidays in the Land of Lincoln.*

Read and ask children to comment on Lincoln's statement, "United we stand, divided we fall."

B. Washington's birthday

What is the date of this holiday?

Locate the date on the calendar.

Read about the greatest Washington celebration of all, the Bicentennial Year, 1932.

Read *Silver for General Washington* by Enid LaMonte Meadowcroft.

Ask children to compare the lives of the two February presidents.

Film: *Special Days in February.*

Read the poem about Washington written by Will Carleton.

2. St. Patrick's Day

Read *St. Patrick's Day* by Mary Cantwell.

What is the date of this holiday?

What prompted the Irish people to honor this saint?

How did this celebration become so important in the lives of Americans?

Individual reports from children on associated legends they can find.

What grounds do we have for believing or disbelieving these legends?

Compare the celebration here with the one in Ireland, using the films *Festival American.*

3. April Fool's Day

Why does this holiday come on the first day of April?

Discuss the vague origin of the holiday.

Do you feel we should have a holiday just for foolish pranks?

Learn some of the nicknames one may earn if one forgets this first day of April.

Encourage children to discuss some of their April Fool's pranks.

Read about some of the more famous April Fool's jokes.

Read to children the lines concerning this holiday from *Poor Robin's Almanac,* 1760.

4. Days to honor family members
   A. Mother's Day

Read *Mothers' Day* by Mary Kay Phelan.

When is this holiday celebrated?

Encourage children to find out what part Miss Anna Jarvis played in establishing this holiday.

Compare the customs of our country with those of others, such as England and Yugoslavia.

Do you feel that department stores, drug stores, and flower shops are justified in commercializing this holiday?

B. Father's Day

When is this holiday celebrated?

How did this custom develop?

Encourage the children to write themes on what fathers have done for them.

Discuss the name "father" as a term of respect.

Explain the origin of last names.

C. Children's day

When is this holiday celebrated?

Who celebrates this holiday?

Locate through reference sources the possible origins of this event.

Compare the original celebrations with the traditions of today.

Discuss some of the major outcomes of this celebration, such as Child Health Day.

5. Legal Holidays
A. Memorial Day

What is the date of this celebration?

What is the purpose of this celebration?

What prompted General Logan, National Commander of the Army of the Republic, to set aside this specific day?

Relate to children the story of the little Southern boy who, during the Civil War, displayed the "True Spirit of Memorial Day." Available: *Why We Celebrate Our Holidays.*

Read *Festivals U. S. A.* by Robert Meyer.

Show slides of the traditional Memorial Day ceremony at the National Cemetery in Arlington, Virginia.

Discuss the ways in which this holiday is remembered in our own communities.

B. Flag Day

Discuss the evolution of our flag.

Children may reproduce many of the original flags of the colonies and the first American flag.

Discuss the establishment of this holiday.

Read *Flag Day* by Dorothy Les Tina.

Children may write stories about their feelings for the flag.

	Discuss flag etiquette and courtesy.
C. Independence Day	What does the word "independence" mean? Record children's thoughts concerning this topic.
	Read *Clancy's Glorious Fourth* by Jane Flory.
	Film: *Celebrating Independence Day.*
	Read "The Story of Our First Celebration." Available: *Why We Celebrate Our Holidays.*
	Read *Fourth of July* by Charles P. Graves.
	What grounds did our forefathers have for refusing to be governed by England?
	What would be different if England still owned our country today?
	Why do we restrict the use of fireworks on Independence Day today?
D. Labor Day	Read *Labor Day* by James Marnell.
	View filmstrip, "Our Holidays and What They Mean."

RELIGIOUS HOLIDAYS GENERALLY MARK THE MEMORY OF IMPORTANT HISTORICAL EVENTS IN THE DEVELOPMENT OF A RELIGIOUS FAITH

1. Chinese holidays A. Say Yang – Say Yin	Teach children the characters for the word "Yang" ( ) and the word "Yin" ( ).
	Discuss what these two words mean and the Chinese belief that is represented by them.
	Discuss the belief that the sun, moon, stars are the dwelling places of gods, heroes, and souls.
	Discuss the rule of these gods, heroes, and souls, and how it affects everyday living.
	Examine a Chinese calendar and begin charts to indicate elements of comparison and contrast.
	Draw or paint the twelve moons which represent the twelve months.
	Film: *China's Festivals.*
B. Spring Is Here	Learn the Chinese meaning for the phrase, "Li Chum."
	Discuss and dramatize the plowing ceremony.
	Construct a processional buffalo, using the symbolic materials and explaining the beliefs associated with it.
	Discuss the other elements associated with this ritual of spring, such as the trip to the temple and the return home for the feast and sacrifice.

	What differences do you see between our celebrations and this one?
C. New Year's Festival	Read about the preparations for this holiday and why it is so festive. Available: *Mei Li.*
	Display a picture of the Kitchen God and explain the circumstances associated with his yearly departure to heaven to report on the behavior of those below. Available: *Holidays Around the World.*
	Compare the elements of American New Year's Eve celebrations with those of the Chinese.
	Discuss the characteristics of the fourteen days of celebration which follow the second day of the New Year.
	What are the main characteristics of this culminating New Year's celebration. Draw a comparison with Li Chum, the spring festival.
D. Pure and Bright Festival	Learn the Chinese meaning for the phrase,, "Ch'ing Ming."
	What other evidences are there that the Chinese love spring?
	Recount the legend behind the custom of eating only "cold food" three days before Ch'ing Ming begins in April. Available: *Holidays Around the World.*
	Read *Take Joy!* by Tasha Tudor.
	Make charts to compare the Chinese Memorial Day, "All Souls Day," and our Memorial Day.
E. Kiteflying Holiday	Learn the Chinese meaning for the expression, "Chung Yang Chieh."
	Recount the legend upon which this celebration is based. Available: *Holidays Around the World.*
	Explain the preparations made by the men and boys and the women and girls.
	Construct kites.
2. Jewish holidays A. Ten Days of Repentence	Film: *Holidays in Israel.*
	When is this holiday celebrated?
	Discuss the reason for the solemnity of this celebration. Available: *Holidays Around the World.*
	Read *Tales of Jewish Holidays* by Charles Bronstein.
	Discuss the rites of this celebration, such as confessions, the blowing of the ram's horn in the

synagogue, the festive meals, and the ceremony at a river or lake shore.

Discuss the characteristics of the last of the ten days, Yom Kippur, the Day of Atonement.

Engage a resource person, such as a local rabbi, to discuss the significance of these celebrations.

B. Festival of Booths

Learn the Hebrew meaning for the expression "Succoth."

Discover through library research the basis for this idea.

Explore its development and evolution into a Jewish Thanksgiving.

Recount for the children the beautiful custom of the succah.

Read about the special significance of the seventh day of this nine-day festival.

Review the preparations and rest on the eighth day for the Torah Festival in honor of the Five Books of Moses, the Torah.

C. Celebration of a Miracle

Learn the Hebrew meaning for the term, "Hanukkah."

When does this celebration occur?

Read about the miracle that took place 2100 years ago in Palestine which makes this celebration possible. Available: *Holidays Around the World.*

Engage a resource person to discuss with children the procedures followed in this eight-day celebration.

Ask children to draw a comparison between this festival and our Christmas celebrations.

D. New Year of the Trees

When does this holiday occur?

For whom is this holiday especially significant?

Learn of the ancient beliefs on which it is based.

Recognize its correlation with Arbor Day.

E. Feast of Esther

When does this holiday occur?

What is the familiar Hebrew word for this holiday?

What preparations for the holiday are made in Jewish homes?

Discuss the ceremonial ritual of the Seder.

Why do the Jewish people feel this ceremony is important?

Display an illustration of the Seder. Available: *Holidays Around the World.*

3. Christian holidays
   A. St. Valentine's Day

When is this holiday celebrated, and what is especially characteristic of this celebration?

What prompted the people to honor St. Valentine with such a holiday? Available: *A Holiday Book: St. Valentine's Day.*

What was the major outcome of St. Valentine's imprisonment? Available: *A Holiday Book: St. Valentine's Day.*
Why do we like to believe these legends about St. Valentine?

How did St. Valentine's Day become a romantic spring festival? Available: *A Holiday Book: St. Valentine's Day.*

Children may conduct library research into old Valentine's Day customs and their development in such countries as England, Sicily, Germany, and France.

Read *Apple Seed and Soda Straws* by Jean Ritchie.

Trace the transformation of Valentine's Day cards from hand-made valentines to those manufactured by the millions in factories around the world.

Read aloud to children during story-hour the legend which the Romans told of Cupid. Available: *A Holiday Book: Valentine's Day.*

Ask children to recount the events which characterized St. Valentine's Day parties which they have attended or which their parents or grandparents attended.

Organize a library display from materials listed in bibliography.

B. *Easter*

Discuss the history of our Easter celebration, including its early relationship to the before-mentioned Jewish Passover, the manner in which it was named, and the part the sun and lights played in early celebrations.

Read aloud to children during storyhour portions of *Easter Fires.*

Encourage children to look for information concerning the various customs of Easter – topics such as the days of Lent, Easter celebrations around the world, and the Easter basket.

Films: *Easter Time Is Your Time* and *The Easter Story.*

Ask children to draw pictures of the objects they associate with Easter — the Cross, the rabbit, the robin, the egg, the palm tree, and the dogwood tree.

Listen to record, "How We Got Our Easter Customs."

Read some of the legends which have grown up around these objects of adoration. Available: *It's Time for Easter.*

Listen to record, "Easter Around the World."

Children may find many poems and stories relating to this season.

Read *Piccolina and the Easter Bells* by Pauline Priolo.

Share with children some of the excellent poems and stories included in *It's Time for Easter.*

C. Halloween

See if children can explain what a superstition is.

Read the story of the Celtic festival which brought about the establishment of our Halloween. Available: *A Holiday Book: Halloween.*

Read *Halloween* by Lillie Patterson.

Help children understand the merging of the Celtic Samhain, with its black cats and evil spirits, and the Roman Pomona Day, with its apples and nuts, and finally the Christian Hallowmas or All Hallows' Day.

Do they know why we often dress in white sheets and pretend to be ghosts on Halloween?

Read *Halloween* by Helan Borten.

Record: "Dance of Death" by Camille Saint-Saens. Read the story associated with the music.

Read the chapter on "Wee Folk" from *A Holiday Book: Halloween.*

Encourage children to find out about Halloween customs in other lands. Ireland, Scotland, Wales, England, France, and Mexico all celebrate this holiday.

How have we Americanized this holiday?

Introduce children to the new "Halloween With a Heart" or "Trick or Treat for UNICEF."

Read *Late for Halloween* by Camilla Fegan.

Organize a library display from materials listed in bibliography.

D. Thanksgiving

Play: "The Thankful Heart" in *A Child's Book of Holiday Plays* by Frances Wickes (New York: Macmillan Co., 1922)

Book: *It's Time for Thanksgiving* by Elizabeth Sechrist (Philadelphia: Macrae Smith Co., 1957)

Book: *Thanksgiving Is For What We Have* by Bettina Peterson (Ives Washburn, Inc., 1959)

Relate the story of the "Two Mayflowers". Available: *A Holiday Book: Thanksgiving.*

Ask children to write their own versions of the *Mayflower's* search for a home.

Read: *Pilgrim Thanksgiving.*

Ask children to find information about the famous persons who were a part of this assemblage, the Mayflower Compact, and the first winter these people spent in their new homeland.

Film: *The First Thanksgiving* by Wilma Hays.

Re-enact the pageantry of the first Thanksgiving.

Listen to Record, "Squanto and the First Thanksgiving."

Tape: *Thankful the Turkey.*

Help children conduct library research on Thanksgiving customs around the world, and construct charts to show comparisons.

Book: *Children's Festivals in Many Lands* by Nina Millen (Friendship Press, 1964)

Discuss with children the events which led to the establishment of Thanksgiving as a legal holiday.

What are the major characteristics of our Thanksgiving celebration today? Why do so many of our holidays have a serious as well as a less serious side to them?

Film: *Turkey Day Parade.*

Organize a library display from materials listed in bibliography.

E. Christmas

Ask children what they know about the beginnings of Christmas.

Listen to record, "Joy to the World," (Christmas Legends told by Ruth Sawyer.)

Help them clarify vague or inaccurate concepts.

Familiarize children with some of the more unfamiliar legends and stories relating to Christmas. Available: *It's Time for Christmas.*

Act out *A Trilogy of Christmas Plays for Children* by Carol Preston.

Urge children to find out all they can about such Christmas customs as the Christmas Chreche, the lights of Christmas (stars, candles, fires, and Yule logs), Christmas greens, the animals of Christmas, and the exchange of gifts at Christmas.

Children may want to look into the stories behind some of our more familiar carols and their composers.

Film: *Christmas Carols.*
Listen to record, "Barbara's Happy Christmas."

Familiarize the children with some of the poems of Christmas.

Travel through other countries and join in their Christmas celebrations by means of a series of films including *Chirstmas in Germany, Christmas in Denmark, Christmas Pioneer Style, Christmas in Sweden, etc.*

View slides, "Christmas in Many Lands."

Supplement this journey with selected information from *Christmas the World Over.*

Read *Starlight in Tourrone* by Suzanne Butler.

Do you feel that merchants are justified in commercializing Christmas? Invite a merchant to discuss this with the class.

Read *New Song for Christmas* by Helen Rayburn Caswell.

Read *The Book of Three Festivals: Stories for Christmas, Easter, and Thanksgiving* by Amy Morris Lillie.

If you could introduce one new Christmas custom, what would it be?

CULMINATING ACTIVITIES

Organize a bibliography of holiday information in a usable form for others who may wish to consult it.

Develop a classroom scrapbook, using the comparison charts designed periodically during the progress of this unit.

Prepare an exhibit, using pictures with original stories, songs, and plays focusing on holidays around the world.

Present an assembly program for other third grade classes, the classroom parents, or P.T.A. Include informative, colorful, and accurate characterizations of the more important information secured through this study.

Write a book about the significance of particular holidays and catalogue it with the other books in the library.

EVALUATION

Group discussion may be used to indirectly appraise the progress of pupils in certain areas of growth, such as listening skills, reading, and creative endeavors.

Individual conferences with each child will yield information concerning his grasp of the concepts presented and his changing attitudes.

Set up a checklist of criteria with the class that may be used to judge the merit of the end products of the unit as well as the procedures used in arriving at these outcomes.

Teacher-made tests may also prove useful in objectifying the performance of each individual. Care should be taken, however, to construct test items which deal with fundamental issues.

Self-evaluation by each pupil of the quality and contribution of his work to the total endeavor may also prove useful.

ADDITIONAL READING

Buell, Hal. *Festivals of Japan.* Dodd, Mead, 1965.
Dobler, Lavinia. *Customs and Holidays Around the World.* Illus. Little. Fleet Pub., 1962.
Millen, Nina. *Children's Festivals From Many Lands.* Illus. Smalley. Friendship Press, 1964.

BIBLIOGRAPHY

1. Birthday celebrations

    A. Reference Material
        Johnson, Lois. *Happy Birthdays Around the World.* illus. Genia. Rand McNally & Company, New York, 1963.

    B. Easy books
        Fischer, Hans. *The Birthday.* Harcourt, New York, 1954.

    C. Fiction books
        Ayars, James S. *Happy Birthday, Mom!* Abelard-Schuman, 1963.
        Ayer, Jacqueline. *A Wish for Little Sister.* Harcourt, New York, 1960.
        Buckley, Helen E. *Little Boy and the Birthdays.* Lothrop Lee and Shepard, 1965.
        Cunningham, Julia. *Candle Tales.* Pantheon Books, 1964.
        Davis, Lavenia. *The Wild Birthday Cake.* illus. Woodward. Doubleday, New York, 1949.
        Fisher, Aileen. *In the Middle of the Night.* Crowell, 1965.
        Guadflieg, Joseph. *The Saints and Your Name.* Pantheon, 1957.
        Hazeltine, Mary Emogene. *Anniversaries And Holidays.* 2nd ed. ALA, 1944.

Heilbroner, Joan. *The Happy Birthday Present.* Harper & Row, New York, 1962.
Kay, Helen. *Snow Birthday.* illus. Barbara Cooney. Ariel Books, New York, 1955.
Lindquest, Jennie. *The Golden Name Day.* illus. Garth Williams. Harper, New York, 1955.
Lowensbery, Eloise. *Martha the Doll.* illus. Werton. Langmans, New York, 1946.
Patterson, Lillie. *Birthdays.* Barrard, 1965.

2. National celebrations

A. Audio-visual aids

Association Films, Inc. *Festivals American.*
Coronet Films, Inc. *Special Days in February.*
Curriculum Materials Co. *Celebrating Flag Day.*
Curriculum Materials Co. *Celebrating Independence Day.*
Filmstrip House, 1965. 8 filmstrips. Color. *Our Holidays And What They Mean*
Illinois Departmental Information Service. *Happy Holiday in the Land of Lincoln*
SVE. 36 fr. sd. 12" rec. 33 1/3 rpm. 8 min. 30 sec. (4-6). *How We Got Our Easter Customs.*

B. Books

Bulla, Clyde Robert. *Lincoln's Birthday.* Crowell, 1965.
Flory, Jane. *Clancy's Glorious Fourth.* Houghton Mifflin, 1964.
Graves, Charles P. *Fourth of July.* Gerrard, 1963.
Les Tina, Dorothy. *Flag Day.* Crowell, 1965.
Meadowcroft, Enid La Monte. *Silver for General Washington.* Crowell, 1957.
Phelan, Mary Kay. *Mothers' Day.* Crowell, 1965.
Waber, Bernard. *Just Like Abraham Lincoln.* Houghton Mifflin, 1964.

3. Religious celebrations

A. Audio-visual aids

Films:
Barr, Arthur, Inc. *Christmas In Denmark.*
Christian Mission Films. *Easter Is Your Time.*
Christian Mission Films. *The Easter Story.*
Christian Mission Films. *The First Thanksgiving.*
Coronet Films. *How the Animals Discovered Christmas.*
D. PM. Productions. *Christmas In Sweden.*
Encyclopedia Britannica. *Christmas Rhapsody.*
Films of the Month. *Our Thanksgiving Day.*
Goodyear Tire & Rubber Company. *Turkey Day Parade.*
Grover-Jennings Productions. *A Christmas Deer.*
Heiz. *Holidays In Israel.*
National Film Board of Canada. *Christmas Carols.*
Republic of China Embassy. *China's Festivals.*
Society of Visual Education. *Mary's Pilgrim Thanksgiving.*

Slides:
ICPP 61 (Social Studies) Set of 24, 9 1/4 X 3/16 bw. (4-6-jh).*Christmas In Many Lands.*

Tapes:
Breitenbach, H. G. *Christmas In Germany.*
_____ . *Frankfurt Christmas Fair.*
_____ . *German's New Year Celebration.*
Indiana School of the Sky. *Christmas Shopping.*
National Film Board of Canada. *Christmas Carols.*
Ohio State Museum. *Christmas Pioneer Style.*
State Historical Society of Wisconsin. *Christmas Treasure.*

Records:

SVE. 40 frames. sd. c 12" record 33 1/3 rpm. 10 min. 30 sec. (4-6-jh). *Barbara's Happy Christmas.*

SVE. 41 frames. sd. 12" rec. 33 1/3 rpm. 12 min. 30 sec. (4-6–. *Easter Around the World.*

SVE. 50 frames. sd. 12" rec. 33 1/3 rpm. 15 min. (4-6-jh). *Squanto And the First Thanksgiving.*

Woston Woods Studio. WW707. (Phonodisc) 2s 12 in. 33 rpm. Christmas Legends told by Ruth Sawyer. *Joy to the World.*

B. Reference Materials

Banks, Marjorie Ann. *How We Celebrate Our Fall Holidays.* illus. Hawkinson. Benefic Press, 1964.

Barksdale, Lena. *The First Thanksgiving.* illus. Lenski. Knopf, New York, 1942.

Borten, Helen. *Halloween.* illus. Borten. Crowell, 1965.

Bronstein, Charlotte. *Tales of Jewish Holidays.* Behrman House, 1959.

Buell, Hal. *Festivals of Japan.* Dodd, Mead, 1965.

Cantwell, Mary. *St. Patrick's Day.* Crowell, 1967.

Dalgleish, Alice. *Christmas.* illus. Woodward. Scribner, New York, 1950.

_____. *The Thanksgiving Story.* Sewell. Scribner, New York, 1950.

Dupuy, Trevor Nevitt, ed. *Holidays of Significance for All Americans.* Watts, 1965.

Eaton, Anne T. *The Animal's Christmas.* illus. Angelo. Viking, New York, 1944.

Folley, Daniel. *Christmas the World Over.* illus. Bowden. Chilton Company, Philadelphia, 1963.

Gardner, Horace. *Let's Celebrate Christmas.* illus. Potter. Ronald, New York, 1950.

Guilfoile, Elizabeth. *A Holiday Book: Valentine's Day.* illus. Lanti. Garrard Publishing Company, Champaigne, Illinois, 1965.

Harper, Wilhelmina. *Easter Chimes.* illus. Jones. Dutton, New York, 1938.

_____. *Ghosts and Goblins.* illus. Jones. Dutton, New York, 1936.

_____. *The Harvest Feast.* illus. Jones. Dutton, New York, 1938.

Hazeltine, Alice. *The Easter Book of Legends and Stories.* illus. Bianco. Lothrop, New York, 1938.

Marnell, James. *Labor Day.* illus. Ross Crowell, 1966.

Patterson, Lillie. *A Holiday Book: Halloween.* illus. Merit. Garrard Publishing Company, Champaigne, Illinois, 1963.

Sechrist, Elizabeth. *Christmas Everywhere.* illus. Fry. MaCrae Smith Company, New York, 1936.

_____. *Heigh Ho For Halloween.* illus. Fry. MaCrae Smith Company, New York, 1948.

_____. *It's Time for Christmas.* illus. Fry. MaCrae Smith Company, New York, 1959.

_____. *It's Time for Easter.* illus. Fry. MaCrae Smith Company, New York, 1961.

Wyntham, Lee. *A Holiday Book: Thanksgiving.* illus. Hoecker. Garrard Publishing Company, Champaigne, Illinois, 1963.

C. Easy Books

Brown, Palmer. *Something for Christmas.* Harper, New York, 1958.

Brunhoff, Jean de. *Babar and Father Christmas.* Random House, New York, 1940.

Duvoison, Roger. *The Christmas Whale.* Knopf, New York, 1945.

Francoise. *Noel for Jean Marie.* Scribner, New York, 1953.

Handforth, Thomas. *Mei Li.* Doubleday, New York, 1931.

Heywood, DuBose. *The Country Bunny and the Little Gold Shoes.* illus. Flack. Houghton, New York, 1939.

Kahl, Virginia. *Plum Pudding for Christmas.* Scribner, New York, 1956.

Seuss, *How the Grinch Stole Christmas.* Random House, New York, 1957.

Tudor, Tasha. *The Doll's Christmas.* Walck, New York, 1950.

_____. ed. *Take Joy!* World, 1966.

D. Other Fiction Books

Bemelmans, Ludwig. *Hansi.* Viking, New York, 1954.

Bulla, Clyde. *The Valentine Cat.* illus. Weisgard. Crowell, New York, 1959.

Butler, Suzanne. *Starlight in Tourrone.* Little, Brown, 1965.

Caswell, Helen Rayburn. *New Song For Christmas.* Van Nostrand, 1966.

Coatsworth, Elizabeth. *First Adventures.* illus. Ray. Macmillan, New York, 1950.

Crowley, Maude. *Azor and the Blue-Eyed Crow.* illus. Sewell. Walck, New York, 1951.

Dickens, Charles. *A Christmas Carol In Prose.* Macmillan, New York.

Dolbeir, Maurice. *Torten's Christmas Secret.* illus. Hanneberger. Little, New York, 1951.

Ets, Marie. *Nine Days to Christmas.* Viking, New York, 1959.

Fegan, Camilla. *Late for Halloween.* Criterion Books, 1966.

Godden, Rumer. *The Fairy Doll.* illus. Adams. Viking, New York, 1956.

Hays, Wilma. *Christmas on the Mayflower.* illus. Duvoisin. Coward-McGann, New York, 1956.

_____. *Easter Fires.* illus. Birchard. Coward-McGann, New York, 1959.

_____. *Pilgrim Thanksgiving.* illus. Weisgard. Coward-McGann, New York, 1955.

_____. *The Story of the Valentine.* illus. Weisgard. Coward-McGann, New York, 1956.

Jones, Elizabeth O. *Big Susan,* Macmillan, New York, 1947.

Massey, Jeanne. *The Littlest Witch.* illus. Adams. Knopf, New York, 1959.

Menotti, Gian Carlo. *Amhal and the Night Visitors.* illus. Duvoisin. McGraw-Hill, New York, 1952.

Milhous, Katherine. *Appolonia's Valentine.* Scribner, New York, 1954.

_____. *The Big Tree.* Scribner, New York, 1950.

_____. *With Bells On.* Scribner, New York, 1950.

Miller, Katherine. *St. George:* a Christmas Muvvers's Play. Houghton Mifflin, 1967.

Politi, Leo. *The Angel of Olvera Street.* Scribner, New York, 1946.

Preston, Carol. *A Trilogy of Christmas Plays for Children;* music selected by John Lanstaff. Harcourt, Brace & World, 1967.

Priolo, Pauline. *Piccolina and the Easter Bells.* Brown, Little, 1962.

Sawyer, Ruth. *The Christmas Anna Angel.* illus. Seredy. Viking, New York, 1944.

Vance, Marguerite. *While Shepherds Watched.* illus. Walker. Dutton, New York, 1946.

Wenning, Elizabeth. *The Christmas Mouse.* illus. Remmington. Holt, New York, 1959.

4. General

A. Audio-visual aids
Film:
R. C. A.'s Films. *Holidays.*

Record:
Sales, L.P. Corporation. *Wonderland Records.*

B. Reference materials
Adams, Florence. *Highdays and Holidays.* illus. Broch. Dutton, New York, 1927.

Burnett, Bernice. *The First Book of Holidays.* illus. Glaubach. Watts, New York, 1955.

Curtis, Mary. *Why We Celebrate Our Holidays.* illus. Morrison. Lyons, New York, 1950.

Dobler, Lavinia. *Customs and Holidays Around the World.* illus. Little. Fleet Publ., 1962.

Douglas, George. *The American Book of Days.* Wilson, New York, 1948.

Gaer, Joseph. *Holidays Around the World.* illus. Jauss. Little, New York, 1953.

Lipkind, William. *Days to Remember, An Almanac.* Obolensky, 1961.

McSpadden, Walker. *The Book of Holidays.* illus. Galster. Crowell, New York, 1958.

Meyer, Robert. *Festivals U.S.A.* illus. Lee Owens. Washburn, 1956.

Millern, Nina. *Children's Festivals from Many Lands.* illus. Smalley. Friendship Press, 1964.

Patterson, Lillie. *Birthdays.* illus. Merkling. Garrard, 1965.

INTERMEDIATE GRADE UNIT
ON ARCHAEOLOGY
HOW WE LEARN ABOUT EARLY MAN

INTRODUCTION TO THE UNIT

Leonard Wooley once said, "knowledge gained by scientific archaeological methods affects us all, becomes part of the general intellectual inheritance, and the justification of archaeology is that it does, in the end, concern everyone."

In a recent (1966) appraisal of archaeology, Joseph Caldwell noted that because of the recent convergence of archaeology with anthropology and social studies, archaeology is now turning to questions of greater generality than those which pertain to a single site or culture. He further suggests that the archaeologist is very much involved with the problems of Western man.

Ashley Montague in the Preface to *Man: His First Million Years* stated, "I believe that anthropology should form the core of the educational curriculum at all levels; grammar school, high school, and college."

Appropriate materials for each topic may be selected from those suggested.

BASIC UNDERSTANDINGS

1. Each society owes more than a small fraction of its present cultural heritage to other times and other places.
2. Tools act as amplifiers of human power; a group of tools perform related tasks and show functional relationships to one another. Tools are indicators of the technological state of the culture.
3. All cultures provide for the essential needs of human group life but differ in the means by which they accomplish the task.
4. The rate of cultural inventions has accelerated as has the speed with which new knowledge spreads around the world.
5. As the world continues to become more interdependent, knowledge of common origins becomes increasingly important.
6. Enlarging the ability to live more harmoniously and more richly results from the understandings derived from many sources.

ATTITUDES TO BE DEVELOPED

1. Appreciation of the patience and skill needed to locate, unearth, catalog, and classify artifacts.
2. Recognition of the gradual nature of change and improvements in technology over a long period of time.
3. Appreciation of the contributions of earlier peoples.

4. Realization that significance of finds depends on knowledge and ability to relate ideas and objects.
5. Appreciation of the contributions of the large number of scholars in many disciplines who make possible each new bit of knowledge.

SKILLS TO BE TAUGHT OR EXTENDED

1. Knowledge of the variety of sources available and the way in which each contributes. Use of books, pamphlets, encyclopedias, almanacs, atlases, specialized indexes, card catalog.
2. Technical knowledge of each source.
   Books — table of contents, index, bibliography, appendix, charts, graphs, diagrams.
   Encyclopedias — arrangement, numbering, finding of names.
   Almanac — index, main and sub headings, cross referencing.
   Atlas — different types of maps available, gazeteer.
   Specialized indexes — which are available in a particular library, limitations of each; the Readers Guide to Periodical Literature.
   Card catalog — how extensive (books only or books + other media), locations of books on shelves.
3. Study skills — note taking, analyzing information, outlining, determining relevance, comparing, summarizing, making conclusions on value of material; maps and globes including kinds, legends, meaning of other geographic lines and interpretation of pictures.
4. Development of critical thinking — defining and analyzing problems, distributing and accepting responsibility, evaluating use of time and values of outcomes of projects, setting criteria, making generalizations, comparing and contrasting, establishing sequence.

INITIATING ACTIVITIES

1. Show the filmstrip, *How We Learn About the Past.*
2. Read *Miss Pickerell Goes on a Dig* to the children.
3. Ask the youngsters to bring things that have been dug up in the back yard or on trips.
4. Look for pictures and books that pertain to archaeology.
5. Ask children to bring color books or comic strips about man and animals in prehistoric times.
6. Show film *Dr. Leakey and the Dawn of Man* Encyclopedia Britannica, 1967.
7. Read *The Walls of Windy Troy* to the children.

I

Each society owes more than a small fraction of its present cultural heritage to other times and other places.

Ideas to be Developed	Terms
1. Archaeology contributes to man's history by making and interpreting excavations.	anthropology
	archaeology
2. Artifacts are buried and preserved in campsites, caves, cities, mounds, and tombs.	artifact
	culture
3. Archaeological sites may be discovered by chance, uncovered by erosion, planned to accord with scientific knowledge of the area, or revealed by aerial photography.	digs
	excavation
	inorganic
	organic
4. The archaeologist may use trenches, pits, quadrants, total excavation, or a combination of these to dig his site.	quadrant
	relic
	site
5. Tools used by archeologists to dig a site include brushes, knives, picks, trowels, shovels, sieves, and baskets.	strata
	technology
	trench

Questions	Activities
	(Throughout the unit 1 denotes activities for the whole class; 2 indicates special projects for group I (high); 3 refers to material for group II (middle); and 4 offers suggestions for group III (less able).
1. What does the term "archaeology" mean?	
2. Of what social science is it a part?	
3. Why has the archeologist named his excavations "digs?"	
4. Why does the archeologist use different methods of excavation?	1. 1 Make an archaeological dictionary using terms suggested for the first section of the unit plus those additional ones that interest each child.
5. What is the difference between organic and inorganic artifacts?	2. 1 Assemble an archaeologists "kit" by bringing various sizes of paintbrushes, a pastry brush, small size shovels, trowels (such as hand garden tools), baskets, and other implements.
6. Would a cave be a better place to find artifacts than a swamp? Why or why not?	
7. What are some other types of areas in which artifacts may be found? In which of these are the artifacts likely to be best preserved?	3. 1 Find pictures suitable to this introductory section and show to the class.
8. What reasons can you give to prove that archaeology is important to man?	4. 1 Take a trip to a museum. If possible plan for an archaeology lesson such as a trip through a specific area with a
9. How would an archeologist's training help him to interpret his finds?	

10. Why should amateurs leave valuable sites alone?

lecture followed by pencil and paper test and questioning period.

5. 1 Make bulletin boards with pictures and drawings of artifacts dated to show their approximate age.

6. 1 Show the filmstrip *Fossils, Keys to the Past,* Ward's, 1965.

7. 2 Tape record pronunciations of archaeological words to help classmates.
Read *America's Buried Past* by Gordon C. Baldwin.

8. 2 Have a panel discussion about the best method of locating a site, each child or small group representing one location method.

9. 2 & 3 Secure a terrarium and place in layers of sand, pebbles, clay, black soil to a depth of several layers. As each layer is deposited put in "artifacts" (old jewelry, bits of glass, bottle caps, etc.) "Excavate" these and make a record of the layer in which each was found.
Show the film *Ancient New World,* rental from University of Illinois, 1965.

10. 2 & 3 Make oral and/or written reports on mounds, especially particular ones that might be found in the state in which the child lives.

11. 2 & 3 Write a story telling what you would do if you were an anthropologist.

12. 2 & 3 Make charts to show combinations of trench, pit, and quadrant methods.

13. 4 Make a chart to show a trench, a quadrant, and a total excavation.

14. 4 Make a game with the new terms on cards. Use game procedure such as is used in other games of similar type.

II

Tools act as amplifiers of human power; a group of tools perform related tasks and show functional relationships to one another. Tools are indicators of the technological state of the culture.

Ideas to be Developed

1. Man's culture changed very little over a period of more than a million years.
2. The geological glacial and interglacial periods, called Pleistocene, correspond with the culture period named Paleolithic meaning old stone.
3. The Holocene geological age covers 10,000 years or less and corresponds to four culture periods: Mesolithic (middle stone), Neolithic (new stone), Bronze, and Iron.
4. Tools in the Lower and Middle Peleolithic ages consisted of core (including pebble, hand axe, and chopper) and flake. These tools were held in the hand. Some differentiation of function was apparent, as the sharp flake tool was used for scraping rather than striking.
5. In the Upper Paleolithic period bone was used to work stone, producing blades and chipping off fine pieces for smoother edges. Burins (stone chisels) were used to make other tools of horn and bone. A spear thrower was developed.
6. In the Mesolithic period microliths (small sharp stones) were developed. These were set in handles and also used as tips on arrows. The fish hook was developed.
7. The Neolithic period shows further refinement of microliths by polishing. There was some use of copper for tools making.
8. During the Bronze Age copper and tin were smelted to make an alloy much stronger than copper alone.
9. Iron was not itself as important or startling a change in toolmaking as some previous developments.

Terms

alloy

awl

blade

bronze

burin

core

chopper

flake

geology

glacial

hand axe

Holocene

Mesolithic

microlith

Neolithic

Peleolithic

Pleistocene

Questions

1. Why were early tools held in the hand?
2. What important advances in toolmaking came about in the Mesolithic period?

Activities

1. 1 Make a scrapbook containing pictures of tools — gather them from color books, old books, magazines, etc. or draw some. Label each accor-

3. Of what importance were microliths?
4. Why were burins considered a big advance in toolmaking?
5. For what reason was bronze considered an advance in technology?
6. Some archaeologists add a steel age after the iron age. Why don't archaeologists agree on the dates and divisions of the various periods?
7. How is it possible to tell whether an ancient stone was worn by nature or purposely cut by man or perhaps both?
8. Where in the world at the present time can we find people who are still in the Paleolithic stage of culture?
9. What source of power is now used for most tools in the U.S.? How is this an improvement over hand tools?
10. Can pottery be classified as tools? Why or why not?

ding to use and the period in which it was found.
Show filmstrip *The Old Stone Age,* Society for Visual Ed., 1956.

2. 1 Put up a blank world map. Draw tools such as were used in prehistoric times and place them on the map at the sites where excavated. Perhaps different colors could be used for different periods.
Read *Science and the Secret of Man's Past* by Franklin Folsom.

3. 1 Make a series of charts classifying various ancient tools according to (1) material (as stone, bone, shell, clay, wood,etc.); (2) function (as knives, axes, scrapers, awls, drills, etc.); (3) various shapes; (4) degree of skill employed.
Read *The First Farmers in the New Stone Age* by Leonard Weisgard.

4. 1 Obtain stones, particularly flint, and attempt to make core and flake tools, Show filmstrip *The New Stone Age.,* Society for Visual Ed. 1956.

5. 2 Make a set of tools to fit a particular job to be done.

6. 2 Write a paper explaining the development of tools from the Paleolithic period to those used by a modern industrial giant.

7. 2 Relate some of our modern tools to the prehistoric ones.

8. 2 & 3 Visit a factory, such as cookie baking or soap making, and note the tremendous change in kind of tools used. Try to classify each of the parts of the whole assembly line as to function.

9. 3 Bring tools from home (modern ones) and classify these as to function.

10. 4 Make drawings of some of the kinds of tools studied in the unit.

III

All cultures provide for the essential needs of human group life but differ in the means by which they accomplish the task.

Ideas to be Developed

1. Man's culture consists of much more than just artifacts, thus the archaeologist must use many different clues.
2. When learning about people, habitation sites such as cities, village, camps, and caves offer many kinds of information. Not only are cooking utensils, dishes, vases etc. important, but remains of houses, public buildings, and bits of clothing also furnish clues to ways of life.
3. Ceremonial sites provide information regarding spiritual development, art forms, and other human practices.
4. Burial sites may help to indicate the state of development of the civilization since these vary from simple holes in the ground to elaborate burial tombs and mounds, and may contain a wealth of artifacts.
5. Cave art contributes to our knowledge of early man's ideas by showing his representation of objects and the relationships of these objects to one another.

Terms

burial

ceremonial

habitation

midden

pottery

preservation

restoration

ritual

Questions

1. Why do archaeoligists consider middens valuable?
2. What things might you find in a burial site which are not found in a habitation site?
3. What will be found in historic sites that is not available in prehistoric ones?
4. Why did ancient peoples bury artifacts with their dead?
5. In a few cases whole cities have been buried. What are some things that can be learned at these sites?
6. Why is the use of pottery associated with the beginning of the farming stage of culture, at the end of the Mesolithic or beginning of the Neolithic periods?
7. How are baskets and pottery alike? How different?

Activities

1. 1 Show slides as *Prehistoric Art,* Cultural Historical Research, Inc.
2. 1 Show filmstrip, *Pre-historic Man — Dawn of Civilization,* Eye Gate House, Inc., — color.
   Show film *Exploring Ancient Mexico: The Maya,* Imperial Film Co., 1964.
3. 1 Make some clay objects and try to decorate them as some ancient peoples did.
4. 1 Suppose that your house were suddenly buried and then excavated 1,000 years from now. What objects would remain in good condition? Which items would no longer be in their present form? What factors would affect the state of preservation? Have a class discussion or a round table talk by a few people who have

8. Do baskets and pottery represent art forms?

9. If people have time for drawing pictures, making designs on pottery, and weaving materials, what does this indicate about the time devoted to making a living?

10. How would you decide if groups of people were in a primitive or advanced state of culture?

worked on the problem ahead of the group discussion.

Read *Treasures of Yesterday* by Henry Garnett.

5. 2 Report to the class on early religions and man's belief in a superior being.

6. 2 Make up your own method of writing or drawing common words. Make a big chart with each character written on it. Use these characters to communicate essential messages.

Show filmstrip, *Exploring Ancient Egypt,* Imperial Film Co., 1964.

7. 2 & 3 Use pictures such as those shown on pages 366-67 and 370 in *Deeds of Men,* Classmate edition, Lyons & Carnahan, 962, to make messages like those earlier peoples might have made.

Show filmstrip, *Exploring Ancient Athens,* Imperial Film Co., 1964.

8. 3 & 4 Collect pictures of ancient art, pottery, basket making, etc. and make an attractive bulletin board.

IV

The rate of cultural inventions has accelerated as has the speed with which new knowledge spreads around the world.

Ideas to be Developed	Terms
1. The development of tools in the last 10,000 years exceeded that of the previous 100 or more 10,000 year periods by a great deal. New knowledge in the few years since 1900 has far exceeded that of the previous millions of years.	absolute dating biology carbon 14 calendrical chronology dendrochronology fauna flora
2. In archaeology, one of the aspects which has especially benefited from the proliferation of knowledge is that of dating.	
3. Methods of *relative* dating such as stratigraphy, seriation, biology, and geology have not changed as much recently as have methods of *absolute* dating.	paleontology potassium-argon radioactive

4. Absolute dating methods depend on recent finds in many other areas of knowledge and include: calendrical, dendrochronology, carbon 14, and potassium-argon.
5. The preservation and restoration of finds can be done with more precision because of new discoveries and inventions.

relative dating

seriation

stratigraphy

Questions	Activities
1. If a cross section of a tree has a thinner or thicker ring, what does this signify?	1. 1 Bring in cross section pieces of trees to note and compare rings.
2. What activities of people might interfere with dating by stratigraphy?	2. 1 Prepare a program to inform other groups about dating. Show various objects made of a variety of materials and explain how a person would go about dating each of these.
3. Are objects at the same depth necessarily the same age? Why or why not?	
4. How do geologists help archaeologists in dating materials?	3. 2 Make an Aztec calendar and compare with our present ones.
5. Why are uncontaminated samples needed for radiocarbon (C14) dating?	4. 2 List invention dates for as many items in the schoolroom as is possible. Then note the accelerating rate of useful inventions.
6. How does the archaeologist decide which dating technique to use?	Read *Carbon 14, and other Science Methods That Date the Past* by Lynn Poole.
7. Why is dating such an important part of the archaeologist's work?	
8. Do you think dating methods will change in the future? Why or why not?	5. 2 & 3 Bring in old pieces of bone, shells, or other objects that have been dug up and discuss which might be older, how one can tell, etc.
9. Why is the work of preservation important?	6. 2 & 3 Make charts to show the ages of objects in years corresponding to various amounts of argon and potassium and different amounts of carbon 14.
10. What is meant by restoration? What kinds of skills are needed for it?	7. 2 & 3 Tell which of the items in 8 have essentially the same function and a closely related form to older artifacts. Name those which are new ideas.
	8. 4 Make a list of items used today. Limit the list to 25 or 50 or some other manageable number.

V

As the world continues to become more interdependent, knowledge of common origins becomes increasingly important.

Ideas to be Developed

1. All races of man appear to have developed from common forebears.
2. Australopithecines are the earliest type of hominids. They were extant during the Early Pleistocene period.
3. Homo erectus appeared in the Middle Pleistocene period. Also during this time Home erectus pekinensis, the first man known to have used fire, came on the scene.
4. Neanderthal Man and Homo sapiens spaebus belong to the late Middle and early Upper Pleistocene. Remains from Home sapiens neanderthalensis have been found in many different sites.
5. Home sapiens, the precursor of modern man, appeared at the beginning of modern times.
6. Since most racial differences are in skin, eye, and hair color and type, fossil, or skeletal, remains do not reveal the relationships of these variations.

Terms

Australopithecine

Cro-Magnon

extinct

fossil

hominid

Homo erectus

Homo erectus pekinensis

Homo sapiens spaebus

Neanderthal

prehistoric

primitive

Questions

1. Why have relics of tools been so much more numerous than fossil remains of man himself?
2. What do you think is the biggest difference between modern man and man 500,000 years ago?
3. Are there the same differences between children of half a million years ago and modern children as there are between ancient and modern adults?
4. Why do you think different artists would draw our ancient ancestors in different ways?
5. What can the teeth of man tell us about his eating habits?
6. Which species forms the link between Australopithecus and the first Home sapiens?
7. How did the size of earlier man compare with the size of present man?
8. Is there any way of telling the eye, hair, or skin coloring of ancient man?

Activities

1. 1 Show the film *Fossils: Clues to Prehistoric Times*, Coronet Films or *Discovering Fossils*, Encyclopaedia Britannica – color.
2. 1 Secure a skeleton (not necessarily full size) and discuss changes from the earliest known hominid to the present time.
3. 1 Do some role playing. Pretend to be members of a Neanderthal or other early-man family.
4. 2 & 3 Make a horizontal time line which can be placed on or above the bulletin board in the front of the room to depict the dates at which various prehistoric men lived. A drawing to represent each of these and placed at the proper point would create even more interest.
5. 2 Read about other fossil remains of man and relate these to the ones already mentioned in the unit.

9. Why would you or would you not have liked to live 500,000 years ago?

Read *The Caves of Great Hunters* by Hans Baumann.

6. 2 Write an imaginary report on the kinds of games early children could have played.

7. 2 & 3 Find out which of the various groups of men named in this part of the unit invented the wheel.

8. 2 & 3 Do some research on animal forms extant at various periods. Discuss or give reports on the kinds of animals to be found.

9. 4 Have a game; let someone in group III name an ancient artifact or animal; have someone in the other groups name something which could have been found at that same time. If correct that team gets a point, if not the other one receives a point.

VI

Enlarging the ability to live more harmoniously and more richly results from the understandings derived from many sources.

Ideas to be Developed	Terms
1. Knowledge from many disciplines contributes to the total information relating to man.	botany
2. Archaeology is closely interwoven with and is dependent upon knowledge in other fields.	customs
3. People are more alike than they are different.	sociology
4. Social sciences are constantly changing and adding new pieces of information which alter our previous conceptions and widen our horizons.	zoology

Questions	Activities
1. What information do botanists and zoologists contribute to the archaeologist to help him describe ancient peoples?	1. 1 Make a chart to show what other social sciences contribute to archaeology and what archaeology, in turn, contributes to each of them.
2. What can archaeologists tell from the arrangement of houses and public buildings about the life of an ancient city?	2. 1 Show the film *How Living Things Change*, Coronet Films.
	3. 2 To demonstrate how things change gradually whisper something to a

3. Why is art work in caves valuable in learning about people?

4. Why does an archeologist sometimes change his ideas about what artifacts indicate to us concerning ancient cultures?

5. How are history and archaeology related?

6. In what way does the archaeologist use geography?

7. In what ways are the races of man alike and in what ways different?

8. Why do people's customs vary? What factors influence the making and changing of customs?

child, have him whisper it to the next person and then write down what he heard. Number the papers and note the changes by writing all of them down and discussing the results.

4. 1 Collect some pictures of the races of man. Discuss the distribution of races over the earth or make a map and put in colored pins to show the distribution.

5. 2 Try to find some new pieces of information that have been added to archaeology or some other social sciences in the last ten years.

CULMINATING ACTIVITIES

1. Give a skit for other rooms depicting man from a million years ago to the present. Each "ancient man" could describe how he lived, the kind of tools he had, etc.

2. Make some games for one another. Write short archaeology words backwards. Write in some letters and make lines for left-out letters for longer words.

3. Do a crossword puzzle such as the one shown on the next page to review terms.

4. Go on a field trip, lay out a site, and stage a "dig." Return to the classroom and make a permanent record complete with photographs taken on the trip.

Read *The Zealots of Masada:* story of a dig by Moshe Pearlman.

EVALUATION

1. Set up criteria at the start of the unit to evaluate progress of children during the unit. Change or add to the criteria as the unit progresses. Such points as these might be suitable for some teachers and/or classes: 1. Did the child exhibit an open mind toward new ideas? 2. Were the concepts of the unit understandable to the child? 3. Was the child motivated to dig deeper, to find things on his own? 4. Did the youngster ask or answer thought questions in such a way as to indicate a reasonable grasp of the material? 5. Did the pupil learn new study skills or improve those techniques with which he was already familiar?

2. Give a test to help inform the student how well he has grasped new terms and meanings.

3. Have children assess the advantages and disadvantages of the unit as it relates to their total learnings.

4. Discuss the ways in which the unit, if repeated, might be strengthened.

5. Have children write a letter to their parents listing the new ideas they have acquired and also the things they might do to acquire more knowledge in this area.

6. Have children evaluate their own strengths and weaknesses in relation to the qualifications required to be an archaeologist.

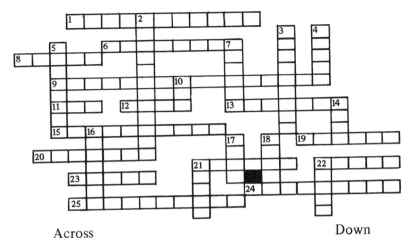

Across

1. The study of the remains of early human culture chiefly through excavations
6. Material remains of human culture
8. Animals living in a given period
9. Dating materials by counting tree rings
11. Pointed instrument for making small holes
12. Type of tool made in Pleistocene Period
13. A member of the family of the primate order
15. The means by which material things are produced
19. Remains of plants and animals produced in the earth's crust
20. The science that deals with the structure of the earth
21. Body of rites or ceremonies
22. Plants living in a given period
23. A tool which can be used to make other tools
24. Dating materials by the characteristics of their workmanship
25. A type of formal ritual

Down

2. The social science of which archaeology is a part
3. Small sharp bits of stone used for tools
4. Combination of metals
5. One fourth of a circle
7. Long, narrow opening in the ground
10. A tool used for digging
14. What archaeologists call their excavations
16. The total behavior patterns of a people
17. The place where an excavation is carried on
18. The sharp edge of a knife or other tool
21. A remaining portion of something that has been destroyed
22. Another type of tool produced in the Pleistocene Period

List of words used in puzzle:

alloy	ceremonial	flora	relic
anthropology	core	fossil	ritual
archaeology	culture	geology	seriation
artifact	dendrochronology	hoe	site
awl	digs	hominid	technology
blade	fauna	microlith	trench
burin	flake	quadrant	

BOOKS FOR CHILDREN

1. Baldwin, Gordon C. *America's Buried Past.* Putnam, 1962.
2. _____ . *Race Against Time: The Story of Salvage Archaeology,* Putnam, 1966.
3. Barr, Donald. *The How and Why Wonder Book of Primitive Man.* Grosset and Dunlap, 1961.
4. Baumann, Hans. *Lion Gate and Labyrinth;* the world of Tyro, Crete, and Mycenae. Pantheon, 1967.
5. _____ . *The Caves of the Great Hunters.* Pantheon, 1962.
6. _____ . *The World of the Pharoahs.* Pantheon, 1960.
7. Bond, Guy L. *Deeds of Men,* Classmate Edition. Lyons and Carnahan, 1962, pages 353-406.
8. Braymer, Marjorie. *The Walls of Windy Troy.* Harcourt, 1960.
9. Brennan, Louis A. *The Buried Treasure of Archaeology.* Random House, 1964.
10. Burland, C. A. *Adventuring in Archaeology.* Hale, 1963.
11. Cleator, Philip. *Exploring the World of Archeology.* Children's Press, 1966.
12. Cottrell, Leonard. *The Secrets of Tutankhamen's Tomb.* New York Graphis Society, 1964.
13. _____ . *Crete: Island of Mystery.* Prentice-Hall, 1965.
14. Curtis, Mary. *How Man Began.* Lyons and Carnahan, 1963.
15. Daugherty, C. *The Great Archaeologists.* Thomas Crowell Co., 1962.
16. Elting, Mary and Folsom, Michael. *The Secret Story of Pueblo Bonito.* Scholastic Book Services, 1963.
17. Fletcher, Helen. *Adventures in Archaeology.* Bobbs, Merrill, 1962.
18. Folsom, Franklin. *Science and the Secret of Man's Past.* Harvey House, 1966.
19. Fortiner, Virginia. *Archaeology as a Hobby.* Hammond.
20. Freed, Stanley A., Freed, Rush S. *Man From the Beginning.* Creative Education, 1967.
21. Friedman, Estelle. *Digging into Yesterday.* Putnam, 1958.
22. Garnett, Henry. *Treasures of Yesterday.* Natural History Press, 1964.
23. Glubok, S. *Art and Archaeology.* Harper, 1966.
24. Gringhuis, D. *The Big Dig.* Dial Press, 1962.
25. Hall, Jennie. *Buried Cities.* 2nd ed. Macmillan, 1964.
26. Holden, R. *Secrets in the Dust.* Dodd, Mead & Co., 1960.
27. Horig, Magazine. *The Search for Early Man.* American Heritage, 1963.
28. Jessup, Ronald. *The Wonderful World of Archaeology.* Doubleday, 1965.
29. Kubie, N. B. *The First Book of Archaeology.* Watts, 1967.
30. Macgregor, E. *Miss Pickerell Goes on a Dig.* McGraw-Hill, 1966, fiction.
31. Pearlman, Moshe. *The Zealots of Masada; Story of a Dig.* Scribners, 1967.
32. Poole, Lynn. *Carbon-14 and other Science Methods That Date the Past.* McGraw-Hill, 1961.
33. Shuttlesworth, Dorothy. *Real Book About Prehistoric Life.* Doubleday, 1957.
34. Silverberg, Robert. *Sunken History: The Story of Underwater Archaeology.* Chilton Books, 1963.
35. _____ . *The Man Who Found Nineveh.* Holt, Rinehart, and Winston, 1964.
36. Sonochson, Dorothy and Joseph. *Good Digging.* Hale, 1966.
37. Stilwell, Hart. *Looking at Man's Past.* Steck-Vaughn, 1965.
38. Suggs, Robert. *Modern Discoveries in Archaeology.* Crowell, 1962.
39. _____ . *The Archaeology of San Francisco.* Crowell, 1965.
40. Watts, Edith. *Archaeology — Exploring the Past.* New York Graphic Society, 1965.
41. Weisgard, Leonard. *The First Farmers in the New Stone Age.* Coward-McCann, 1966.
42. White, Anne. *All About Archaeology.* Random, 1959.
43. _____ . *Lost Worlds: The Romance of Archaeology.* Random, 1941.

BOOKS FOR TEACHER

1. Braidwood, Robert. *Archaeologists and What They Do.* Watts, 1960.
2. Broderick, Alan. *Man and His Ancestry.* Premier Books, Fawcett World Library, 1960.

3. Caldwell, Joseph R. *New Roads to Yesterday*. Basic Books, Inc., 1966.
4. Ceram, C. W. *The March of Archaeology*. Alfred A. Knopf, 1958.
5. Childe, V. Gordon. *Man Makes Himself*. Mentor Books, 1963.
6. Cottrell, Leonard. *Digs and Diggers*. World Publishing Co., 1964.
7. _____. *The Horizon Book of Lost Worlds*. Dell Pub. Co., 1962.
8. Dietz, James. *Invitation to Archaeology*. Rinehart & Winston, 1967.
9. Eydoux, Henri-Paul. *The Buried Past*. Frederick A. Praeger, 1962.
10. Gorenstein, Shirley. *Introduction to Archaeology*. Basic Books, Inc., 1965
11. Hole, Frank and Heizer, Robert. *An Introduction to Prehistoric Archaeology*. Holt, Rinehart, and Winston, 1965.
12. Heizer, Robert F. (ed.) *The Archaeologist at Work*. Harper and Bros., 1959.
13. Hibben, Frank. *Digging Up America*. Hill and Wang, 1960.
14. Honigman, John J. *The World of Man*. Harper and Row, 1959.
15. Marek, Kurt W. *Gods, Graves, and Scholars*. Knopf, 1967.
16. Mollett, John William. *An Illustrated Dictionary of Art and Archaeology*. American Archives of World Art, 1966.
17. Oakley, Kenneth P. *Man, the Toolmaker*. The University of Chicago Press, 1964.
18. Shapiro, Harry L. (ed.) *Man, Culture, and Society*. Oxford University Press, Inc., 1956.
19. Shepherd, Walter. *Archaeology*. New American Library, 1965.
20. Suggs, Robert C. *Modern Discoveries in Archaeology*. Thomas Crowell, 1962.
21. Watson, Jane Werner. *The Sciences of Mankind*. Golden Press, 1960.
22. Wooby, Sir Leonard. *The Beginnings of Civilization*. Mentor Books, 1965.

FILMSTRIPS

1. *Discovering Fossils*. Encyclopedia Britannica. Color.
2. *Epic of Man*. Life Filmstrips. Color. There are several filmstrips in this series.
3. *Exploring Ancient Athens*. Imperial Film Co., 1964.
4. *Exploring Ancient Egypt*. Imperial Film Co., 1964.
5. *Exploring Ancient Mexico; The Maya*. Imperial Film Co., 1964.
6. *Exploring Rome and Pompeii*. Imperial Film Co., 1964.
7. *Fossils, Keys to the Past*. Lamar State College of Technology, Beaumont, Texas, Words 1965.
8. *How We Learn About the Past*. Filmstrip of the Month Club, 1965. Color.
9. *Man of Long Ago*. Curriculum Films, Inc. Color.
10. *The Nature of Fossils*. Lamar State College of Technology, Beaumont, Texas, Words 1965.
11. *The New Stone Age*. Society for Visual Education, 1956.
12. *The Old Stone Age*. Society for Visual Education, 1956.
13. *Story Fossils Tell*. Encyclopedia Britannica. Color.

FILMS

1. *Ancient New World*. Rental from University of Illinois, 1965.
2. *Cave Dwellers of the Old Stone Age*. Encyclopedia Britannica Films.
3. *Dr. Leakey and the Dawn of Man*. Encyclopedia Britannica, 1967.
4. *Exploring Ancient Civilizations*. Imperial Film Co., 1964. Color.
5. *Forty Centuries*. Pictura Films Distribution Co.

SLIDES

1. *Art Treasures of Prehistoric Man*. (Cultural Historical Research, Inc.)
2. *The Story of Ancient Man*. (American Museum of Natural History)
3. *Prehistoric Art*. (Cultural Historical Research, Inc.)

Upper Grade Unit
CANADA

SKILLS TO BE DEVELOPED

1. Problem-solving skills involving the ability to identify questions, find information concerning related topics, pick out key ideas, and organize the information for presentation.
2. The ability to use, interpret, and understand maps, charts, graphs, and globes.
3. Improved listening, reading, and speaking skills involving an understanding of sequence, cause-and-effect relationships, and the ability to construct valid generalizations.
4. Skills in group work involving the planning of tasks to be completed, the equitable distribution of responsibilities, and the coordination of individual efforts.
5. Skills in establishing criteria which may be used in judging the procedural activities and final products.
   Appropriate materials for each topic may be selected from those suggested.

UNDERSTANDINGS

1. The history of a country greatly influences the political, social, and economic development of its people.
2. Geographic factors and natural resources play an important part in shaping the lives of a people.
3. Relationships among countries are affected by social and political customs, economic conditions, and mutual interests.
4. The religious, educational, and recreational activities within a nation often reflect the basic interests of its people.

ATTITUDES

1. An appreciation of the importance of cooperation among nations.
2. Respect for the ideas and opinions of others.
3. Appreciation and acceptance of differences in people.

SUGGESTED APPROACHES

1. Obtain and prepare a display of books and book jackets in the library corner. Suitable books are recommended in the bibliography.
2. Invite a person who has lived and traveled in Canada to come and speak to the class. He may illustrate his talk with colored slides or pictures.

3. Arrange a collection of pictures of Canada and Canadian activities on a bulletin board with accompanying questions which will generate interest.
4. Encourage the children to bring and exhibit souvenirs of Canada or Canadian currency.
5. Mount newspaper clippings relating to Canadian affairs.
6. Send for travel folders and information concerning Canadian industries (See Bibliography).
7. Show a film about Canada (See list of suggested films in Bibliography).

The History of a Country Greatly Influences the Political, Social, and Economic Development of Its People

Understandings

Leif Ericson may have touched the shores of Newfoundland and Labrador about the year 1000.

Five hundred years later, John Cabot, an Italian in search of a water route to the Far East, explored what is now the east coast of Canada and claimed the land for England.

French explorers also attempting to reach the Far East discovered and explored the St. Lawrence River and some of the Great Lakes. These men, Jacques Cartier, and Samuel de Champlain, claimed the land for France.

Both French and English settlers moved into Canada.

Activities

Questions:

1. What stimulated interest in Canada?
2. Why was Champlain called "The Father of New France?"
3. How did the rapids found by Cartier affect the settlement of the New World?
4. How would the population have been different if the rapids had not been there?
5. How would the exploration of Canada have been affected if the St. Lawrence River had not existed?
6. Why was exploration considered important?

Encourage children to read from a variety of books to learn about the settlement of Canada. Among them: *Drums in the Forest* (Allan Dwight) and *The Pageant of Canadian History* (Anne Peck)

The teacher may read about the early days of the French settlers in *Madeleine Takes Command*, Brill (Montreal, 1962)

Questions:

1. What was the main problem faced by the settlers?
2. What would you have brought along if you were an early settler?
3. How did rivalry in the fur trade affect the settlers and the Indians?
4. What kind of government did the French provide?

5. What was the place of the church in colonial affairs?

Add to vocabulary chart.
Wuorio's *Return of the Vikings*

Pupils may participate in a play about Canadian history. See Stephen, *Classroom Plays from Canadian History.*

Develop a chronology line which shows the settlement of Canada.

Construct dioramas showing life in the early settlements.

View a filmstrip, *Colonial Family of New France* or *The Rise and Fall of New France.*

The disputed claims of England and France were settled when the English defeated the French in the French and Indian War.

Questions:

1. What were the causes of the conflict between England and France?

2. What were the major outcomes of the war?

3. What were the effects on the French settlers?

4. What might have been a better way to settle the dispute between England and France?

Read from a variety of references about the war:

The Fort in the Forest, by Helen Lobdell.
Land of Promise by John Field.
A Picture History of Canada by Clarke Hutton.
The Canadian Story by May McNeer.

France gave up all claims to land in North America.

Questions:

1. How did the peace treaty of 1763 change the map of North America?

2. What territories were annexed?

3. How did the Quebec Act of 1774, which allowed the French to retain their language and customs, affect the country then and now?

4. How might the history of our country have been changed if this act had not been passed?

5. How would Canada be different if the French had won?

Dramatize events from the war.

Plot the conflicting land claims on an historical map. Read *Exploring American Neighbors,* Gray, pp. 282-283.

Add to vocabulary chart.

View the filmstrip *Canada: A Nation Grows* or view film *People of Canada* (traces the migrations of various ethnic groups to Canada)

Geographic Factors and Natural Resources Play an Important Part in Shaping the Lives of a People

Today Canada is a member of the British Commonwealth of Nations.

Questions:

1. What is meant by Commonwealth?

2. Who is the head of Canada's government?

3. Why did Canada never have to fight for independence from England?

Send for: *Invitation to Canada*

Read and observe maps in the following books about the British Commonwealth of Nations:

Compton's Pictured Encyclopeida, Vol. B.
Neighbors in the United States and Canada, by Smith et al.

Read *The First Book of Canada* by Lineaweaver, *This is Canada* by Sally Lindsay, or *Canada and Her Northern Neighbors* by Frances Carpenter. *Canada* by Dorothy Wood.

Overview of the Country:

Canada, often called the Land of the Maple Leaf, is a vast expanse of land stretching from the Atlantic Ocean to the Pacific and from the northern boundary of the United States far up into the Arctic Ocean almost to the North Pole.

Examine a political-physical wall map of North America. Note the location and size of Canada. Point out the bodies of water that border it. Note the location of our country in relation to Canada.

View the filmstrip – *Canadian Regional Geography* (set one)

Questions:

1. How does the size of Canada compare to that of other countries?

2. How does the population compare with that of other countries in size: Brazil, Australia, the United States?

View the motion picture *Canada*

The surface features of the United States and Canada are somewhat alike.

The Eastern Coastlines of both countries are deeply indented.

In the east, the Appalachians extend into Canada.

Questions:

1. Why would you expect the west coast to be damp and the plains dry?

2. How useful are the rivers as travel routes?

3. Why is the Canadian population distributed so unevenly?

The Laurentian Plateau around Hudson Bay covers two-thirds of Canada's surface. It is a forested area with many lakes.

The lowlands of the St. Lawrence Valley and around the Great Lakes have fertile soil for farming activities similar to those in Ohio and Michigan.

The prairie lands to the west are a continuation of the prairie and plain region of our country.

In the far west the Rockies, the Cascades, and the Coast Ranges extend into Canada and form one range called the Canadian Rockies.

To the far north are highland plains and Arctic islands.

The climate of the United States and Canada is much the same along the common boundary.

Northern Canada is much colder than any part of our country. The southern part of the United States is much warmer than any part of Canada.

Because the climate is more desirable, most of the people of Canada live in a narrow strip of land in the south-central and southeastern parts of the country just north of our border. Here the climate, together with fertile

Observe, study, and discuss various types of detailed maps and globes of North America and Canada to discover the major features of terrain within the country.

Make a relief map of salt and flour or papier mache to show the surface features of Canada. Color to indicate the physical divisions.

Play "Place Geography" on a large unmarked globe to locate various surface features.

Add to vocabulary chart.

View the Filmstrips: *Canadian Regional Geography* (Set two)

Questions:

1. What natural features in Canada are the same as those in the United States?

2. What effect would an irregular coastline have on Canada?

3. How is the region of the far north different from any part of our country?

4. What do the maps tell us about the effect the Rockies have had on the development of Canada?

5. How are the Great Lakes and St. Lawrence River important to Canada?

6. What are the major physical divisions of Canada?

7. What kind of life would you expect in the lowlands? In the far north? On the prairies?

Construct a map using colored mapping pins to show the distribution of the population.

Draw pictures depicting the cold climate.

View the filmstrip *The Polar Bear* or *The Arctic Islands.*

Add to vocabulary chart.
Teachers Kit on Canada (free)

Questions:

1. How does the climate appear to vary from region to region?

2. What causes the wide variety of climates?

3. How would the climate influence the life of the people?

soil, makes it a good land for agriculture.

Canada is divided into provinces rather than states.

The people of the four Maritime Provinces of the east coast get most of their wealth from the sea. Dairying, farming, and lumbering are leading occupations in this section.

The two large provinces of Ontario and Quebec lie just west of the Maritimes. They have rich farms to the south and much lumbering and mining in the north. The largest cities of Canada are located in the southern

Find information in *Canada and Her Northern Neighbors* and *The First Book of Canada.*

Questions:

1. What are some jobs that depend upon fishing resources? on lumbering?

2. How have modern inventions helped the fishing industry?

3. What factors have caused Newfoundland to have one of the largest pulp and paper mills in the world and to be called "The Crossroads to Continents"?

4. Why are Labrador and Newfoundland so cold compared to England and France, which are in the same latitude?

View film: *Avalon Holiday*

Divide into four groups and give illustrated reports or booklets (maps, collections, charts, graphs, original sketches) on each of the four Maritime Provinces. Other provinces may be included, and this can be a continuing activity throughout the unit.

Listen to a travel talk by anyone who has visited one of the Maritime Provinces.

View a motion picture or filmstrip which shows what life is like in the Maritime Provinces.

The Atlantic Region (film)
Maritime Provinces of Canada (film)
Fishermen of Nova Scotia (filmstrip)

Add to the vocabulary chart.

View filmstrips: *Canadian Regional Geography* (Set three)
View slides: *Trans-Canada West*

Paint a frieze which shows the major ways of making a living in the Maritime Provinces.

Collect various types of woods produced in Canada.

Questions:

1. Why is the St. Lawrence important?

2. Why is Quebec a famous city?

3. What factors have caused Montreal to become an important city?

4. What makes French Canada different?

part of these provinces. Much of Canada's manufacturing is carried on in this section.

5. What can we say about the way the people make a living in Quebec and Ontario?

6. Why do most of the people live in southern Canada?

Read references in the *World Book Encyclopeida* related to Quebec — also *St. Lawrence Seaway* by Judson and *Through the Locks — Canals Today and Yesterday* by Buehr.

View the filmstrip *Farm and City in Ontario.*

Collect pictures of life in Ontario and Quebec.

View a filmstrip relating to the French Canadians, *Villages in French Canada.*

Write an imaginary letter to a friend, telling what you saw on a French Canadian farm in Quebec. Draw pictures of interesting things you saw there.

Add to vocabulary chart.

Send for pamphlet: *Prince Edward Island.*

The Prairie Provinces, westward from Ontario, make up the vast wheat region of Canada: The southern part of these provinces is a region similar to our Wheat Belt. Fur-trapping is a valuable industry in the northern part of these provinces. Much coal and oil are found here.

Questions:

1. What factors make this a suitable area for growing wheat?

2. Why are there few large cities in this region?

3. What is the chief occupation of the people?

4. What other work is done there?

5. What factors caused Winnipeg to become a great mail-order center?

6. Why is Canada eager to export wheat?

7. Is it right for Canada to send wheat to Russia and Communist China?

Read accounts of life in Manitoba, Saskatchewan, and Alberta. *Golden Tales of Canada* by May Becker.

View a motion picture or filmstrip to gain a clearer picture of these provinces. *The Great Plains* (film); *Wheat Farmers in Western Canada* (filmstrip)

Children can imagine that they are living on a wheat farm in the Prairie Provinces and compare their life there with their real-life activities.

Have a special report on how coal and oil are formed.

On a map or diagram, trace the route which wheat or oil would take for export.

On the Pacific Ocean is the province of British Columbia. Lumbering is the leading industry. This province is the second-largest mining region of Canada. Fur-trapping and fishing are outstanding, also.

Questions:

1. What effect do the mountains have on this province?
2. What occupations result from the fishing?
3. What has made Vancouver a great seaport?
4. Why is a large aluminum manufacturing plant located at Kitimat, even though there is no bauxite?

View a motion picture or filmstrip about the western part of Canada. *Pacific Canada* (film); *Vancouver and the Western Mountains* (filmstrip); *Logging in Canada* (filmstrip).

Draw a panel picture that tells the story of lumbering, fur-trapping, or fishing in British Columbia.

Enjoy a motion picture that tells a Canadian folk tale. *Ti Jean Goes Lumbering.*

Add to vocabulary chart.

To the north are two territories, the Yukon and the Northwest Territories. The northernmost parts of these regions are frozen tundra and, therefore, sparsely populated. Two valuable minerals, uranium and radium, are mined in the far north. Lumbering and fur-trapping are carried on here. This region is the home of the Indian and Eskimo.

Questions:

1. What methods of transportation are used to meet the demands of the climate?
2. How are the lives of the Eskimo and the Indian alike?
3. Why could this area be called a "land of tomorrow"?
4. How did the Royal Mounted Police bring law and order to the West?

Read legends of the north. (*Glooskap's Country and Other Indian Tales,* by MacMillan)

Listen to records:
    "Call of the Seal" (Eskimo Chant)
    "Folk Songs of Canada"

Read *The First Book of Eskimos* by Brewster.

Learn an Indian song (*"I Travel On"*)

Prepare a report on the "Land of the Midnight Sun."

Filmstrips:
    The Caribou Eskimo
    Eskimo Prints
    Eskimo Sculpture
    The Modern Eskimo
    Eskimo of St. Lawrence Island — A Series

Trace the Alaskan Highway on a map or diagram.

Some children may want to read rather extensively about the life of the Royal Canadian Mounted Police. References:

Return of Silver Chief by Jack O'Brien

The Real Book About the Mounties, Irwin Block.

Royal Canadian Mounted Police, Richard Neuberger.

The Living Legend, Alan Phillips.

The Friendly Force, Douglas Spettigue.

The Scarlet Force, Thomas Longstreth.

The Real Book About the Mounties, Benjamin Brewster.

Filmstrip: *The Yukon*
Film: *Gold*

Questions:

1. What are the greatest natural resources of the United States?

2. How do our resources compare with those of Canada?

3. How do these abundant resources affect life in our country? Life in Canada?

4. What are the possibilities for future development?

5. What efforts are made toward conserving our resources?

Send for: *Facts on Canada*

Questions:

1. The United States gave some powers to the federal government and reserved the rest for the states. Canada gave some powers to the provinces and reserved the rest for the central government. Which plan do you think is better? Why?

2. Some of the French-Canadians would like to separate from Canada and establish a separate country. Should they be allowed to do this?

3. What are the important functions a government performs for its people?

Have a group of capable students find information about the government of Canada and share the information in a special report.

Canada can be called a rich country because of its great natural resources. Chief among the resources are these:

1. fertile soil for agriculture, Canada's greatest resource

2. abundant forests
3. valuable fur-bearing animals
4. extensive mineral resources, including uranium and radium

5. abundant water power
6. a wealth of fish off both coasts

The government of Canada resembles ours in some ways.

Canada is a self-governing country which elects its own officials, just as the United States does.

The law-making body, called Parliament, is similar to our Congress.

Canada does not have a President. The Prime Minister is really the head of the government.

Canada, as a member of the British Commonwealth of

Nations, recognizes the British Queen as its leader. The Governor-General represents the ruler of Great Britain.

Find pictures in magazines and newspapers of Canadian leaders. Prepare a bulletin board.

Watch for articles in the newspapers or children's magazines about the Canadian government.

Draw a picture of the Canadian flag.

Film: *Ottawa: Canada's Capital*

Relationships Among Countries Are Affected by Social and Political Customs, Economic Conditions and Mutual Interests

The United States and Canada are good neighbors. The two countries work together and help each other.

There are no forts and no guards along the 3,000 mile border between the two countries. Many monuments have been erected along the boundary line. One of the most famous is located at Blaine, Washington, called the "Portal of Peace." On the American side is inscribed "Children of a Common Mother." On the Canadian side the inscription reads: "Brothers Dwelling Together in Unity."

Both nations are working toward building and maintaining the strong defenses of North America. Both Canada and the United States guard the Artic Radar Line.

The two countries cooperated in the building of the Alaskan Highway.

They worked together on the St. Lawrence Seaway Project.

Both use electric power from Niagara Falls.

Questions:

1. Do we have to work to keep good relations between the United States and Canada?

2. What problems are presented by the international hydroelectric development in the Pacific Northwest?

3. What are some of the problems in the international sale of wheat?

4. What are some of the joint United States-Canadian committees for studying problems?

5. What factors have contributed to the peace between the United States and Canada?

Read accounts of the peaceful relationship between our country and Canada.

Listen to the record, "The Undefended Border," narrated by Raymond Massey.

Look for articles in newspapers and magazines about the relationship between Canada and the United States.

Mount newspaper headlines, pictures, and clippings about the various projects.

Questions:

1. Would it be a good idea to unite the United States and Canada?

2. How has the St. Lawrence Seaway affected our relationships?

Read about the cooperation between the United States and Canada on the projects in encyclopedias or textbooks.

Read *The Friendly Frontier* — the story of the Canadian-American Frontier, by Meyer.

Start a mural showing the story of "Good Neighbor" activities between the two countries.

Have a panel discussion: "In What Ways Do Canada and the United States Help Each Other?"

Filmstrip: *The St. Lawrence Seaway*

Read for reference: *Canada and Our Latin American Neighbors 1968.*

Canada and the United States are interdependent. Canada produces many products that we need. We rank with Great Britain in being Canada's best customer. Among the products we import are:

asbestos	aluminum
nickel	furs
uranium	iron ore
copper	wood
	paper pulp

Questions:

1. What basis is there for the Canadian fear that the United States may dominate Canada economically?

2. What rules might be developed for American businesses operating in Canada?

3. Is the export of Alberta's abundant natural gas to the United States in the long-range interest of Canada?

4. How can Canada's lopsided trade deficit with the United States be remedied?

5. How did improved transportation make it possible for Canadians to discover and make use of the riches of land and water?

6. Why is Canada a great trading nation?

7. Should we let Canadian lumbermen compete with our lumber industry?

8. Is it good to have competition?

9. If you were starting a business in Canada today, what would you choose?

10. Why are Canadians able to produce a great surplus of food?

11. What are the reasons for Canada's becoming a great industrial nation?

Look up product maps in several references. Quinn, *Picture Map Geography of Canada and Alaska.*

Sketch a large wall map of Canada. Draw pictures or place samples of the leading products on the map.

Add to vocabulary chart.

Make a chart listing products, where found, and how used.

Check references for exports and imports of Canada and the United States. Draw bar graphs to illustrate the value of minerals, agricultural products, and other items.

Send for: *Across Canada; Canadian National Railways*

Exhibit various products made from aluminum, copper, etc.

Develop a transportation-facilities map.

View a film or filmstrip. *Industrial Canada* (film); *Water Serves Canada* (filmstrip)

Make a map showing imports and exports.

Panel discussion: "Should Canada Export Natural Gas?"

The people of Canada and the United States on the whole can trace their ancestry to European countries. One of the official languages of Canada is English, just as ours is. The other is French.

Questions:

1. What contributions has each nationality made to the culture of Canada?

2. In what ways are the people in the United States and Canada alike? In what ways are they different?

View a motion picture about the different nationalities of people among the Canadians. (*Peoples of Canada*)

Read a story showing the French influence on Canadian life. *Up Canada Way,* Dickson.

The teacher may read a folk tale (Carlson, *Alphonse, That Bearded One*) or poem "Canadian Boat Song," "The Kayak"

Listen to records. "O Canada" (unofficial French national anthem)

Draw a circle graph to show the distribution of population by national origins and compare it with a similar graph of American ethnic groups.

Read for reference: *Canada: Young Giant of the North*

The Religious, Educational, and Recreational Activities Within a Nation Often Reflect the Basic Interest of its People

Education in Canada resembles that of the United States in many ways.

The provinces have their own school systems just as the states do.

In all provinces except Quebec, the schools are taught in English.

Questions:

1. What would you expect to find if you visited a school in Canada today?

2. In what ways are the schools in Canada like ours?

Read accounts of schools in references such as *The Train School,* by Acker.

The religions of Canada, with the exception of the United Church of Canada and the Anglican Church of Canada, are the same as ours. Six million people are Roman Catholic, descendants of the French.

Canada serves as a great playground for the people of our country. Canadians are dependent upon our tourist trade as an important source of income.

Our tourists enjoy Canada's beautiful scenic mountains, national parks, many lakes, and mountain streams for:

camping   skiing
sightseeing   tobogganing
fishing   ice-skating
hunting

Canada and the United States enjoy many of the same sports.

Ice hockey, the national game of Canada, is also popular in our country.

Ice-skating, skiing, water sports, fishing, and hunting are popular in both countries.

The recreational interests of Canadian children and American children are very similar.

Games such as football, baseball, hopscotch, marbles, and other common games are much the same as ours.

If possible, exchange letters with Canadian children. The Friends Service Committee aids in this effort.

Questions:

1. What are the religious affiliations of the people?

2. What problems are created by religious differences?

3. How are minority groups treated?

Find information in general reference books relating to the religions of Canada.

1. What are the greatest tourist attractions in Canada?

2. Should Americans "See America First?"

View a filmstrip to better understand how Canada is a playground for tourists.

Film: *Attractions for Visitors*

Read how Canada serves as a great vacationland. Government bulletin: *Canada: Vacations Unlimited.*

Draw pictures of interesting things you might see on a trip through Canada. Make a bulletin board advertising Canadian Attractions.

Send for: Highway Map: Canada and Northern United States.

Make a booklet, *Vacation Fun,* including post cards and travel posters.

1. How are Canadian children like American boys and girls?

2. What games do they share in common? Read books about Canadians at play. Children may particularly enjoy *Young Canada,* by Anne Peck.

Read true-to-life stories of children in Canada today:
Bice, *Across Canada, Stories of Canadian Children*
DeAngeli, *Petite Suzanne*
Harrington, *Oo look, the Eskimo Girl*

Enjoy songs that the Canadian children sing.

The American Singer, "My Husky Dog," "The Saw," and "Roll, My Ball."
Music in Our Country, "Bells."

Because of the colder climate, opportunities for winter sports far exceed ours. In winter, many school-yards are used for ice-skating, ice hockey, and tobogganing.

In summer, tennis, golf, football, swimming, boating, and canoeing are common sports.

Lacrosse is a popular game.
Baseball has not reached the stage of popularity that it has in our country.

Canada is facing several present-day problems:

Farm recession
Unemployment
World tensions
Increased urbanization and industrialization
Separatist movement in Quebec.
Travel in the far north

Draw pictures of children at play.

Find out how lacrosse is played by reading about it in the encyclopedia.

Questions:

1. If a region of a country is not useful, should the government help to expand it?
2. If one part of the country is wealthy and another poor, should the wealthy help the poor?
3. What is being done to promote unity among the Canadians?
4. What is Canada's relation with the world? (United Nations, N.A.T.O., atomic energy, boundary waters, D.E.W. Line)
5. Should the immigration policy be changed?

Read descriptions of Canadian problems in encyclopedias and *The National Geographic*.

Look for articles of interest in newspapers and magazines.

CULMINATING ACTIVITIES

The group may plan one or more of the following:

1. Tell or dramatize your favorite story about Canada.
2. Use the "Continuing Story." A student is chosen to start by relating pertinent information concerning one topic on Canada. He designates another pupil to continue the story, and so on until all classmates have had an opportunity to contribute. Students must listen carefully in order not to repeat. They may start a new topic if there is no more relevant information.
3. Play the game "Where Am I?" A child describes a place orally or in written form, and the other children guess where in Canada the place is located.
4. Make a class bibliography of the best references concerning Canada.
5. Make a chart of the ten provices, showing their capitals, location, main attractions and products.
6. Plan and prepare an informal program for another class or a parents group. Present "What We Have Learned and Done in Our Study of Canada." Display maps, charts, art work, graphs, and booklets. Sing some songs, relate stories, give reports, and present a dramatization.

EVALUATION

Evaluation should be a continuous process. However, the teacher will want to ask herself such additional questions as:

1. Have the pupils understood the most important concepts underlying the unit of study?
2. Have the pupils grown in such skills as:
   a. Locating and gathering information
   b. Evaluating, analyzing, and organizing information
   c. Using and interpreting maps, charts, graphs, and globes
   d. Writing and speaking clearly and logically
3. Have the pupils shown increased ability in thinking through problems and issues?
4. Do the pupils show a willingness to share ideas and materials with others.
5. Were the pupils challenged by the activities of the unit?
6. Have the pupils increased their understanding and appreciation of what it means to be a citizen of the United States and of the world?
7. Have the pupils grown in their willingness to accept responsibility?

Answers to these questions may be acquired by

1. Observing pupils in work groups, dramatizations, and reporting. (Anecdotal records.)
2. Giving written tests.
3. Using pupil self-check lists for habits, attitudes, and behavior in class.
4. Individual conferences with the teacher.
5. Checking the quality of pupil work completed during the study of Canada.

TEACHER'S BIBLIOGRAPHY

Arbuthnot, May Hill. *Time for Poetry.* Chicago: Scott, Foresman and Co., 1951.

Beattie, John W., et al. *The American Singer.* New York: American Book Co., 1955.

Boni, Margaret. *Fireside Book of Folk Songs.* New York: Simon & Schuster, 1947.

H. W. Wilson Co., *The Children's Catalog, 1961.*

Educational Media Index-Intermediate (4-6). New York: McGraw-Hill Book Co., 1964.

The Elementary School Library Collection. Newark, N.J.: The Bro-Dart Foundation, 1966.

Ferris, Helen. *Favorite Poems, Old and New.* Doubleday, 1957.

Gustafson, Ralph. *The Penguin Book of Canadian Verse.* Hamondsworth: Penguin Books, 1958.

Millen, Nina. *Children's Games from Many Lands.* New York: Friendship Press, 1943.

Mursell, James L., et. al. *Music in Our Country.* Chicago: Silver Burdett Co., 1956.

Pitts, Lilla Belle, Mabelle Glenn, and Lorrain E. Watters. *Singing Together.* Boston: Ginn and Co., 1957.

Readers Guide to Periodical Literature. New York: the H. W. Wilson Co.

Smith, Janet Adam. *Looking Glass Book of Verse.* Random House, 1959.

Stephen, A. M. *Classroom Plays from Canadian History,* Dent, 1929.

Subject Index to Children's Plays. Chicago: American Library Ass'n., 1940.

Unit Planning and Teaching in Elementary Social Studies, U.S. Department of Health, Education and Welfare. U.S. Government Printing Office, 1965.

Wade, Mason. "New Relations of the U. S. with Canada," *The United States and the World Today.* New York: Rand McNally and Co.

FREE AND INEXPENSIVE MATERIALS

Requests for the following materials may be written by the teacher or by individual pupils under the guidance of the teacher.

Canadian Government Travel Bureau
Ottawa, Canada

1. *Game Fish in Canada*
2. *Canada*
3. *Canada: Vacations Unlimited*

The Canadian Shredded Wheat Company

1. *The Exciting Story of Wheat*
   Prince Edward Island Travel Bureau
   Queen Street
   Charlottetown, P. E. Island
   Canada
1. Prince Edward Island

Aluminum Company of Canada, Ltd.
11700 Sun Life Building
Montreal, Quebec

1. *Kitimat, A Saga of Canada*
2. *Shipshaw Power Development*

Grand Truck Railway System
105 West Adam Street
Room 900
Chicago, Illinois 60603

1. *Across Canada*
2. *Canadian National Railways*

MacMillan and Bleedel, Ltd.
837 West Hastings Street
Vancouver 1, B. C. Canada

1. *Miracle in Wood*

Department of Fisheries
Ottawa, Ontario, Canada

1. *Fisheries Fact Sheets*
2. *Science in Fisheries*
3. *Purse Seine to Lobster Pots*
4. *Canada's Pacific Salmon*
5. *Oceanography – Science of the Sea*
6. *Canada's Atlantic Salmon*

Superintendent of Government Publication
The Queen's Printer
Ottawa, Ontario

1. *Our Transportation Services*
2. *Native Trees of Canada*
3. *Canadian Eskimo Arts*
4. *The St. Lawrence Seaway and Power Project*

The Canadian Consul General
Canadian Consulate General
1407 Tower Building
Seattle 1, Washington

A teacher's packet may be procured by writing to the nearest Canadian Consul General.

Teacher's Kit on Canada (Free)
Canadian Consulate General
310 S. Michigan Avenue
Chicago, Illinois 60604

Free and Inexpensive Learning Materials

Facts on Canada, 1967. Queen's Printer and Controller of Stationery, Ottowa, Canada. 50¢.

Invitation to Canada, 1968. Canadian Government Travel Bureau, Ottowa, Canada (free).

Highway Map: Canada and Northern United States, 1968. Canadian Government Travel Bureau, Ottowa, Canada.

CHILDREN'S BIBLIOGRAPHY

Textbooks

Barrows, Harland H., Edith Putnam Parker, and Clarence W. Sorensen. *The American Continents.* New York: Silver Burdett Co., 1956.

Brown, Gertrude Stephens, Ernest W. Tiegs, and Fay Adams, *Your Country and Mine, Our American Neighbors,* Boston: Ginn, 1960.

Bruner, Herbert Bascom; Bathurst, Effie G.; Bruner, Lucile. *Canada and Our Latin American Neighbors.* River Forest, Illinois: Laidlow Bros., 1968.

Carls, Norman Frank E. Sorensen, and Margery D. Howarth. *Neighbors in Canada and Latin America.* Philadelphia: The John C. Winston Co.

Carpenter, Francis. *Canada and Her Northern Neighbors.* New York: American Book Co., 1946.

Compton's Pictured Encyclopedia and Fact Index. Chicago: FEE. Compton and Co., 1968.

Cutwright, Prudence, et al. *Living Together in the Americas.* New York: The Macmillan Co., 1958.

Gray, William H., et. al. *Exploring American Neighbors.* Chicago: Follet Publishing Co., 1958.

Hanna, Paul R., Clyde F. Kohn, and Robert A. Lively. *In the Americas.* Chicago: Scott, Foresman and Co., 1962.

Jones, Emlyn D., J. Warren Nystrom, and Helen Harter. *Within the Americas; North and South America.* New York: Rand and McNally and Co., 1957.

Meyer, J. G., and O. Stuart Hamer. *The New World and Its Growth.* New York: Follett Publishing Co., 1952.

Smith, J. Russell, and Frank E. Sorensen. *Neighbors Around the World.* Philadelphia: The John C. Winston Co., 1952.

_____. *Neighbors in the United States and Canada.* Philadelphia: The John C. Winston Co., 1952.

Tiegs, Ernest W., Fay Adams, and Gertrude Stephens Brown. *Your Country and Mine.* Boston: Ginn and Co., 1958.

World Almanac, New York World-Telegram, New York, 1965.

World Book Encyclopedia. Chicago: Field Enterprises Education Corporation, 1968.

Non-Fiction

Averill, Esther. *Cartier Sails the St. Lawrence.* Harper, 1956.

Block, Irvin. *The Real Book About the Mounties.* New York: Garden City Publishing Co., 1952.

Bonner, Mary. *Canada and Her Story.* New York: Knopf, 1950.

_____. *Made In Canada.* New York: Knopf, 1943.

Boswell, Hazel. *French Canada* The Viking Press, 1938.

Brewster, Benjamin. *The First Book of Eskimos.* New York: Franklin Watts, Inc., 1952.

Brindze, Ruth. *The Story of the Totem Pole.* Vanguard Press, 1951.

Brown, George W. *The Story of Canada.* D. C. Heath, 1949. Buehr, Walter.

Buehr, Walter. *Through the Locks — Canals Today and Yesterday.* New York: F. P. Putnam's Sons, 1954.

Ferguson, Robert. *Fur Trader: The Story of Alexander Henry.* MacMillan, 1961.

Field, John. *Land of Promise.* New York: Abelard-Schuman, 1962.

Harris, Leila G., and Walter K. Harris. *Let's Read About Canada.* Grand Rapids: Fideler Co., 1949.

Hill, T. L. and S. J. Hill. *Canada.* Grand Rapids: Fideler Co., 1959.

Hutton, Clarke. *A Picture Story of Canada.* New York: Franklin Watts, Inc., 1956.

Judson, Clara Ingram. *St. Lawrence Seaway.* Chicago: Follett Publishing Co., 1959.

Leitch, Adelaide. *Canada; Young Giant of the North.* Nelson, 1964.

Lineaweaver, Charles, and Marion Weaver. *The First Book of Canada.* New York: Franklin Watts, Inc., 1955.

Lindsay, Sally. *This Is Canada.* New York: Grosset & Dunlap, 1965.

Longstreth, Thomas. *The Scarlet Force.* New York: Macmillan, 1953.

McNeer, Mae. *The Canadian Story.* Ariel, 1958.

Myer, Edith Patterson. *The Friendly Frontier, the Story of the Canadian-American Border.* Boston: Little, Brown, 1962.

Neuberger, Richard L. *Royal Canadian Mounted Police.* Random House, 1953.

Peck, Anne. *The Pageant of Canadian History.* Toronto: Longmans Green, 1943.

———. *Young Canada.* Toronto: Longmans Green, 1945.

Phillips, Alan. *The Living Legend.* Boston: Little, Brown, 1947.

Quinn, Vernon. *Picture Map Geography of Canada and Alaska.* Philadelphia. J. B. Lippincott, Co., 1954.

Ross, Frances. *The Land and People of Canada.* Philadelphia: J. B. Lippincott Co., 1947.

Schull, *The Saltwater Men: Canada's Deep-Sea Sailors.* Macmillan, 1957.

Smith, A. J. M., ed. *The Book of Canadian Poetry.* University of Chicago Press, 1943.

Smith, Frances C. *The World of the Arctic.* Lippincott, 1960.

Spettigue, Douglas. *The Friendly Force.* Toronto: Longmans Green, 1955.

Syme, Ronald. *Boy of the North.* Morrow, 1950.

———. *Champlain of the St. Lawrence.* Morrow, 1952.

———. *Henry Hudson.* Morrow, 1954.

Tharp, L. H. *Company of Adventures – The Story of the Hudson's Bay Company.* Little, 1946.

Watson, Virginia. *Flags Over Quebec.* New York: Coward McCann, Inc., 1941.

Wood, Dorothy. *Canada;* illus. by Harvey Shelton. Children's Press, 1964.

Wood, Kerry. *The Great Chief: Maskepetoon: Warrior of the Crees.* Macmillan, 1957.

Legends and Folklore

Barbeau, Marius. *The Golden Phoenix.* Walk, 1958.

Becker, May. *Golden Tales of Canada.* New York: Dodd, Mead & Co., 1938.

Carlson, Natalie Savage. *Alphonse, That Bearded One.* Harcourt, Brace and Company, 1954.

———. *The Letter on the Tree.* New York: Harper and Row, 1964.

———. *The Talking Cat and Other Stories of French Canada.* Harper and Brothers, 1953.

Fisher, O., and C. Tyner. *Totem, Tipi, and Tumpline.* Dent, 1951.

Fraser, Frances. *The Bear Who Stole the Chinook.* Macmillan, 1959.

Gillham, Charles E. *Beyond the Clapping Mountains.* Macmillan, 1943.

Hooke, Hilda Mary. *Thunder in the Mountains.* Toronto, Oxford, 1958.

Macmillan, Cyrus. *Glookaps Country and Other Indian Tales.* Oxford University Press, 1955.

Martin F. *Nine Tales of Coyote.* Harper, 1951.

Fiction

Acker, Helen. *The School Train.* New York: Abelard Press, Inc. 1953.

De Angeli, Marguerite. *Petite Suzanne.* New York: Doubleday, 1937.

Bice, Clare. *Across Canada, Stories of Canadian Children.* New York: Macmillan, 1949.

———. *The Great Island.* Toronto: Macmillan, 1954.

Bingley, Barbara. *The Story of Pit'Be and His Friend Mouffette.* Abelard Press, 1962.

Brill, Ethel C. *Madeleine Takes Command.* New York: McGraw-Hill Book Co., 1946.
Burnford, Sheila. *Incredible Journey.* Little, 1961.
Carlson, Natalie Savage. *Letter in the Tree.* New York: Harper and Row, 1964.
Clipperfield, Joseph E. *Baru, Dog of the O'Molley.* McKay, 1966.
Craig, John. *The Long Return.* Bobba, 1959.
Crisp, W. G. *Oop-pik, The Story of an Eskimo Boy.* Dent, 1952.
Dickson, Helen. *Up Canada Way.* Boston: D. C. Heath and Co., 1942.
Dwight, Allan. *Drums in the Forest.* Toronto: Macmillan, 1936.
Gaither, Frances. *Painted Arrow.* Toronto: Macmillan, 1931.
Hayes, John F. *Land Divided.* Toronto: Copp Clark, 1951.
Henderson, Lewis M. *Amik, The Life Story of a Beaver.* Morrow, 1948.
Holling, H. C. *Paddle-to-the-Sea.* Houghton Mifflin, 1943.
Jones, Adrienne. *Wild Voyageur.* Little, Brown, 1966.
Lathrop, West. *Northern Trail Adventure.* New York: Random House, 1944.
Leitch, Adelaide. *The Great Canoe.* Toronto: Macmillan, 1962.
Little, Jean. *Mine for Keeps.* Boston: Little, Brown & Co., 1962.
Longstreth, T. Moris. *The Calgary Challengers.* Macmillan, 1962.
McClelland, Hugh. *The Magic Lasso.* Macmillan, 1963.
McCracken, Harold. *Pirate of the North.* J. B. Lippincott, 1953.
_____. *The Biggest Bear on Earth.* Lippincott, 1943.
_____. *Sentinel of the Snow Peaks.* J. B. Lippincott, 1945.
Malkus, Alida. *Outpost of Peril.* New York: Day, 1961.
Meader, Stephen. *River of the Wolves.* New York: Harcourt, 1948.
Montgomery, L. M. *Anne of Green Gables,* Page, 1908.
Murphy, Robert William. *Wild Geese Calling.* Dutton, 1966.
Nye, Harriet K. *Uncertain April.* New York: Dodd Mead, 1958.
O'Brien, Jack. *Return of Silver Chief.* Holt, Rinehart & Winston, 1962.
_____. *Silver Chief, Dog of the North.* Winston, 1941.
Phillips, Ethel. *Gay Madelon.* Houghton Mifflin. Boston: Houghton, 1931.
Pinkerton, Katherine. *Adventure North.* Harcourt, Brace & World, Inc., 1940.
_____. *Farther North.* New York: Harcourt, Brace, 1944.
Reynold, G. and D. Reynold. *Brother Scouts.* New York: Thomas Nelson, 1952.
Riley, Louise. *Train for Tiger Lily.* Viking Press and Macmillan, 1954.
Sauer, Julia L. *Fog Magic.* Viking Press, 1943.
Swayze, Beulah Garland. *Father Gabriel's Cloak.* Macmillan, 1962.
Van Stockum, Hilda. *Canadian Summer.* Viking Press, 1948.
Ward, Lynd. *Nic of the Woods.* Houghton Mifflin, 1965.
Wood, Kerry. *The Boy and the Buffalo.* Macmillan, 1963.
Wuorio, Eve-Liz. *The Canadian Twins.* London: Jonathan Cape, 1956.
_____. *Return of the Vikings.* Hale, E. M., 1964.

Magazines

The Beaver. Winnipeg, Canada: Hudson's Bay Co.
Canadian Audubon. Toronto, Canada: Canadian Audubon Society.

MOTION PICTURES AND FILMSTRIPS

The following motion pictures and filmstrips can be obtained from various sources. Local film guides should be consulted for those available in the community.

Motion Pictures

1.	The Atlantic Region East coast region of Canada; life, industry of its people.	NFBC	1957	22 min. sd., b&w
2.	Avalon Holiday Visits picturesque places of Blow Me Down, Bald Head, Break-Heart Point and Heart's Desire, A rugged country of the Avalon Peninsula of Newfoundland.			13 min. sd. color Canadian Travel Film Library
3.	Canada Canada's natural resources, industrial development, water power	NF	1953	17 min. sd., b&w
4.	Canada's History: Colony to Commonwealth	CORF	1962	13 min. sd., color
5.	Colonial Family of New France	CORF	1958	13 min. sd., color
6.	Family Tree History 1763-1791. Animated.	NFBC	1949	15 min. sd., color
7.	Gold Modern gold mining as practiced in the Yukon is vividly contrasted with primitive methods of the early gold seekers.			11 min. sd., color McGraw-Hill
8.	The Great Lakes–St. Lawrence Lowlands	NFBC	1957	23 min. sd., b&w
9.	The Great Plains Canada's prairie region: occupations of farmers, townsmen throughout the year; development from settlement days to recent oil industry	NFBC	1957	24 min. sd., color
10.	Industrial Canada Canada's change over the past fifty years from agricultural country to major industrial nation.	CORF	1958	16 min. sd., b&w
11.	Land of the Maple Leaf Canada's cities, countryside, wild life.	TFC	1939	10 min. sd., b&w
12.	Maritime Provinces of Canada	Erpi	1943	11 min. sd., b&w
13.	Ottawa: Canada Capital Pictures Ottowa in the full bloom of tuliptime. Explores beauty spots in and around the city and shows how it has capitalized on its natural endowments.			14 min. sd., color Canadian Travel Film Library
14.	Pacific Canada	Erpi	1943	11 min. sd., b&w
15.	Peoples of Canada How different racial groups contribute to national character of Canada. Similarity of Canada's and United States' development.	IFB	1947	21 min. sd., b&w
16.	Physical Regions of Canada Relation of each region to the occupations of its inhabitants	NFBC	1957	23 min. sd., b&w

17.	Ti-Jean Goes Lumbering	CNFB	1953	16 min. sd., color
18.	Winter in Canada Winter activities of boys in a Quebec Laurentian town and the Alberta foothills.	NFBC	1953	18 min. sd. b&w

Filmstrips

1. Attractions for Visitors — E-GH

2. Canada: A Nation Grows — N. Y. Times Current Affairs Filmstrip 55 fr.

3. Canada: Regions and Resources — SVE   49 frames
   Four geographical regions of Canada, provinces, leading cities in each region. Shows natural resources, industries, people. Questions at the end of each filmstrip test comprehension.

4. Canada's North — A Series — Encyclopedia Britannica
   Examines the geography of Canada's North, the culture and art forms of its people and the developments that are changing both.

The Artic Islands	38 fr. color
Canada's North — Introduction	46 fr. color
The Caribou Eskimo	38 fr. color
Eskimo Prints	43 fr. color
Eskimo Sculpture	50 fr. color
The Mackenzie River	42 fr. color
The Modern Eskimo	42 fr. color
The Yukon	45 fr. color

5. Canadian Regional Geography (set one) — McGraw Hill Book Co. 6 strips 42 frames each.
   Photographs and interpretive maps present an overall geography of Canada.

6. Canadian Regional Geography (set two) — McGraw Hill Book Co. 6 strips 42 frames each.
   Topography, climate, economy, human and natural resources, cattle ranches, railway cities, timber cities, wheat farming.

7. Canadian Regional Geography (set three) — McGraw Hill Book Co. 6 strips 42 frames each.
   Deep sea fishing, the sea, individual cities, port cities, the seaway, ships and power.

8. Discovery and Exploration of America — Popular Science Publishing Co.   46-53 fr. each
   Series of eight filmstrips describing the founders of colonies in America.

9 Eskimos of St. Lawrence Island — A Series — HANDY
   Tells how the Eskimos of St. Lawrence Island hunt and fish for food. Describes their daily life, festivals and recreational activities.

Fun and festivals with the Eskimos	40 fr. color
Hunting with the Eskimos	48 fr. color
Life in an Eskimo Village	40 fr. color

10.	Farm and City in Ontario Describes farming and industries	Encyclopedia Britannica	50 fr., color
11.	Fishermen of Nova Scotia Explains fishing industry of Nova Scotia	Encyclopedia Britannica	49 fr., color
12.	Growth of Canada Historical, economic, political influences shaping development of Canada	BOW	29 frames
13.	Historic Background	E-GH	
14.	Logging in Canadian Forests Describes lumbering in British Columbia, Ontario, Quebec	Encyclopedia Britannica	49 fr., color
15.	The Polar Bear Describes life cycle and adaptation to en- vironments	Canadian Films Board	35 fr.
16.	Rise and Fall of New France Describes work of French explorers, settlers, and rivalry for dominance	Yale University Press	40 fr., b&w
17.	The St. Lawrence Seaway Depicts the St. Lawrence Seaway and describes the history, geography and eco- nomics of the areas adjacent to the waterway	POPSCI	40 fr., color 1960.
18.	Vancouver and the Western Mountains Describes forest workers, farmers and fishermen of British Columbia	Encyclopedia Britannica	49 fr., color
19.	Villages in French Canada Explains how farmers live and work in eastern Canada.	Encyclopedia Britannica	46 gr.
20.	Water Serves Canada Fresh-water lakes and rivers of Canada — their use for commerce and recreation; how they provide sources of cheap hydroelectric power and sheltered sites for industry along the coastline.	CUMC	32 fr.
21.	Wheat Farmers in Western Canada Deals with life and work in the prairie lands of western Canada.	Encyclopedia Britannica	48 fr., color

RECORDINGS

"Call of the Seal," (Eskimo Chant) Victor 22329.
"Folk Songs of Canada," Stanley Bowmar Records.
"French-Canadian Folksongs," FW6929.
"O Canada," Victor set, 2170
"The Undefended Border" with Raymond Massey. Recording Division, N.Y. University Film Library,
3-0901 A-F.

SLIDES

Trans-Canada West (Slides) Mile Zero, Victoria, B. C.

B. C. Parliament, grain elevators, fishing in Victoria, salt encrusted pond near Kamloops.

H. E. Badik Films & Slides
39 slides
color
1964

PICTURE FILE

Canada Classroom Pictures. Hills, Theo L. and Hills, Sarah J. 1963. Information Classroom Picture Publishers, Inc.   U. S. A.

Upper Grade Unit
PROGRESS IN UNDERSTANDING EACH OTHER

UNIT ORGANIZATION

Attitudes and Values to be Fostered

Skills to be Developed

Initiating Activities

I. Introduction and Overview
   Generalizations
   Understandings
   Activities
   Vocabulary
   Questions

II. Kinds of Problems — Physical
   (the five parts under each section are identical)

III. Kinds of Problems — Environmental

IV. Who Helps and How?

V. Institutions
VI. Conclusions

Culminating Activities

Evaluation

Examples of Service Projects in Various Areas of Social Problems

Reference List of Some Persons Who Relate to the Unit

Bibliography for Children

Filmstrips, Pictures, Plays, Records

Bibliography for Teachers

ATTITUDES AND VALUES TO BE FOSTERED*

Concern for others is an important part of American life.

Each person can contribute in some way to the betterment of social conditions.

Social reform is worthwhile, since it leads to the lessening of human suffering.

Improving conditions for one group of people or kind of disability will develop sensitivity to other types of problems needing attention.

*Objectives are incorporated with attitudes, values, and understandings.

Service to others provides satisfaction to the individual performing the service.

Progress in the amelioration of social problems is dependent upon dissatisfaction and desire to effect change.

Social reform aids in promoting the dignity of man by striving to allow each individual to develop to his fullest potential.

A deep feeling, almost an empathy, for others is basic in a society such as we now live in.

Appropriate materials for each topic may be selected from those suggested.

SKILLS TO BE DEVELOPED

1. Gathering information from many sources
   card catalog
   social studies books
   fiction
   biographies
   encyclopedias
   pamphlets
   literature from organizations
   pictures
   charts
   tapes
   films
   filmstrips
   magazines
   newspapers
   people

2. Listening

   keeping attention on the speaker
   thinking about what is said
   relating what is heard to what one already knows
   following directions
   making judgments about what is relevant
   deciding what is most important to remember
   deciding when to take notes
   preparing to make intelligent criticism

3. Speaking

   contributing to discussions
   giving oral reports
   asking pertinent questions
   giving clear directions
   serving as a committee or discussion leader
   giving concise summaries

4. Vocabulary

   special words appropriate to this area of study
   new meanings of already-familiar words
   words helpful in interpreting reading

5. Organizing and presenting information

   note taking
   outlining
   report writing
   relevance of pictorial material
   care to use sequential development
   use of aids such as graphs and charts
   listing of sources
   fitting a report into a class series of reports on a subject

6. Critical thinking

   assessing worth of contribution
       type or background of contributor
       date of material
       limit of its applicability
   inference making
   extrapolation
   assessment of emotional involvement in aspects of subject
   making of judgments
   relating and reassessing of values

7. Evaluation

   assessment of the learning from the unit which is related more specifically to the
       forming of values than to the acquisition of facts
   development of the ability to separate emotional, attitudinal, and factual components
       of material.

INITIATING ACTIVITIES

1. Read a story to the class about handicapped children.

2. Plan the unit at a time when a united drive is being carried on in the school.

3. Read *Shutterbug* by Lou Shumsky.

4. Have children read biographies of people who were engaged in helping others and improving social conditions.

5. Read *Pablo Casals; Cellist for Freedom* by Aylesa Foresee.

6. Ask children to bring in newspaper reports of happenings which relate to social problems.

7. Read *Great Women Teachers.* by Alice Fleming.

8. Show the UNICEF filmstrip, *Children of the Cities.*

9. Show *Let there Be Bread* from the United Nations.

10. Have the children write a short piece on some handicapped person. Several of the best ones may be read to the class.

11. Read *Long Way Up; The Story of Jill Kinmont* by Evans Valens.

I. INTRODUCTION AND OVERVIEW

Generalizations relating to history, political science, sociology, anthropology, and psychology:

1. Man's struggle for freedom and human dignity has occupied a relatively brief period of time as compared to the total span of man's existence.
2. Change has been a universal condition of human society. The tempo of change has increased markedly in the recent past.
3. Brotherhood is one of man's worthiest and earliest experiences.
4. People have struggled through the ages to achieve a better life.
5. A democratic society invites its members to subscribe to basic values; at the same time it presents the responsibility to protest arrangements that have outlived their usefulness, to challenge instances where society is not living up to its ideals, and to formulate improved methods of realizing the potentials of democracy.

Understandings

1. Reform indicates dissatisfaction with the status quo.

2. Reform aims at the betterment of conditions and usually is concerned with what is right, good, or desirable.

3. Desire for change may sometimes be motivated by resentment.

4. Reform is accomplished by people who are dedicated to a cause.

5. Some periods in history show more active agitation for change than others.

6. Social reform in the United States has been especially prominent in three decades: the 1840's, when the rash of activity involved almost every aspect of American life; the 1900's when "educating the public" became of primary importance; the 1930's when legislation sought to alleviate many of the ills created by the depression of the late 1920's.

7. Social reform focuses on changing the situation rather than the individual or the group.

8. Awareness of human needs is essential if each individual is to contribute his

Activities

1. Have each person make a list of the social problems that he thinks need change and improvement. Compile these individual lists into one for the entire group.

2. Show pictures on human rights to establish background (such as the picture story supplied by the National Association of Manufacturers).

3. Show filmstrips on Jane Addams.

4. Pupils may wish to keep a personal list of words encountered in the unit or they may choose to set up a class unit dictionary in which each contributes as he sees a need.

5. Youngsters may collect pamphlets and other material such as folders listing objectives of organizations and groups that have worked for social reform. These may later be presented to the Materials Center or Library as part of a permanent collection.

6. Buttons and insignia of various groups may be collected, or, if this is not feasible, perhaps drawings of some of these insignia might be made.

share to the human relations of the community.

9. Social reform is both an outgrowth and a necessary component of democracy.

Vocabulary

philanthropy

concern

humanitarianism

reform

social

agitation

dissatisfaction

insignia

democracy

7. Bring in some persons from the community who are concerned with or interested in the area of social reform and social problems. Introduce them as resource persons to be consulted as the unit progresses.

8. Have a discussion relating to sources of material and information on the unit, stressing the need for wide searching.

9. Write letters to organizations that supply free materials.

Discussion

1. Why do we need reforms at times?
2. How does one decide what needs changing?
3. What might be some ways of getting changes made?
4. Who is responsible for problems needing change?
5. When and by whom should undesirable conditions be changed?
6. What factors especially influence reform movements?

II. KINDS OF PROBLEMS – PHYSICAL

Generalization

All societies are confronted with the problem of persons who are afflicted with physical disabilities.

Understandings

1. Through the devoted efforts of interested people, the blind are able to get an education and hold jobs.
2. Concern for the deaf has resulted also in the improvement of communications for those who hear.
3. Aiding crippled persons to lead as near a normal life as possible has helped to show that handicaps can be overcome.
4. Continuing efforts in the area of mental health have brought about cures in cases that were formerly considered hopeless.

Activities

1. Invite a blind or deaf person to class to discuss these handicaps.
2. Read *Wild Horse of Santander* by Helen Griffiths.
3. Have children list ways in which they can personally help blind and deaf people.
4. Read *The Dark of the Cave* by Ervie Rydberg.
5. Read *Windows for Rosemary* by Marguerite Vance.

5. Constant, patient attention to the problems of educating the mentally retarded has shown that much can be done to improve their condition.

6. Because medicine has provided the means by which people can live longer, the problems of older people have needed more attention.

7. Increased concern for those people with relatively severe handicaps has resulted also in the amelioration of conditions for those with light or fringe disabilities.

8. Those persons with disabilities of many kinds have much to contribute to a democratic society.

9. In previous years and in less enlightened cultures those with handicaps were discarded as an unbearable burden.

10. Because mental illness was not understood, persons afflicted with this unfortunate malady were regarded as witches, as possessed of the devil, as the residing place of evil spirits, etc.

11. With the advent of increased understanding of mental illness and retardation, a new compassion has been evident throughout most of the world.

Vocabulary

handicapped

retarded

disabled

braille

mute

multiple handicaps

infirm

prosthetics

partially sighted

deaf and dumb

hearing aids

seeing eye dog

eye banks

6. Show film, *The Visually Handicapped Child*. (29 min)

7. Secure Braille books and/or talking records.

8. Make a copy of the Braille alphabet.

9. Read *The Black Symbol* by Annabel Johnson.

10. Punch out messages in Braille by using a pencil and ordinary paper. See if you can read the messages with your eyes shut.

11. Show film *The Auditorially Handicapped Child; The Deaf*.

12. Find out about the education of blind and deaf persons. Present an oral report to the class.

13. Read *About Glasses For Gladys* by Mary K. Ericsson.

14. Read *Let the Best Boat Win; The Story of American's Greatest Yacht Designer*. by Constance Buel Burnett.

15. Show film, *Land of Real Believe*.

16. Write letters to organizations which specialize in helping less fortunate persons.

17. Read *Warrior Scarlet* by Rosemary Stucliff.

18. Read *Sink it Rusty* by Matthew F. Christopher.

19. Read *Nacar, the White Deer* by Elizabeth Brown Trevino.

20. Take a trip to a place such as a neighborhood service center. Find out how it goes about improving conditions in the neighborhood by aiding those with problems.

21. Read *Helen Keller and Her Story* by Nancy Hamilton.

22. Read *Laughter in the Lonely Night* by H. C. Viscardi.

23. Show film *Why They Can't Stay Home*

24. Put on a play or do some role playing illustrating the problems faced by those with disabilities.

Some Questions for Discussion

1. In considering the various areas of reform and improvement of conditions, which do you think is the most important?

2. Which area of physical disability should be attacked first?

3. Can solutions be found for the problems of physically impaired persons? How?

4. Can physical disabilities be prevented? How?

5. What persons or groups address themselves to these problems?

6. Should persons with handicaps be cared for in their own homes or in institutions? Give reasons for your answer.

7. Why have the mentally ill and mentally retarded been regarded as witches and possessors of evil spirits?

8. Why have some societies found it necessary to ignore those not well and strong?

25. Read *Parton's Island* by Paul Darcy Bales.

26. Visit a school or schoolroom which cares for handicapped children only.

27. Bring pictures of persons who have overcome handicaps.

28. Play tape, *Heroes For Our Time.*

29. Read *I Have A Dream* by Emma Gelders Sterne.

30. Write or present orally reports on biographies of handicapped persons with special emphasis on how others helped them to overcome difficulties.

31. Read *Breakthrough to the Big League* by Jackie Robinson.

32. Read *Pioneers and Patriots; the Lives of Six Negroes of the Revolutionary Era* by Lavinia Dobler.

33. Have a discussion on Seeing Eye Dogs and the training which is given the blind in Morristown, N.J.

34. Read *A Weed is a Flower: The Life of George Washington Carver.* by Aliki.

35. Read *David, the Story of Ben Gurion* by Maurice Edelman.

36. Discuss eye banks and their possibilities for restoring or giving sight to blind persons.

37. Read *Odyssey of Courage; the Story of Alvar Nunez Cabeza de Vaca* by Maia Wojciechowska.

38. Read *The Triumph of the Seeing Eye* by Peter Putnam.

39. Have someone demonstrate hearing aids and discuss their potentialities.

III. KINDS OF PROBLEMS — ENVIRONMENTAL

Generalization

The environment in which a person lives and his opportunities for personal growth have profound effects upon the development of every individual. When these are limited by cultural poverty or repressive action, society is as much a loser as the individual.

Understandings

1. The poor are sometimes responsible for their condition because of not trying. At other times their condition is due to misfortune and illness.

2. Many attempts have been made and are continuing to be made to help the poor to help themselves and to change their conditions.

3. Sometimes people need assistance because of disasters over which they have no control. Reform movements then concentrate on controlling these conditions when possible, or providing emergency help when natural disasters can't be controlled.

4. Reform has often focused on migrant problems because the mobility of the people does not allow them to alleviate their poor living and educational conditions.

5. Unemployment and consequent suffering is often due to technological causes, thus retraining is necessary. Often this is beyond the ability of the individual.

Questions

1. Can poverty be prevented?

2. Why do some people have so much less than others?

3. In tornadoes and floods should reform be concerned with prevention or with providing aid? Why?

4. Why do we need to be concerned with those who are unemployed if there are jobs available which are not filled?

5. Why are people migrant workers when living and educational conditions are not desirable for them?

6. How can we help young persons to stay out of crime and delinquency?

Activities

1. Interview children who have been or are migrants. Present their reactions to the class.

2. Read *That Bad Carlos* by Mina Lewiton.

3. Give oral book reports on fiction books about migrant children.

4. Read *Anyplace But Here* by Arna Bontemps.

5. Find out if your state has a program for migrant children.

6. Put on a play such as *The Bean Pickers* or *Change of Heart* (both by Lois Lenski and available from the National Council of Churches).

7. Read *White Harvest* by Lela Waltrip and Rufus Waltrip.

8. Try to find cartoons which apply to this area (current magazines and newspapers or books showing cartoons). Explain their value and relationship to social reform.

9. Show film *Desk For Billie* from National Educational Association.

10. Let members of the class draw cartoons illustrating some phase of social reform.

11. Show film *Home is a Long Road* from University of Wisconsin.

12. Design posters to involve people in helping others who have suffered from a tornado, flood, or fire.

13. Show film *Fate of a Child* from United Nations.

14. Find out about a community that has suffered from a disaster and report on the various kinds of help that was available.

15. Make a mural or series of pictures to illustrate how a community can be devasted by a tornado or flood and then gradually be rebuilt.

Vocabulary

delinquency

disaster

juvenile

migrant

indigent

probation

16. Visit your state employment service to find how they help people.

17. Ask your juvenile court officer to talk to the class about problems in this area.

18. Follow up the talk above by listing on a chart ways to use one's time constructively to avoid delinquency problems.

IV. WHO HELPS AND HOW?

Generalization

Interdependence has been a constant and important factor in human relationships everywhere.

Understandings

1. Reform begins with the dissatisfactions of individuals but is carried out with the cooperation of many individuals.

2. Although the government is involved in many areas of helping distressed people, it does not do the job alone.

3. Private business has been responsible for many contributions toward the improvement of the conditions of human beings.

4. Fund raising has tended recently to be consolidated into fewer but combined appeals.

5. Many organizations such as UNICEF operate on a world-wide basis.

6. Social reform uses many methods in carrying out its objectives including campaigns to educate the public, making social surveys, conducting congressional investigations, and passing regulatory legislation.

7. Foundations supported by private funds supply many useful services to persons needing aid.

Some Questions

1. How can we get all people involved in the betterment of social conditions? Is this desirable?

Activities

1. Assign topics such as:
   American Red Cross
   UNICEF
   National Foundation
   American Cancer Society
   American Heart Association
   National Society for Crippled Children
   National Tuberculosis Association
   National Association for Mental Health
   Arthritis and Rheumatism Foundation
   U.S. Public Health Service
   Have a round-table or panel discussion.

2. Read one of the UNICEF books on children of other nations and report to the class what is being done for children in some other country.

3. Read *The Pool of Knowledge; How the United Nations Share Their Skills* by Katherine Binney Shippen.

4. Display UNICEF Christmas cards or pictures and discuss UNICEF purposes in making these available.

5. Give a report on the UNICEF campaign at Halloween.

6. Find out how money is used from the Community Chest in your city. Make graphs to show its distribution.

2. Why do people create foundations whose purpose is philanthropic?

3. Is it the business of the government to provide for all social needs?

4. Why is it valuable for each of us to be involved in programs to help others?

5. Why do we have such a large number of national associations to deal with social problems?

6. Why is social reform carried on by so many different agencies and organizations?

Vocabulary

legislation

charity

distress

investigation

foundation

survey

7. Make a chart on various government agencies or services to individuals or groups suffering from poverty, disabilities of age, illness, physical handicaps, mental illness, and disasters such as floods and fires. Add to this chart as new services are discovered through reading.

8. Have each child list the name of the organization which he feels has contributed most to improving the conditions of people, and then give three reasons for his choice. Compile the list of organizations and discuss reasons. An outline might be useful.

9. Play tape, *CARE is there* from Kent State University.

10. Read *It's Time For Brotherhood.* by E. H. Sechrist.

11. Read *Getting to Know UNESCO* by Ella Griffin.

12. Show filmstrip on UNICEF.

13. Show filmstrip and play record on Clara Barton or other persons working with organizations.

14. Make a map showing the countries receiving UNICEF aid. (See the *Hi Neighbor* book).

15. Show film, *A Grain of Sand* from UNICEF.

16. Show film, *Children of the Sun* from UNICEF.

17. Make a time line to indicate when many of the helping organizations were begun and which ones are still operating.

18. Play tape, *Jane Hoey's — I Was There* from Kent State University.

19. Find out about the Russell Sage Foundation and its work in the area of social reform.

V. INSTITUTIONS

Generalization

Modern societies tend to provide specialized institutions for the care of persons whose behavior is considered deviant according to that society's standards.

Understandings

1. Large public buildings were erected to care for the specific needs of persons with disabilities.

2. The institutions which were created to give maximum service by gathering persons with like disabilities in one place became so large, in many cases, as to make themselves objects of reform.

3. Institutions have always been a target for reform inasmuch as their functions are at least quasi-public.

4. Institutions have further provided material for reformers by being slow to respond to the forces of change.

5. Institutions belong to the public, hence are considered as a proper sphere for criticism and change.

Vocabulary

institution

penitentiary

atypical

asylum

settlement house

detention

Questions

1. What services do schools commonly have?

2. Are special schools better for handicapped persons?

3. Why have jails and other places such as mental hospitals been a target for reformers?

4. Should children be placed in orphanages?

5. What is a more modern way of caring for children who do not have parents?

Activities

1. Discussion:
   How do institutions such as schools, hospitals, children's homes, jails, homes for the aged, etc. serve the people?
   Work in teams, each team be responsible for listing the services of one type of institution.

2. Play tape *The Story of Bill.*

3. Play tape *Delinquency and Adjustment.*

4. Choose two institutions from the list above. Tell how they are alike and how they are different.

5. Play tape *Make Way for Youth.*

6. Play tape *A Criminal is Born.*

7. Duplicate a short article presenting two or three views on the values of institutions for segregating persons who are atypical. Have children write a comment on their view of the problem.

8. Play tape *Easy Life.*

9. Make a list of the institutions in your neighborhood that are concerned with caring for less fortunate members of society.

10. Read *Thunder Road* by William Campbell Gault.

11. See if you can discover how churches share in the problem of helping unfortunate persons.

12. Read *Ellen and the Gang.* by Frieda Friedman.

13. Show film *Boy With a Knife.*

14. Make a model community (using blocks or other easy construction materials) showing what institutions are

6. Should the church share in alleviating social ills? How do its services fit in with those of other agencies?

necessary and helpful toward taking care of social needs and problems.

15. Ericsson, Mary K. *About Glasses For Gladys.* Melmont, 1962.

VI. CONCLUSIONS

Generalizations

1. National emergencies and conditions of social disruption provide special incentives to invent new techniques and to strike out boldly for solutions to practical and social problems.

2. A society must continuously evaluate and modify its culture in order to adjust to changing conditions; failure to do so leads to social disorganization or the absorption or exploitation of the society by more agressive and rapidly developing cultures.

Understandings

1. History has demonstrated that human beings do shape and influence the direction of social change through social reform.

2. There are no "cures" for social problems; social reform merely alleviates some of the undesirable situations.

3. Social problems in an age of scarcity tend to be associated with physical pain and survival; in an age of abundance they involve stresses and strains related to idleness, boredom, and tensions associated with personal relationships.

4. Awareness has been developing that people all over the world have similar problems; that sometimes they welcome help in solving them; that America has a world role to fulfill.

5. Our ways of regarding social problems have changed drastically in the last hundred years or so. More and better solutions are possible because of enlightened interest in the whole area of human relations.

Questions

1. Is social reform a good or bad thing?

2. What has social reform accomplished in the United States?

Activities

1. Bring in clippings from newspapers relating to the area of social reform. Classify these under specific headings and display them on a bulletin board.

2. Divide the class into groups and assign a magazine or magazines to each group to assess for interest in or attention to the area of social reform.

3. Have a debate on the merits of government vs. private administration of health insurance or aid to handicapped or other topic in which the class is interested.

4. Find some poetry relating to the unit and display on bulletin board or read to class.

5. Divide into groups. Let each group choose a social problem or area that it feels needs attention. Let the group tell how it would solve the problem.

6. Read to find out more about the Peace Corps. Compare this example of social reform on an international scale with those within the United States.

7. Discuss the trend toward involvement with social problems on an international scale. (Peace Corps, UNICEF, UNESCO, WHO)

3. Can social reform help eliminate war?

4. Does social reform have any connection with racial problems?

5. Does social reform have a connection with strikes and labor relations?

8. Review perceptual development by:
   1. listing areas of concern for social reform (blind, migrants, mentally retarded), etc.
   2. noting the characteristics that (a) distinguish one above problem from another; (b) the elements that are similar.
   3. relating these separate areas to a meaningful whole as physical problems versus environmental; in a larger sense problems that ameliorate conditions (the physical and environmental) as opposed to those reform movements which seek to acquire new rights: voting for women or for more people, improved conditions for labor, etc.

9. Report to the class current television or radio programs relating to the area of social reform. (Children are afforded an opportunity to evaluate points of view, reasons behind presentation, peripheral areas and to make inferences and judgments relating these presentations to pamphlets, books, etc.)

10. Again make a list of social problems. Compare with original list.

CULMINATING ACTIVITIES

1. Make a mural depicting the scope of social reform in the United States.
2. Give a skit for another room indicating the accomplishments of social reform.
3. Form a committee (perhaps three or four altogether in the room). Select a social problem. Outline how you would "solve" it (apply social reform to it) (Learner should not remain on a committee whose "problem" he does not regard as a social problem area).
   1. "Problem" probably should be identified as an issue in which some aspect is disturbing or attention-attracting.
   2. Group may then make a tentative list of facts relating to the problem, as these are seen at the moment.
   3. Further reading may be done, particularly with regard to facts on which there was disagreement.
   4. Several courses of action may be listed with the possible or probable consequences of each.
   5. A solution may be proposed which appears to be the most desirable solution to the problem.

6. Conditions may be noted under which other solutions would be more feasible.
7. Children will need to evaluate the procedure noting the strengths and weaknesses.
8. If possible the knowledge gained or solution offered should be tested in an actual situation; for example, actually helping to provide materials for a handicapped child.

4. Children may wish to gather all of the material from the unit and set up a display in the hall for others to see or set up a display in the room and invite other rooms to visit.
5. Devise a community setup which will minimize the need for social reform. Then cite situations which might conceivably occur in the future to upset the pattern and once again make social reform necessary.

EVALUATION

1. Save the lists of social problems compiled at the beginning of the unit to compare with those made at the end of the unit. Have children indicate changes in perceptions of problems.
2. Make a list of persons (encountered in this unit) who were important in bringing about changes in social conditions or improvement in some aspect of life.
3. Have children set up evaluation procedures at the start of the unit. Then in the concluding phase, they may evaluate their procedures as well as the unit.
4. Have a discussion session and answer such questions as:

   Why have a unit like this one?
   What was good about the way it was carried out?
   What would you change if the unit was repeated?
   Which kinds of resources and information were most valuable to you?

5. Make a checklist showing points on which teacher would like to evaluate. List these at the left. Then check each specific point at the beginning, in the middle, and at the end of the unit.
6. Have children write a note to parents listing the important things they have learned in the unit, or have a class discussion first and head the written note, *Things We Have Learned in This Unit*.

EXAMPLES OF SERVICE PROJECTS IN VARIOUS AREAS

Blind or Visually Handicapped

Transcribing into Braille
Safety glasses for school shops
School vision — testing machines
Eye bank
Guide dogs for the blind
Nursery school for the blind
Purchase of Braille books
Traveling eye health unit
Recording for the blind
Purchase of white canes for the blind

Deaf and Hard of Hearing

Audiometer to test hearing
Language master equipment
Establishment of a speech and hearing center
A desk amplifier for the classroom
Starting a hearing-testing program
Preparation of scrapbooks and pictures
Securing funds for a speech therapist
Nursery school for hard of hearing and deaf

Juvenile Delinquency

Aid for social workers in Juvenile Division
Development of codes of conduct
A youth forum in television
Providing of aid for first offenders
Handicraft supplies for juvenile centers
Services to parents of delinquent children
Establishment of help-others program for delinquents

Mental Health

Establishment of mental health center
Recreation program for mental health patients
Mental health displays and exhibits
Foster homes for mentally ill

Mental Retardation

Development of recreation center for mentally retarded
Organization of opportunity workshop
Scout troop for mentally retarded
Provision of library material and audio-visual aids
Special recreation programs for mentally retarded
Scholarships for persons who wish to be trained to work in this area

Social Welfare

Clothes closet for the needy (where they can secure free garments)
Publicity on welfare programs
Recognition of foster parents
Service center for migrants
Help to travelers
Volunteer services in child welfare work
Recruitment of adoptive parents

REFERENCE LIST OF SOME PERSONS WHO RELATE TO THE UNIT

People with Handicaps

Ludwig Beethoven
Sarah Bernhardt
Laura Bridgeman

Those Involved in Social Reform

Jane Addams
Clara Barton
Clifford Beers

Lord Byron	Alexander Bell
Glen Cunningham	Louis Braille
Ben Hogan	Dorothea Dix
Helen Keller	Thomas Gallaudet
John Milton	Samuel Howe
Franklin Roosevelt	Florence Nightingale
Alec Templeton	Benjamin Rush
	Edouard Seguin
	Anne Sullivan
	Booker Washington

BIBLIOGRAPHY FOR CHILDREN*

Blind

*Bowden, Nina. *The Witch's Daughter.* Lippincott, 1966.
*Canty, Mary. *The Green Gate.* McKay, 1965.
Carter, Gordon. *Willing Walkers: The Story of Dogs for the Blind.* Abelard-Schuman, 1965.
*Chipperfield, Joseph. *A Dog to Trust.* McKay, 1963.
Ericsson, Mary K. *About Glasses For Gladys.* Melmont, 1962.
*Garfield, James. *Follow My Leader.* Viking Press. 1957.
Griffiths, Helen. *Wild Horse of Santander.* Doubleday, 1966.
Johnson, Annabel. *The Black Symbol.* Harper, 1959.
Putnam, Peter. *The Triumph of The Seeing Eye.* Harper, 1963.
*Rydburg, Ervie. *The Dark of the Cave.* McKay, 1965.
*Vance, Marguerite. *Windows for Rosemary.* Dutton, 1956.
*Vinson, Kathryn. *Run with the Ring.* Harcourt, Brace and World, 1965.

Deaf

*Farley, Carol. *Mystery of the Fog Man.* Watts, 1966.
*Robinson, Vermica. *David in Silence.* Lippincott, 1965.
*Woods, Hubert C. *Child of the Arctic.* Follett, 1962.

Juvenile Delinquency

*Alcock, Gudrun. *Run, Westy, Run.* Lathrop, Lee & Shepard, 1966.
*Armer, Alberta. *Troublemaker.* World, 1966.
*Friedman, Frieda. *Ellen and the Gang.* Morrow, 1963.
_____. *Dot for Short.* Morrow, 1947.
*Gault, William Campbell. *Thunder Road.* Dutton, 1952.
*Winterfield, Henry. *Trouble at Timpetill.* Harcourt, Brace, & World, 1965.

Mentally Handicapped

*Bales, Paul Darcy. *Parton's Island.* Macmillan, 1958.
*Faber, Nancy W. *Cathy's Secret Kingdom.* Lippincott, 1963.
*Friis, Babbis. *Don't Take Teddy.* Scribner, 1967.

*Starred books are fiction.

Migrants

Bontemps, Arna. *Anyplace But Here.* American Century, 1966.
*Gates, Doris. *Blue Willow.* Viking Press, 1940.
*Lenski, Lois. *Judy's Journey.* Lippincott, 1947.
*Lewiton, Mina. *That Bad Carlos.* Harper, 1964.
*Shotwell, Louisa. *Roosevelt Grady.* McKay, 1965.
*Snyder, Zelpha. *Velvet Room.* Athaneum, 1965.
*Waltrip, Lela and Waltrip, Rufus. *White Harvest.* Longmans, 1960.

Physically Handicapped

*Burnett, Francis. *The Secret Garden.* Lippincott, 1938.
*Caudill, Rebecca. *A Certain Small Shepherd.* Holt, Rinehart, & Winston, 1965.
*Christopher, Mathhew F. *Sink It Rusty.* Little, 1963.
*De Angeli, Marguerite. *The Door in the Wall.* Doubleday, 1949.
*Essex, Raymond. *Into the Forest.* Coward-McCann, 1963.
*Faber,Nancy W. *Cathy at the Crossroads.* Lippincott, 1962.
*Friis, Babbis. *Kristy's Courage.* Harcourt, Brace, & World, 1965.
*Hodges, Cyril Walter, *The Namesake.* Coward McCann, 1964.
*Little, Jean. *Mine for Keeps.* Little, Brown, 1962.
*Reynolds, Marjorie. *A Horse Called Mystery.* Harper & Row, 1964.
*Shumsky, Lou. *Shutterbug.* Funk 1963.
*Sutcliff, Rosemary. *Warrior Scarlet.* Wallk, 1958.
*Trevino, Elizabeth Brown. *Nacar, the White Deer.* Farrar, 1963.
Viscardi, H. *Laughter in the Lonely Night.* Hill and Wang, 1961.
*Weik, Mary Hays. *The Jazz Man.* Athaneum, 1966.

Red Cross

Epstein, Beryl. *The Story of the International Red Cross.* Nelson, 1963.
Sechrist, E. H. *It's Time for Brotherhood.* MaCrae Smith, 1962.

United Nations – Children's Fund

Breetveld, Jim. *Getting to Know United Nations Crusaders.* Coward-McCann, 1961.
CARE is There. A-V Center, Kent State University, Kent, Ohio. (Tapes for Teaching, 14 min.).
Griggin, Ella. *Getting to Know UNESCO.* Lothrop, 1961.
Shippen, Katherine Binney. *The Pool of Knowledge; How the United Nations Share Their Skills.* Harper,1965.
Shotwell, Louisa. *Beyond the Sugar Cane Field.* World, 1964.
Speiser, Jean *UNICEF and the World.* Day, 1965.
*Summerfelt, Aimee. *The Road to Agra.* Criterion Books, 1961.
UNICEF, *Hi Neighbor.* Hastings, House.
   (There are 8 of these covering various countries of the world and published at different times since 1960.)

Biography

Jane Addams: Pioneer of Hull House by Helen Stone Peterson. Garrard, 1965.
Clara Barton, Founder of the American Red Cross by Helen D. Boyleston. Random House, 1955.
Clara Barton: Soldier of Mercy by Mary Catherine Rose. Garrard, 1960.
Out of Silence Into Sound (Life of *Alexander G. Bell*) by Roger Burlinggame. Macmillan, 1964.
Alexander Graham Bell: Man of Sound by Elizabeth Rider Montgomery. Garrard, 1963.
Seeing Fingers, the Story of *Louis Braille* by Etta De Gering. McKay, 1962.
Child of the Silent Night (Story of *Laura Bridgman)* by Edith Fisher Hunter. Houghton-Mifflin, 1963.

*Starred books are fiction.

Let the Best Boat Win; the Story of America's Greatest Yacht Designer by Constance Buel Burnett. Houghton, Mifflin, 1957.

A Weed is a Flower; the life of *George Washington Carver.* by Aliki. Prentice-Hall, 1965.

Pablo Casals; Cellist for Freedom. by Aylesa Forsee. Crowell, 1965.

Down from the West: The Story of *Genevieve Caulfield* by Margaret Ron. Hawthorne, 1964

Pioneers and Patriots; the lives of Six Negroes of the Revolutionary Era by Lavinia Dobler. Doubleday, 1965.

Gallaudet: A Friend of the Deaf by Etta De Gering. McKay, 1964.

David; the Story of *Ben Gurion* by Maurice Edelman. Putnam, 1965.

A Light in the Dark: the Life of *Samuel Gridley Howe* by Milton Meltzer. Crowell, 1964.

Helen Keller: Toward the Light by Stewart and Polly Anne Graff. Garrard, 1965.

The *Helen Keller* Story by Catherine Peare. Crowell, 1959.

The Long Way Up; the Story of *Jill Kinmont* by Evans Valens. Harper, 1966.

The Silent Storm by Marion Brown and Ruth Crone. Abingdom, 1963. (Helen Keller's teacher *Anne Macy* (Sullivan)

Florence Nightingale; War Nurse by Anne Culver. Garrard, 1961.

Breakthrough to the Big League by Jackie Robinson. Harper. 1965.

Franklin D. Roosevelt: Four Times President by Wyatt Blassingame. Garrard, 1966.

Odyssey of Courage; the Story of *Alvar Nuney Cabeza de Vaca* by Maia Wojciechowska. Atheneum, 1965.

Great Women Teachers by Alice Fleming. Lippincott, 1965.

I Have a Dream by Emma Gelders Sterne. Knopf, 1965.

Booker T. Washington: Leader of His People by Lillie Patterson. Garrard, 1962.

Booklets

Kenworthy, Leonard. *Speaks Series* (biographical booklets; 18 for $1.00) (includes Jane Addams, Albert Schweitzer and other persons active in the social reform area) City College, New York.

Filmstrips

Jane Addams. Jim Handy.
Clara Barton. Eyegate.
Alexander G. Bell. Jim Handy.
UNICEF and the Children of the Cities; Faces and Places in UNICEF'S World (1b — w, 1c)

Pictures

Flight for Freedom National Association of Manufacturers.

Plays

The Bean Pickers by Lois Lenski from the National Council of Churches.
Change of Heart by Lois Lenski from the National Council of Churches.

Records

Clara Barton, Founder of the American Red Cross. Phono-disc ERL 12, by Helen D. Boyleston.
Delinquency and Adjustment.
Heroes for Our Time.
Jane Hoey's — I Was There. A-V Center, Kent State University, Kent, Ohio. (Tapes for Teaching. 40 min)
The Story of Bill.

Films

A Criminal Is Born.
A Grain of Sand. UNICEF.
Boy With a Knife.

Children of the Sun. UNICEF.
Desk For Billie. National Educational Association.
Easy Life.
Fate of a Child. United Nations.
Helen Keller In Her Story. Nancy Hamilton.
Home is a Long Road. University of Wisconsin
Land of Real Believe 16mm – 13 min.
Let There Be Bread. United Nations.
Make Way For Youth.
Mentally Handicapped Children; Why They Can't Stay Home.
The Auditorially Handicapped Child: The Deaf.
The Visually Handicapped Child: The Blind.

BIBLIOGRAPHY FOR TEACHER

Books

Allen, Steve. *Ground is our Table.* Doubleday 1966.
Bremner, Robert. *American Philanthropy.* University of Chicago Press, 1960.
Carter, Richard. *The Gentle Legions.* Doubleday & Co., Inc. 1961.
Crosby, Muriel. *Adventures in Human Relations.* Follett, 1965.
_____. ed. *Reading Ladders for Human Relations.* American Council on Education, 1963.
DeGrazia, Alred. *Grass Roots Private Welfare.* N. Y. University Press, 1957.
Filler, Louis. *American Social Reform.* Philosophical Library, 1963.
French, Edward L. *Child in the Shadows.* Lippincott, 1960.
Hickerson, Nathaniel. *Education for Alienation.* Prentice-Hall, 1966.
Horton, Paul B. and Leslie, Gerald R. *The Sociology of Social Problems.* Appleton-Century-Crofts, 1965.
Laubach, Frank C. *The World is Learning Compassion.* Fleming H. Revell Co., 1958.
Lowe, Jeanne R. *Cities in a Race with Time.* Random House, 1967.
McKown, Robin. *Pioneers in Mental Health.* Dodd, Mead & Co., 1961.
Michaelis, John. *Social Studies in Elementary Schools.* National Council for the Social Studies, 1962.
Moore, Truman. *Slaves We Rent.* Random House, 1965.
Public Affairs Committee, 381 Park Ave., New York, N.Y.
Ryan, Orletta and M. F. Greene. *Schoolchildren.* Signet, 1967.
Smith, Henry. *Sensitivity to People.* McGraw-Hill, 1966.
Spoerl, Dorothy. *Tensions Our Children Live With.* Beacon Press, 1959.
Viscardi, Henry. *...a letter to Jimmy.* Eriksson, 1962.

Pamphlets

Basic Human Values for Childhood Education. Association for Childhood Education International, 1963.
Children with Impaired Hearing, Publication No. 326, Children's Bureau, Washington, D. C.
Implications of Basic Human Values for Education. Follow up of 1963 publication, ACE, 1964.
Newton, Mary Griffin. *Books For Deaf Children.* Bell, 1962.
Our Changing World. American Education Publications, Inc., 1965.
Public Welfare. 1963.
That No Man Shall Hunger. 1960.
The Poor Among Us...Challange and Opportunity. 1964.
What Everybody Should Know About Blindness. The American Foundation for the Blind.
Who is Your Neighbor? So You Want to Help Migrants – Handbook for Volunteers. The Migrant Ministry, National Council of Churches.

Films

The U.N.'s Concern with Blindness
In This Dark World

BIBLIOGRAPHY

Bacon, Phillip, "Changing Aspects of Geography and the Elementary Curriculum," *Social Education*, XXXI:609-611, November 1967.

Ballinger, Stanley E., "Social Studies and Social Controversy," *School Review*, 71:97-111, Spring 1963.

Baumgarten-Tramer, Franziska, "Une Methode Nouvell D'Education Morale." *Enfance*, 6:152-57, (1953).

Bently, Joseph, "Creativity and Academic Achievement," *Journal of Educational Research*, 59:269-271, February 1966.

Berg, Harry D., *Evaluation in Social Studies*, Washington, National Council for the Social Studies, 1965.

Biber, Barbara, "Premature Structuring as a Deterrent to Creativity," *American Journal of Orthopsychiatry*, 29:280-290, 1959.

Blackwell, Gordon W., "Impact of New Social Patterns upon Education," *Teachers College Record, 42:396, March 1956.*

Bower, William Clayton, *Moral and Spiritual Values in Educationn;* Lexington, University of Kentucky Press, 1952.

Bradley, R. C., "Suggestions for Improving the Social Studies Curriculum at the Elementary School Level," *The Social Studies*, LIX, 63-67, February 1968.

Brubaker, Dale L., "Normative Value Judgments and Analysis," *Social Education*, XXXII:489-492, May 1968.

Bruner, Jerome, "The Act of Discovery," *Harvard Educational Review* XXXI: 21-32, Winter 1961.

Buros, Oscar K., *The Fifth Mental Measurements Yearbook*, Highland Park, N.J., Gryphon Press, 1959.

Calvin, A. D., Hoffman, F. K., and Harden, E. L., "The Effect of Intelligence and Social Atmosphere on Group Problem—Solving Behavior," *Journal of Social Psychology*, 45:61-74, 1957.

Carpenter, Helen McCracken, *Skill Development in Social Studies*, Washington, National Council for the Social Studies, 1963.

Cassirer, Ernst, *The Philosophy of Symbolic Forms:* New Haven; Yale University Press, 1953.

Corey, Fay L., *Values of Future Teachers: A Study of Attitudes Toward Contemporary Issues*, New York, Bureau of Publications, Teachers College, Columbia University, 1955.

Cluckhorn, Clyde, *Mirror for Man*, New York, McGrawHill Book Co., Inc., 1949.

Eberle, R. F., *Teaching for Creative Productive Thinking Through Subject Matter Content;* Edwardsville, Illinois; Edwardsville Community Schools, 1966.

Educators Progress Service, *Educators Guide to Free Social Studies Materials.* Randolph, Wisconsin, The Service, 1963.

Fair, Jean, and Shaftel, Fannie R., *Effective Thinking in the Social Studies.* Washington, National Council for the Social Studies, 1967.

Fenton, Edwin, *The New Social Studies,* New York; Holt, Rinehart and Winston, Inc., 1967.

Flanders, Ned A., "Teacher Influence in the Classroom," *Theory and Research in Teaching, New York, Bureau of Publications, Teachers College, Columbia University,* 1963.

Fraenkel, Jack R., "Building Anthropological Content into Elementary School Social Studies," *Social Education*, XXXII:251-253, March 1968.

Frazier, Alexander, "Lifting Our Sights in Primary Social Studies," *Social Education*, 23:7, 337-338, November, 1959.

Gibson, John S., *New Frontiers in the Social Studies,* I and II, New York, Citation Press, 1967.

Guenther, Richard, "Anxiety and Its Relation to Cognitive Processes," *Child Study Center Bulletin*, 1966.

Halek, Loretta, "Atmosphere for Creativity," *Delta Kappa Gamma Bulletin,* Vol. 31:10-14, Summer 1965.

Huelsman, Charles B., Jr., "Promoting Growth in Ability to Interpret When Reading Critically: In Grades Seven to Ten," *Promoting Growth Toward Maturity in Interpreting What Is Read* (Supplementary Educational Monographs, No. 74), Chicago, University of Chicago Press, 1951).

James, Preston E., "Geography," *The Social Studies and The Social Sciences,* American Council of Learned Societies and the National Council for the Social Studies, New York; Harcourt, Brace & World, Inc., 1962.

Jarolimek, John, "Curriculum Content and the Child in the Elementary School," *Social Education,* XXVI, No. 2:117, February, 1962.

_____. *Social Studies Education: The Elementary School.* Washington, National Council for the Social Studies, 1967.

Jones, Vernon, *Character and Citizenship Training in the Public School – An Experimental Study of Three Specific Methods,* Chicago; University of Chicago Press, 1936.

Joyce, Bruce R., *Strategies for Elementary Social Science Education,* Chicago Science Research Associates, Inc., 1965.

Klevan, Albert, "An Investigation of a Methodology for Value Clarification: Its Relationship to Consistency of Thinking, Purposefulness and Human Relations" (Unpublished Ed. D. thesis) New York University, 1958.

Lewis, Ben W., "Economics," *The Social Studies and the Social Sciences,* American Council of Learned Societies and the National Council for the Social Studies; New York: Harcourt, Brace & World, Inc., 1962.

Lowenfeld, Viktor, and Brittain, W. Lambert, *Creative and Mental Growth,* New York, Macmillan Company, 1967.

Maier, N. F. and R. A., "An Experimental Test of the Effects of Developmental vs. Free Discussions on the Quality of Group Decisions," *Journal of Applied Psychology,* 41:320-323, 1957.

Massialas, Byron, and Zevin, Jack, *Creative Encounters in the Classroom: Teaching and Learning Through Discovery,* New York, John Wiley and Sons, Inc., 1967.

McAulay, J. D., "Social Responsibility – A Modern Need of the Social Studies," *The Social Studies,* 58, 3:120, March, 1967.

_____, "Criteria for Elementary Social Studies," *Educational Leadership,* 25:651-655, April 1968.

McCutcheon, Samuel P., "A Discipline for the Social Studies," *Readings for Social Studies in Elementary Education,* New York, The Macmillan Company, 1965.

Meier, Arnold *et al., A Curriculum for Citizenship – A Report of the Citizenship Education Study,* Detroit, Wayne State University, 1952.

Michaelis, John W., and Johnston, A. Montgomery, *"The Social Sciences: Foundations of the Social Studies,"* Boston, Allyn & Bacon, Inc., 1965.

Michaelis, John U., "New Directions in Social Sciences Education," *Influences in Curriculum Change,* Washington Association for Supervision and Curriculum Development, 1968.

Miel, Alice, "Social Studies with a Difference," *Readings for Social Studies in Elementary Education,* 357-359, New York, The Macmillan Company, 1965.

Morris, Van Cleve, *Philosophy and the American School,* Boston, Houghton Mifflin, 1961.

Mowlton, Muriel, "Controversy in the Classroom" *Social Education,* XXXII:39-40, January, 1968.

National Council for the Social Studies, "Criteria for an Adequate Social Studies Curriculum," *Readings for Social Studies in Elementary Education,* New York, The Macmillan Company, 1965.

Nichols, Richard, "Developing Cognitive Abilities with Social Studies Trade Books," *Reading and Thinking,* Garden City, Doubleday & Co., 1967.

Ozmon, Howard, *Challenging Ideas in Education,* Minneapolis, Burgess Publishing Company, 1967.

Peck, Robert, and Robert Havighurst, *The Psychology of Character Development,* New York, Wilcy, 1960.

Rath, James, "A Strategy for Developing Values," *Educational Leadership,* 21:509-514, 554, May 1964.

Raths, Louis E., Harmin, Merrill, and Simon, Sidney B., *Values and Teaching,* Columbus; Charles E. Merrill Books, Inc., 1966.

Reissman, Frank, *The Culturally Deprived Child*, New York, Harper & Row, 1962.

Rokeach, Milton, *The Open and Closed Mind*, New York, Basic Books, Inc., 1960.

Russell, David, *Children's Thinking*, Boston, Ginn & Company, 1956.

Sand, Ole, and Joyce, Bruce, "Planning for Children of Varying Ability," *Social Studies in Elementary Schools*, N.C.S.S., 1962.

Shotka, Josephine, "Critical Thinking in the First Grade," *Childhood Education*, 36, 9:405, May, 1960.

Smith, B. O., Stanley, William O., and Shores, J. Harlan, *Fundamentals of Curriculum Development*, New York: Harcourt, Brace & World, 1957.

Smith, James, *Creative Teaching of the Language Arts in the Elementary School*, Boston, Allyn & Bacon, Inc., 1967.

Stimson, Lillian W., "Geography," *The Social Sciences*, Boston, Allyn & Bacon, Inc., 1965.

Stein, M. I., "Creativity and Culture," *Journal of Psychology*, 36:311-322, 1953.

Stewart, G. W., "Can Productive Thinking Be Taught?" *Journal of Higher Education.* 2,4;-4;4; 1950.

Tests in Print, Highland Park, N. J.; Gryphon Press, 1959.

Thurstone, L. L., *Applications of Psychology*, New York, Harper & Row, 1952.

Torrance, Paul, *Creativity*, National Education Association, 1963.

Weber, Del, and Haggerson, Nelson L., "Broad Trends and Developments in the Social Studies Today," The Social Sciences, 58:1-6, January, 1967.

Wheeler, Eldon G., *Developing the Social Studies Curriculum for Citizenship Education;* Manhattan, Kansas; Kansas State College, 1952.

Williams, Frank, "Reinforcement of Originality," *Reinforcement in Classroom Learning;* Washington, D. C.; U. S. Department of Health, Education and Welfare, 1964.

_____."Teach for . . .Creative Thinking," *The Instructor*, 76:88-89, May, 1967.

_____."Training Children to be Creative May Have Little Effect on Original Classroom Performance − Unless the Traits of Creative Thinking Are Taught Within a Structure of Knowledge." *California Journal of Educational Research, 17:73-79, 1966.*

Wolf, Ronald H., *"Economics," The Social Sciences*, American Council of Learned Societies and the National Council for the Social Studies, New York: Harcourt, Brace & World, Inc., 1962.

APPENDIX

MAJOR GENERALIZATIONS WITHIN THE SOCIAL STUDIES

(Generalizations are thought of as "large, central ideas" around which learning in the social studies is to be organized, patterned, and made meaningful.)

GENERALIZATIONS RELATING TO GEOGRAPHY

Generalizations Relating to Physical Geography

1. Life on the earth is influenced by the earth's (global) shape, its size, and set of motions.
2. The shape of the earth causes the unequal distribution of sunlight, or energy from the sun, which in turn influences the circulation of the atmosphere and differentiates climate and natural vegetation into regional types.
3. Earth movements of rotation and revolution are basic to understanding climate and time: rotation of the earth on its axis is a measure of time and causes night and day; seasons are caused by a combination of revolution, inclination, and parallelism of the axis.
4. Weather, climate, and earth crustal movements affect the surface of the earth and cause regional differences in land forms, minerals, drainage, soils, and natural vegetation.
5. Climate is determined by sunlight, temperature, humidity, precipitation, atmospheric pressure, winds, unequal rates of heating and cooling of land and water surfaces, irregular shape and distribution of land and seas, ocean currents, and mountain systems.
6. Major climatic regions coincide approximately with major vegetation zones because vegetation is related to climatic conditions. Natural vegetation is a great resource utilized by man.
7. Soils are altered by nature and man. Nature combines the action of climate, vegetation, and animals on parent materials to produce regional variations in soils.

Generalizations Relating to Cultural Geography

1. Man constantly seeks to satisfy his needs for food, clothing, and shelter and his wants; in so doing he tries to adapt, shape, utilize, and exploit the earth to his own ends. Some aspects of the natural environment, however, are not significantly altered or utilized by man.
2. The significance of the physical features of the earth is determined by man living in his environment. The natural environment may set the broad limits of economic life within a region, but it is man who determines its specific character within the limits of his culture.
3. To exist, man must utilize natural resources. Groups develop ways of adjusting to and controlling the environment in which they exist. Human change and even the whole structure of civilization may depend upon the nature and extent of man's available supply of energy and his ability to control it.
4. Man's utilization of natural resources is related to his desires and his level of technology.
5. The economic processes of production, exchange, distribution, and consumption of goods are economic concepts which have a geographic orientation and vary in part according to geographic influences. The nature of the organization of economic processes within an area (spatial organization) results from the kinds of resources, the stage of technology, and the sociopolitical attitudes prevailing.
6. The location of production is related to factors of production: land (natural resources of the physical environment), labor, and capital. In most cases the attainment of maximum efficiency, motivated by competition for the factors of production, determines location of production. In some cases, location of production is determined by political or other social-control groups rather than by economic efficiency.
7. Land, a basic factor in production, is less mobile than other factors, labor and capital, and has a dominant position in the location of production. Since people, in general, prefer to live near their work, the location of production becomes significant in the location of people.

8. The kinds of climate, soil, native vegetation, animals, and minerals influence the nature and extent of man's achievements within each region. The amount and the kind of food needed for health vary with climatic conditions and man's technology.

9. Factors of production, including technology, are subject to change; therefore, geography is concerned with changing patterns of land use.

10. Understanding the location of political or other social institutions is not complete without an understanding of the economy of an area. Since understanding of the economy of an area depends in part upon understanding the natural environment of that area, it follows that political and social institutions are related to the natural environment.

11. The sequence of human activities and culture patterns are related to the geographic accessibility, location, and the particular time in which human beings live. People in different stages of civilization react differently to similar environments.

12. Man may, by his activities, upset the balance of nature. He is not unlike other animals in this respect. Man is different, however, in that he may do something—as the practice of conservation—to correct the problem.

13. Competition for the acquisition of the earth's natural resources sometimes results in political strife, and even war.

14. Geographic positions of nation states are also related to political co-operation and strife.

GENERALIZATIONS RELATING TO HISTORY (CHRONOLOGY, SEQUENCE, CHANGES, MAIN TENDENCIES IN THE GROWTH OF CIVILIZATIONS, HISTORICAL INTERPRETATION)

1. Space and time form a framework within which all events can be placed. All of man's experience has occurred within a space and time framework; however, the same relationship does not necessarily apply to events as they have occurred in various parts of the world.

2. Man's struggle for freedom and human dignity has occupied a relatively brief period of time, as compared to the total span of man's existence.

3. The historical past influences the present. The present cannot be adequately understood without knowledge of the past. Life goes on against the intricate tapestry of the past. History does not repeat itself, but events tend to occur in some sort of sequence. Events in nature usually occur uniformly. Human events are predictable but to a lesser extent.

4. Change has been a universal condition of human society. Change and progress are, however, not necessarily synonymous. Numerous civilizations have risen and fallen, some of which have contributed greatly to our present civilizations. The tempo of change has increased markedly in the recent past.

5. History reveals a degree of homogeneity in mankind of all periods of recorded time. Environments in many places and regions have been altered physically, but human motives or drives within them have remained nearly the same.

6. Brotherhood, in the social sense of peaceful co-operation, is one of man's worthiest and earliest historical experiences. Conflict and hostility are also within man's experience. Men of all races have many basic physical similarities. Geographical variations and time variations in man's environments help explain his past behavior and continue to do so.

7. In the contemporary world historical events have a significance which reaches far beyond the limits of a state or province or the place of their origin. In such circumstances the world-wide relationship of events must be understood.

8. Although certain historical customs and institutions have characterized individual civilizations or nations of the past, men in every age and place have made use of basic social functions in adjusting themselves to their world.

9. Past and present civilizations represent our cultural heritage. The races, cultures, and civilizations in most areas of the world and of most historical periods, beginning with the dawn of recorded history, have made some contributions to the growth of our present civilizations.

10. Interdependence has been a constant and important factor in human relationships everywhere.

11. Such factors as the passing of time and advances in historical scholarship have brought new perspectives and understandings of history. The new interests and controversies of our own day and

of past centuries have had marked effects also on the interpretation of events and ideas. Use of the historical method in fact-finding and problem-solving has made possible the discovery and use of new interpretive data.

12. Human motives, drives, and ideas of various sorts, whether correct or incorrect in terms of historical progress and human improvement, have marked influence upon action on a local, national, and international scale. The interpretation of these is one of the most critical tasks of historical analysis.

13. There are various special interpretations, traditional or contemporary, regarding historical processes and movements of a national and international scope, which may for some people illuminate the study of history. Such historical processes are sometimes referred to by such terms as action and reaction; rise and fall; growth and decline within civilizations, nations, empires and the like.

14. The efforts of people, great material achievements, and important ideas are delineated, assessed, interpreted, and given a relative place by historians.

15. History demonstrates that mankind has been motivated by morals and ideals and by material wants and needs. The demand for moral standards has persisted throughout man's experience. The ideals of men in all parts of the world and in all ages have been rooted in the value systems of large and small groups.

GENERALIZATIONS RELATING TO GOVERNMENT AND DEMOCRACY

1. Throughout history the peoples of the world have experimented with a wide variety of governments. While Americans are wrestling with their own governmental problems, the peoples of all other countries are doing the same thing.

2. Government is but one of the institutions serving society. The state or government is essential to civilization and yet it cannot do the whole job by itself. Many human needs can best be met by the home, the church, the press, and private business.

3. Two essential functions of government are to serve and to regulate in the public interest. The ultimate responsibilities of government fall into five big fields: (a) external security, (b) internal order, (c) justice, (d) services essential to the general welfare, and (e) under democracy, freedom. Perhaps the clearest indication of the importance of the state in the twentieth century lies in the fact that although it has exclusive responsibility in none of these fields, it has residual responsibility in all.

4. In a democracy, government is the servant of the people; people are not the servants of government. Government is by right an institution made by man for man. The source of authority resides in the people.

5. It is the business of government to do for the people what they cannot do for themselves or, in any event, cannot do as well for themselves. The functions of government range from a bare minimum called laissezfaire, which hardly goes beyond maintaining peace and order, to totalitarian collectivism. Government is indispensable for ensuring external security and achieving internal order. Since order is indispensable if freedom is to have any genuine meaning, indeed, if life itself is to be tolerable, its establishment and maintenance are prime tasks of government.

6. No one yardstick is adequate for comparing different political systems. It is particularly important for citizens in a free society to understand the ideas and techniques characteristic of authoritarian political systems and to develop attitudes which will permit them to cope objectively with problems arising from the real or potential hostility of those systems.

7. In organizing government, it is essential to endow rulers with power and make provision for holding them responsible for its use.

8. Government cannot be effective unless it has the flexibility to cope with new conditions. Adaption, social invention, and gradual change provide the best safeguards against political revolution. To fulfill its role in a democracy government ought to be so organized as to meet the changing conditions of a growing nation. The Constitution of the United States provides for flexibility to meet changing conditions.

9. Political parties and special interest groups perform certain necessary services in the governing process. The political parties of this country and of every free land were formed so that citizens having common beliefs and interests may seek to mold the key policies and choose the key personnel of government. Parties and interest groups both play a check-and-balance, force-and-counterforce

role, which leads to evolutionary changes and growth. The politician generates and musters popular or legislative support necessary for formal approval or adoption of policy.

10. All nations in the modern world are part of a global interdependent system of economic, social, cultural, and political life. The evolution of the international law of war has been paralleled by the effort to develop an international law of peace and by the attempt to devise and build international political institutions and organizations capable of making such laws effective. Consideration for the security and welfare of the people of other nations remains the mark of the civilized man and has now become the price of national survival as well.

11. Democracy implies a way of life as well as a form of government.

12. Democracy is based on certain fundamental assumptions. Among these are the integrity of man, the dignity of the individual, equality of opportunity, man's rationality, man's morality, man's practicality, and man's ability to govern himself and to solve his problems co-operatively.

13. Man develops his fullest potential in a climate of freedom. Much of civilization's advance can be traced to man's search for a larger measure of freedom. For the truly civilized man, no amount of material wealth can ever compensate for the lack of freedom. Since freedom allows individuals to develop their creative talents, a society benefits when its individual members are relatively free.

14. Human beings are creatures of self-interest. For democracy to function, self-interest cannot be the dominating force. Rather, it must be curbed in favor of public interest.

15. A chief end of democracy is the preservation and extension of human freedoms. Freedom is unworkable unless balanced by a corresponding responsibility. The line of advance in freedom appears to run from legal freedom to political freedom, and from political freedom to genuine economic and social freedom.

16. Civil liberty—freedom of thought, speech, press, worship, petition, and association—constitutes the central citadel of human freedom. With it all other kinds of freedom become possible; without it, none of them can have any reality.

17. Basic to democracy is belief in progress. A free society is hospitable to new ideas and to change and encourages the unfettered search for truth. Peaceful action rather than violence is one of its hallmarks.

18. Certain factors are necessary for democracy to succeed. These include (a) an educated citizenry, (b) a common concern for human freedom, (c) communication and mobility, (d) a degree of economic security, (e) a spirit of compromise and mutual trust, (f) respect for the rights of minority groups and the loyal opposition, (g) moral and spiritual values, (h) participation by the citizen in government at all levels.

19. Opportunity sufficient to allow every individual voluntarily to choose the division of labor in which he will perform is a concept that has flourished under democratic philosophy and practice and the capitalistic system.

GENERALIZATIONS RELATING TO ECONOMICS

1. Economic welfare is a goal in most, if not all, modern economic societies. It is believed to be beneficial for people to have more economic goods rather than less, that poverty *per se* is not a desirable state of affairs. Many economists believe that not only economic welfare is one of the important qualities of a good society, but also that economic progress makes the other qualities of that society easier to attain, that the creative arts—such as painting, music, and literature—are more apt to flourish in a highly productive economy than in a poverty-stricken one.

2. Productive resources are scarce and human wants unlimited. Inasmuch as man cannot satisfy all of his desires for material goods, he has to make choices. The essence of "economy" lies in making wise choices in economic matters, such as between saving and spending, the object of expenditure, the kind of investment, and the choice of job. The "real cost" of any end-product is thus the alternatives sacrificed in producing it. This is known in economics as the "opportunity cost principle."

3. The size of the Gross National Product (consisting of the total value of all economic goods—products and services—produced annually) depends upon many conditions. Included are (a) the extent and richness of natural resources; (b) the number, quality, and motivation of the working population; (c) the amount and nature of the capital goods (factories, houses, bridges, roads, machines and tools of all kinds) created through saving and investment; (d) the effectiveness of investors and entrepreneurs

in organizing and energizing productive activity; (e) the existence of a large free-trade area in which the free flow of goods permits each locality to specialize in the production of those goods in which it has the greatest relative advantage and to obtain other goods by trade, which in economics is known as the "principle of comparative advantage"; and (f) the presence of economic and political institutions which are conducive to, and encourage, creative and productive effort on the part of all human beings. To preserve these several conditions upon which high productivity (and consequently our high plane of living) rests, conservation must be practiced.

4. The size of both the GNP and the population greatly influence economic welfare. Economic welfare depends upon the race between population growth and resource exhaustion on the one hand, and the improvement in techniques of production and expansion of capital goods, on the other. The economic optimum would be that size population relative to other resources as would produce the largest output per man-hour of labor, other things being equal. As population grows relative to other resources (land and capital goods) beyond this point of diminishing returns, output per worker declines, in the absence of improvements in technology. This principle is known in economics as the "law of diminishing return."

GENERALIZATIONS RELATING TO ANTHROPOLOGY

1. Many people believe that man has developed to his present form through the same processes of biological evolution as the rest of the animal kingdom; that he is a product of some one and one-half billion years of biological evolution that has resulted in the multitude of plant and animal forms inhabiting the earth.
   a. Physical anthropologists generally believe that man's separate stem of evolution goes back several million years; however, in the scale of biological time man is a relatively new phenomenon.
   b. Fossil remains of early man illustrate the ultimate evolution of the distinctively human characteristics. The most important include large brains, upright posture, manipulative hands, keen vision, and the development of mouth and throat structures that make speech possible.
   c. Man had attained essentially his modern biological attributes many thousands of years ago; his development since then has been overwhelmingly cultural. Man's survival no longer depends chiefly on his further biological evolution but rather on his cultural development.
2. Although man is a member of the animal kingdom, he differs profoundly from all other creatures by virtue of his development of culture. Culture is a product of man's exclusive capacity to comprehend and communicate symbolically (e.g., via language). Culture is socially learned and consists of the knowledge, beliefs, and values which human groups have invented to establish rules of group life and methods of adjusting to and exploiting the natural environment. The variety of cultures, to whose rules different human soicieties adhere, affords man more diverse ways of living than any other animal enjoys. Every society at a specific time and place has a culture to some degree different from that of any other society, past or present. Culture can be altered rapidly to cope with new conditions and a society can borrow ideas readily from an alien culture. Both these facts emphasize the superiority of man's cultural adaptions to the slowly developing and constrictive biological adaptions to which the lower animals are restricted. (Man didn't have to evolve wings to fly.) They also suggest the desirability of encouraging the continuance of many different cultural streams and of fostering sympathetic understanding of them: this diversity enriches all of human life.
3. No modern society has invented more than a small fraction of its present cultural heritage—each owes tremendous debts to cultural inventors of other times and other places.
   a. Recognizable men have left relics of their presence in the Old World, both skeletal fragments and artifacts, for at least the past 500,000 years. Paleolithic (Old Stone Age) men invented and developed languages, made crude tools of chipped stone and probably other less durable materials, eventually developed primitive clothing, and learned to control fire, and still later domesticated the dog.
   b. Some nine or ten thousand years ago men living around the east end of the Mediterranean Sea first conceived the idea of domesticating food plants and animals, thus beginning the Neolithic ("New Stone") Age. This control of the food supply constituted one of the most far-reaching revolutions in human history. Populations increased rapidly in those areas that adopted farming,

and permanent towns sprang up. The increased density of population plus the security and leisure made possible by the relatively assured food supply gave man his first opportunity to invent the cultural ramifications that are the basis of civilization: writing; mathematics and science; specialized technologies such as weaving, pottery making, and metallurgy; organized philosophy and religion; legal, political, and economic organizations. These inventions and their elaboration began soon after the agricultural base was established.

   c. No real break exists between the cultures of the ancient Neolithic farmers and the great civilizations of today. But the rate of cultural inventions has accelerated as has the speed with which new knowledge spreads around the world. This speed-up—particularly in science and technology—has created new opportunities for man, and also new and pressing problems. Everyone should be aware that the uses to which such advances are put is a cultural problem—the most urgent problem in the modern world.

4. The culture under which a person is reared exerts a powerful influence on him throughout his life.

   a. Since the culture of an individual's own society becomes thoroughly instilled in his innermost personality, he feels, thinks, and acts according to its imperatives—not only in order to be accepted by his fellows, but to be able to maintain a good opinion of himself. The world into which every individual must fit is the world as defined by his culture.

   b. Language is an essential, effective, and exclusively human tool for the invention and transmission of culture. Art, music, and other symbolic and aesthetic expressions are also effective means of transmitting culture.

   c. Culture, the creation of human activities, may be altered by human activities; norms of culture are derived historically but are dynamic, and thus they may be subjected to planned change.

   d. All cultures provide for the essential needs of human group life but differ, sometimes markedly, not only in the means by which they do this, but also in the individual feelings, modes of thought, and modes of action prescribed by the cultures in comparable situations. People generally prefer the culture of their own society, but they should recognize that, had they grown up under a different culture, they would probably prefer that one.

   e. Anthropologists have been unable to discover scientifically objective grounds for evaluating cultures as absolutely inferior or superior to one another.

   f. A major problem in the modern world is to discover ways in which social groups and nations with divergent cultures can co-operate for the welfare of mankind, and yet maintain respect for one another's cultural patterns.

5. All human beings, since long before the beginning of written history, have been members of a single biological species, *Homo sapiens*. For convenience of description and classification, anthropologists divide the species into "races," aggregates of men possessing more or less distinctive observable physical traits which distinguish them from other aggregates of men. These physical traits, however, merge imperceptibly into one another os that most men are intermediate between two or more types.

   a. Populations have seldom remained isolated long enough nor have they been subjected to sufficiently intensive natural selection to become homogeneous races. Modern world-wide interdependencies and rapid transport make it clear that such isolation cannot be expected in the future.

   b. Anthropologists distinguish three main stocks or extreme limits of human biological variability: Mongoloids, Caucasoids, and Negroids. The great bulk of humanity is intermediate between the extremes.

   c. Physically all human beings are much more alike than different. Geneticists estimate that all human beings have more than 99 per cent of their genes in common; that the most extreme variation results from genetic differences in less than one per cent of the genes. Differences between members of the same main stock are frequently greater than differences between persons of different groups.

   d. A common misconception is to label groups as "races" on the basis of language, religion, or nationality. These are all cultural, non-biological factors. So-called "ethnic groups" are generally defined on the basis of one or a combination of these characteristics. Even when biological traits are said to be an identifying feature, wide physical variations are likely to be found among members of an ethnic group. Such a group is, in general, a minority group, either in numbers or in power, whose culture differs to some degree from that of the majority group of the locality. If cultural differences are to be cherished for their enrichment of human life, ethnic groups should not suffer disadvantages or discrimination merely because they vary culturally from the norm of the majority.

6. Human beings, regardless of their racial or ethnic backgrounds, are nearly all capable of participating in and making contributions to any culture.
   a. The environment in which a person lives and his opportunities for personal growth have profound effects upon the development of every individual. When these are limited by cultural poverty or repressive action, society is as much the loser as the individual.
   b. So-called "race problems" are cultural problems arising from conflicts between ethnic groups or an ethnic group and the majority population. If the positive social value of cultural diversity is recognized, ethnic differences can add to the general richness of life.

GENERALIZATIONS RELATING TO PSYCHOLOGY

1. Human behavior is purposive and goal-directed. The individual may not always be aware of basic purposes and underlying needs that are influencing his behavior. The study of psychology attempts to bring about a better awareness of the underlying causes of behavior.
2. Individuals differ from one another in personal values, attitudes, personalities, and roles; yet at the same time the members of a group must possess certain common values and characteristics.
3. Social groupings develop as a means of group co-operation in meeting the needs of the individuals. The basic society of the family makes it possible for two individuals to co-operate in producing and rearing children. Similarly other social groupings (communities, social organizations, nations) enable individuals to work together toward satisfaction of common needs. The nature and structure of groupings tend to change and become more complex with the circumstances under which man lives.
4. Differences are important in the personality structure and behavior of individuals, and make possible the infinite variety of work and recreation activities that characterize modern culture. Differences also furnish a basis for flexibility and creativity which is essential to bring about social change and development. In any social group, differences among individuals in the group are likely to be greater than the differences between any two groups.
5. Socialization processes (for example, child-rearing practices) differ markedly in different social classes, groups, and socieities. Personality structure and behavior are largely influenced by these practices. Value standards developed by individuals reflect their experiences with such practices as they seek to relate themselves to the group and to satisfy their personal needs.
6. The satisfaction of social needs is a strong motivating force in the determination of individual behavior. Values placed on learning, as well as individual levels of aspiration, are in large part attributable to the mores of those groups that are "reference groups" for individuals. What sometimes appears to be nonconforming behavior may be in reality conforming behavior in terms of a particular group in which an individual seeks status. The strong human tendency to conform to social pressures often prevents individuals from seeking reality. The stereotyping of individuals because of racial or cultural backgrounds is another example. In general, nonco-operative aggressive behavior is a sign that the need for social acceptance has been frustrated. The individual displaying such behavior usually has been forced, through repeated rejection experiences, to develop an attitude of defeat and inferiority.
7. The behavior of individuals is related to the structure and organization of the group in which they are placed. A range of roles such as leadership, followership, aggression, submission may be exhibited by the same individual in different groups. The "need-satisfying" quality of a group and the member-to-member relationship influence behavior.
8. For preservation of group identity, a social group resists change through the phenomena of cultural lag and conservatism of members. A social group also changes in various degrees in the light of new conditions to preserve group identity.

EXPERIMENTAL STUDY TO DETERMINE THE PERCENTAGE OF FOURTH GRADE CHILDREN WHO ARE CAPABLE OF IDENTIFYING GENERALIZATIONS

INTRODUCTION

Through experience we learn what to expect of the people and things around us. We expect honey to be sweet, ice cream to be cold, and children on a playground to be noisy. But no one has ever tasted all the honey in the world, any more than he had listened to all the playing children in the world. We simply make the guess that whatever has been true in a number of cases will probably be true in other cases of the same kind. Such a guess is called a generalization.

Each of the stories on the following pages will help students form a guess or a generalization about people or things around them. After you read each story to them, they should be given time to write down generalizations.

SAMPLE STORY: Tom's Cocker Spaniel has long ears, a short tail, and curly hair. Jill's blond Cocker Spaniel has long ears, a short tail, and curly hair. Bill's spotted Cocker Spaniel has long ears, a short tail, and curly hair. Jeff's black Cocker Spaniel has long ears, a short tail, and curly hair.

SAMPLE GENERALIZATION:_____

_____

_____

If students said something like "Cocker Spaniels have long ears, a short tail, and curly hair, no matter what color they are," THEY ARE RIGHT!

NAME_____ DATE_____

AGE_____

STORY 1

Think for a moment of the Flintstones' supermarket and shopping center . . . Abba-dabba-doo!

The cave man, who lived on our earth many years ago, hunted wild animals for food. For a while he used his bare hands to capture his prey. Later he used crude weapons made of wood and stones to help him capture or kill other animals. Fred, and others like him, used the meat as food for his family, then helped his wife shape the hide into a pair of furry overalls—poor Wilma!

Fred and Wilma used a cave for a house. Not until years later did some clever cousins of their great-great-great grandchildren think of using the wood and baked clay to build houses wherever they wanted them. If the children wanted more clothes, they found out how to use wool and other fibers to make them. They even learned how to raise crops and how to preserve or save some kinds of food so that they wouldn't run out of things to eat.

Wilma and Fred would certainly be surprised and proud to see our modern supermarkets and shopping centers! But the Flintstones would probably notice that the mountains around the town still look almost the same as they did many years ago. What does this story tell you about man?

GENERALIZATION 1: *Man constantly seeks to satisfy his needs for food, clothing, and shelter and his wants; in so doing he tries to adapt, shape, utilize, and exploit the earth to his own ends. Some aspects of the natural environment, however, are not significantly altered or utilized by man.*

STORY 2

Hi, boys and girls! My name is Sam Soil. As you probably know, I am just one in a large family. Some of my relatives whom you know are Rock, Mud, and Dirt. We all live close together on the surface of the earth and do a lot of travelling. Water, ice, and wind are our means of transportation. I would like to tell you about some of the things that happen to me on my travels.

I was once part of a huge white boulder hidden under several inches of dirt and grass. But one day there was a huge explosion, and I landed on the top of a pile of gravel where I could see sunshine for the first time! A man with a giant shovel came and scooped me up into a big red gravel truck. The smooth pebbles riding with me said that they were going to live in a special place and that some of us would be used to help build roads and driveways.

Just as I was getting comfortable, a strong wind blew me from the truck to the hard road. I broke into several pieces and rolled down a hill to a sandy beach. I stayed with this Soil family for several years and we were rubbed smooth and round by the wind and water as we bumped against each other in the sun.

When my friends and I became fine enough, a man came again and shoveled us into a truck. He dumped us into a big field and sprinkled nourishment on us to make us healthy. After a few weeks, tiny plants began to stretch their roots around us and through us. Animals walked over us and dug their noses into us. In the fall, the decaying parts of plants and animals enriched us and we felt good. That winter, the snow and ice froze the ground and broke some of us into smaller pieces of Soil. This summer, after a nice rain, I'm going to break loose from the other Soil around me and dive into a stream of water, which will take me on a new adventure. It was nice talking with you. Good-bye!

GENERALIZATION 2: *Soils are altered by nature and man. Nature combines the action of climate, vegetation, and animals on parent materials to produce regional variations in soils.*

STORY 3

In science this year Tom learned a lot about our natural resources. He studied about the water cycle and about the way the sunshine, air, water, soil, minerals, forests, and wildlife work together to keep the earth and its people healthy.

His teacher asked, "Can you explain the balance of nature?"

Tom said, "That is the way that the numbers of plants and animals are controlled by nature. Most plants and animals have natural enemies that kill some of them, so that there won't be too many of one certain kind of plant or animal. Birds eat flying insects, snakes eat birds, and plant lice eat plants.

Can you give an example of the balance of nature?

Tom noticed in his little garden that the healthy weeds and insects were killing his new vegetables. The vegetables could do nothing to protect themselves, but Tom could. Tom pulled the weeds and sprayed the air to kill the insects that were hurting the vegetables.

In geography, Tom learned that the Nile River was flooding and washing away valuable soil in some areas of Egypt. The soil could do nothing to protect itself. The men who lived in Egypt did something to solve this problem, though. They built the Aswan Dam to control the mighty river.

Dangerous chemicals and waste products are killing the fish in Lake Michigan, and the fish can't do anything to protect themselves. But men are working very hard to solve this problem.

GENERALIZATION 3: *Man may, by his activities, upset the balance of nature. He is not unlike other animals in this respect. Man is different, however, in that he may do something—as the practice of conservation—to correct the problem.*

STORY 4

Many years ago in Greece, the people who lived there tried out a type of government called a Democracy. Every man who owned land held some kind of public office and met with his friends to vote on important matters.

A few years later, the Romans of Italy decided to try the kind of government called a Republic. The people voted for senators to represent them. These senators had meetings where they discussed public problems and voted on ways to solve them.

The people in some countries were very busy working in the fields. They had to raise enough food to feed their families and also give some to their rulers. They let one man and his family rule them. Whatever the emperors said, the people tried to do. The emperors became very powerful and fought neighboring countries to get more wealth and power.

Just a few years ago, a German named Hitler tried to build a super race. He believed it was even right to kill the people who did not measure up to his standards. Other countries joined forces to stop this government.

In Africa, the new nations are working hard to set up a government that will be just right for them. In Viet Nam, the people do not agree on what sort of government is best for them. And, in America, some people question some of the ideas of our government.

GENERALIZATION 4: *Throughout history the peoples of the world have experimented with a wide variety of governments. While Americans are wrestling with their own governmental problems, the peoples of all other countries are doing the same thing.*

Percentage of fourth grade children who were able to formulate an appropriate generalization following each story. (93 children tested — average I.Q. 105)

First Story	50%
Second Story	30%
Third Story	45%
Fourth Story	45%

A DIRECTORY OF SOCIAL STUDIES PROJECTS

Wallace Anderson. Intercultural Studies (K-16). State College of Iowa, Cedar Falls, Iowa 50613 (Ford).

Robert C. Angell. Sociological Resources for Secondary Schools. 503 First National Building, Ann Arbor, Michigan 48108 (National Science Foundation).

Gregory R. Anrig and Lawrence H. Vadnais, Jr. Development of a Pilot Program for Cultural Approach to the Study of History in Grades Seven and Eight. Mt. Greylock Regional High School, Williamstown, Massachusetts.

*Melvin Arnoff. The Development of First Grade Materials on "Families of Japan." Kent State University, Kent, Ohio.

Wilfred Bailey and Marion J. Rice. Development of a Sequential Curriculum in Anthropology for Grades 1-7. University of Georgia, Athens, Georgia.

James M. Becker. An Examination of Objectives, Needs and Priorities in International Education in U.S. Secondary and Elementary Schools. Foreign Policy Association, New York, New York.

Edgar Bernstein. A Study to Develop Instructional Materials for a Ninth and Tenth Grade World History Curriculum Integrating History and the Social Sciences. University of Chicago, Chicago, Illinois.

Bary K. Beyer. Development and Testing of Instructional Materials, Teaching Guides and Units on the History and Culture of Sub-Saharan Africa, Ohio State University, Columbus, Ohio.

Richard H. Brown and Van R. Halsey, Jr. Construction and Use of Source Material Units in History and Social Studies. Amherst College, Amherst, Massachusetts.

Paul E. Cawein. Harvard-Newton Project in Business History and Economic Concepts. Newton Public Schools, Newton, Massachusetts 02159 (Harvard, Newton Schools, Industries).

B. J. Chandler. Sounds of Society: A Demonstration Program in Group Inquiry. Northwestern University, Evanston, Illinois.

Allan B. Cole. Survey of Asian Studies in Secondary Schools in New England. Tufts University. Medford, Massachusetts.

James S. Coleman. Research Program in the Effects of Games with Simulated Environment in Secondary Education. Department of Social Relations, Johns Hopkins University, Baltimore, Maryland.

Malcolm C. Collier. Anthropology Curriculum Study Project (Secondary). 5632 South Kimbark Avenue, Chicago, Illinois 60637 (National Science Foundation).

Charlotte A. Crabtree. Teaching Geography in Grades One Through Three: Effects of Instruction in the Core Concept of Geographic Theory. University of California at Los Angeles, California.

O. L. Davis, Jr. Effectiveness of Using Graphic Illustrations with Social Studies Textural Materials. University of Texas, Austin, Texas.

*Robert W. Edgar. Impact on Learning and Retention of Specially-Developed History Materials for Culturally Deprived Children. Queens College, City University of New York, New York, New York.

Richard W. Elliott. A study of the Effectiveness of Taped Lessons in Geography Instruction. Westfield Public Schools, Westfield, Massachusetts.

Shirley H. Engle and Howard D. Mehlinger. A High School Curriculum Center in Government. Indiana University, Bloomington, Indiana.

Raymond English. The Greater Cleveland Social Science Program (K-12). Educational Research Council of Greater Cleveland, Rockefeller Building, 614 West Superior Avenue, Cleveland, Ohio 44113 (The Council).

Edwin Fenton. The Development of a Sequential and Cumulative Curriculum in the Social Studies for Able Students. Carnegie Institute of Technology, Pittsburgh, Pennsylvania.

*Robert S. Fox and Ronald Lippitt. Teaching of Social Science Material in the Elementary School. University of Michigan, Ann Arbor, Michigan.

*Norman H. Fries. An Exploratory Study in Teaching World History in German. Board of Education, Common School District Joint No. 16, Sussex, Wisconsin.

*Dale M. Garvey and William H. Seiler. A Study of Effectiveness of Different Methods of Teaching International Relations to High School Students. Kansas State Teachers College, Emporia, Kansas.

*John S. Gibson. Development of Instructional Materials Pertaining to Racial and Cultural Diversity in America. Tufts University, Medford, Massachusetts.

John S. Gibson. Development of Instructional Units and Related Materials on Racial and Cultural Diversity in America (continuation of above project). Tufts University, Medford, Massachusetts.

Clark C. Gill and William B. Conroy. Development of Guidelines and Resource Materials on Latin America for Use in Grades I-XII. University of Texas, Austin.

Jacqueline Grennan. Curriculum Innovation in the Fields of History, Science, Music, and Art Within a Single Institute. Webster College, St. Louis, Missouri.

Donald W. Hardy. Inland Valley Elementary School Archeology Project. University of California, Berkeley, California.

*Robert S. Harnack. The Use of Electronic Computers to Improve Individualization of Instruction Through Unit Teaching. State University of New York at Buffalo.

Robert J. Havighurst and Robert L. McCaul. The Interaction Between Education and Society in Chicago. University of Chicago, Chicago, Illinois.

Glenn W. Hawkes. A Philosophical and Historical Rationale for a New Approach to "Problems of Democracy." Harvard College, Cambridge, Massachusetts.

Nicholas Helburn. High School Geography Project. 2450 Broadway, Box 1095, Boulder, Colorado 80302 (National Science Foundation) (Selected Classroom Experiences, unit on Urban Geography available from NCGE Publications Center, Illinois State Normal University, Normal, Illinois).

Howard M. Hennebry. Conservation Education Improvement Project. University of Wyoming, Laramie.

Robert D. Hess and David Easton. The Development of Basic Attitudes and Values Toward Government and Citizenship During the Elementary School Years, University of Chicago, Illinois.

*Carl S. Johnson and Charles A. Dambach. Survey of Printed Materials on Conservation Education. Ohio State University, Columbus, Ohio.

Bruce R. Joyce. Use of a Data Storage and Retrieval System to Teach Elementary School Children Concepts and Modes of Inquiry in the Social Sciences. Teachers College, Columbia University, New York, New York.

*Harold H. Kastner, Jr. Knowledge of Economics of Eleventh Grade U.S. History Students, Florida State Department of Education, Tallahassee, Florida.

*Ida B. Lalor and Maurice L. Hartung. To Study Insights Gained from a High School Social Studies Course. University of Chicago, Chicago, Illinois.

Marvin Lee. Economics Education Committee on the Southern States Work Conference (Secondary). College of Human Resources and Education, West Virginia University, Morgantown, West Virginia 26506 (Joint Council on Economic Education).

John R. Lee. Social Studies Curriculum Study Center: A Sequential Curriculum on American Society for Grades 5 - 12. Northwestern University, Evanston, Illinois.

Ella C. Leppert. A Sequential Social Studies Course for the Secondary School. University of Illinois, Urbana.

*Meno Lovenstein. The Development of Economic Curricular Materials for Secondary Schools. Ohio University, Athens, Ohio.

Harold M. Long. Improving Teaching of World Affairs (K-12). Glens Falls Public Schools, Glens Falls, New York 12801 (National Council for the Social Studies). Improving the Teaching of World Affairs available from the Council.

*William T. Lowe. A Study of the Objectivity of Materials Used in Current Events Instruction in Secondary School Social Studies Classrooms, Cornell University, Ithaca, New York.

John E. Maher. Developmental Economic Education Program (K-12). Joint Council on Economic Education, 1212 Avenue of the Americas, New York, New York 10036 (various associations and groups).

Milton O. Meux. Evaluative Teaching Strategies in the Social Studies. University of Utah, Salt Lake City, Utah.

John U. Michaelis. Preparation of Teaching Guides and Materials on Asian Countries for Use in Grades 1 - 12. University of California, Berkeley, California.

Jerry Moore. Experimental Statewide Seminars in Teaching About Democracy and Totalitarianism. Northwestern University, Evanston, Illinois.

Elting E. Morison. A Program of Curriculum Development in the Social Studies and Humanities (1-12). Educational Services, 44-A Brattle Street, Cambridge, Massachusetts 02183 (various foundations).

* Irving Morrissett. To aid in the Development of Social Science Education. Purdue University, Lafayette, Indiana.

* Rose Mukerji and Helen F. Robinson. Demonstration of Concept and Language Development in a Kindergarten of Disadvantaged Children, Brooklyn College, Brooklyn, New York.

Louis Nicolosi. Preparation of Teaching Guides and Materials on World Geography, North American Geography, and Louisiana Geography of Use in Grades I-XII. Louisiana State Department of Education, Baton Rouge, Louisiana.

Donald Oliver. A Law and Social Science Curriculum Based on the Analysis of Public Issues. Harvard University, Cambridge, Massachusetts.

* Vito Perrone. Image of Latin America: A Study of American School Textbooks and School Children Grades Two Through Twelve. Northern Michigan University, Marquette, Michigan.

* Frank A. Pinner. Relationships Between High School Group Structures and the Development of Orientations Toward Public Affairs. Michigan State University, East Lansing, Michigan.

Roy A. Price. Identification of Major Social Science Concepts and Their Utilization in Instructional Materials. Syracuse University, Syracuse, New York.

William D. Rader. Elementary School Economics Program (4 and 5). Industrial Relations Center, University of Chicago, 1225 East 60th Street, Chicago, Illinois 60637 (The Center).

Edwin C. Roswenc. Basic Concepts in History and Social Science (Secondary). Department of American Studies, Amherst College, Amherst, Massachusetts 01002 (The College). Pamphlets available from D. C. Heath.

Lawrence Senesh. Elkhart Indiana Experiment in Economic Education (1-12). Department of Economics, Purdue University, Lafayette, Indiana 47907.

Judson T. Shaplin. Development of a Model for the St. Louis Metropolitan Social Studies Center, Grades K-12. Washington University, St. Louis, Missouri.

James P. Shaver. A Secondary School Social Studies Curriculum Focused on Thinking Reflectively About Public Issues. Utah State University, Logan, Utah.

Ridgway F. Shinn, Jr. A Study of Geo-Historical Structure for a Social Studies Curriculum. Rhode Island College, Providence, Rhode Island.

* Ridgway F. Shinn, Jr. An Investigation Into the Utilization of Geography and History as Integrating Disciplines for Social Studies Curricular Development in a Public School System. Rhode Island College, Providence, Rhode Island.

John G. Sperling and Suzanne E. Wiggins. Development and Evaluation of a 12th Grade Course in the Principles of Economics. San Jose State College, San Jose, California.

* Ursula K. Springer. Recent Curriculum Developments at the Middle Level of French, West German, and Italian Schools. Brooklyn College, City University of New York, New York.

L. S. Stavrianos. World History Project (Secondary). Department of History, Northwestern University, Evanston, Illinois 60201. (The University and Carnegie) Books available from Allyn and Bacon.

Hilda Taba. Development of a Comprehensive Curriculum Model for Social Studies, Grades 1-8, Including Procedures for Implementation. San Francisco State College, San Francisco, California.

* Hilda Taba. Thinking in Elementary School Children. San Francisco State College, San Francisco, California.

Henry Toy, Jr. Civic Education Project (5-12). Council on Civic Education, 300 East 33rd Street, New York, New York 10016 (Danforth). A consortium that inclues groups that work on curriculum and materials, research and theory, promising practices and interdisciplinary programs.

* Merle W. Vance. Demonstration to Improve the Teaching of Social Studies - Grades 1-6. Sacramento State College, Sacramento, California.

Edith West. Preparation and Evaluation of Curriculum Guides and Sample Pupil Materials for Social Studies in Grades K-14. University of Minnesota, Minneapolis, Minnesota.

Richard L. Wing. The Production and Evaluation of Three Computer-Based Economic Games for the Sixth Grade. First Supervisory District Schools, Yorktown Heights, Westchester County, New York.

Robert L. Zangrando. The Identification of Criteria for the Effective Use of Films in Teaching History in the Classroom, in a Variety of Teaching Stiuations, Grades 7-12. American Historical Association, Washington, D.C.

INDEX